by JESSICA MITFORD

Daughters and Rebels
The American Way of Death
The Trial of Dr. Spock

The Trial of Dr. Spock

The Trial of
DR. SPOCK

The Rev. William Sloane Coffin, Jr.,
Michael Ferber,
Mitchell Goodman,
and Marcus Raskin

by JESSICA MITFORD

 *ALFRED A. KNOPF, New York, 1969*

THIS IS A BORZOI BOOK
PUBLISHED BY ALFRED A. KNOPF, INC.

FIRST EDITION

Library of Congress Catalog Card Number: 69–10682

Acknowledgment is gratefully made to Atlantic-Little, Brown
and Co. for permission to reprint from *The Autobiography
of Bertrand Russell.* Copyright 1951, 1952, 1953, © 1956
by Bertrand Russell. Copyright © 1968 by George Allen and
Unwin Ltd. *The Yale Review* and Professor Joseph L. Sax
have granted permission to reprint from an article in the
June 1968 issue. Copyright © 1968 by *The Yale Review.*

To my husband,

Robert Treuhaft,

who counseled, aided, and abetted
the writing of this book,
and who appears in its pages as
the Old Trial Hand

Trust yourself. You know more than you think you do. . . . Don't take too seriously all that the neighbors say. Don't be overawed by what the experts say. Don't be afraid to trust your own common sense. . . .

Benjamin Spock, M.D.,

The Common Sense Book of Baby and Child Care,
First edition, 1946

Contents

Part I V

NOTE

As this book goes to press, the four defendants found guilty (Spock, Coffin, Ferber, and Goodman) are at liberty on their own recognizance pending the outcome of their appeal, which was argued in the United States Court of Appeals for the First Circuit in January 1969.

The likelihood is that no matter what the decision of the First Circuit Court, there will be further appeals and the fate of the defendants will eventually be decided by the United States Supreme Court.

J. M.
May 1969

Part **I**

1

The Accusation

All of the defendants first learned they had been indicted from the press. The Justice Department, with a fine flourish of incivility, hand-delivered its releases to the media and then mailed the indictments to the defendants' homes.

Thus Marcus Raskin, co-director of the Institute for Policy Studies, got a phone call at his office in Washington from a UPI man: "We wondered if you would care to make a comment?"

"A comment on what?"

"On the indictment."

What indictment?"

"Well—it says here—let's see—you've been indicted along with Dr. Spock; Rev. William Sloane Coffin, Jr., chaplain of Yale University; Mitchell Goodman, a New York writer; and Michael Ferber, a twenty-three-year-old Harvard graduate student, for 'a continuing conspiracy to aid, abet, and counsel violations of the Selective Service law.' "

"You've *got* to be kidding!"

And so it was with three of the others. No fleet-footed courier double-knocked on their doors crying, "Open up, open up in the name of Ramsey Clark!" UPI, AP, and *The New York Times* stood in for the harbinger of tidings, with the assistance of Ma Bell.

But Dr. Spock had been out all day on various errands and could not be reached by telephone. Coming home in the afternoon on the subway he saw a headline over his seatmate's shoulder: SPOCK INDICTED. "I was *dying* to read it, but the man kept twitching it away just out of my sight. I felt like saying to him, 'But that's *me!* I want to see what I've been indicted for!' "

Michael Ferber, who grades English papers at Harvard University, sat down to correct his indictment when it arrived. Offended by the redundancies ("combine, conspire, confederate, and agree"), the split infinitives ("to unlawfully, knowingly, and wilfully counsel, aid, and abet"), the misspelling of "fabricoid" (spelled with a "k" in his dictionary), and the word "co-conspirator," which he could not find in *any* dictionary, he gave the document a C–, and wrote in the margin, "You should do better. See me." Which they eventually did.

The indictment,* returned by a federal grand jury in Boston on January 5, 1968, charges that the five conspired "with each other, and with diverse other persons, some known and others unknown to the Grand Jury," to counsel, aid, and abet violations of the Selective Service law and to hinder administration of the draft. In addition, the elder four are charged with conspiring to "sponsor and support a nation-wide program of resistance" to the draft.

It cites a number of "overt acts" committed in furtherance of the conspiracy:

In August, 1967, Coffin and Spock "distributed and caused to be distributed . . . a statement entitled 'A Call to Resist Illegitimate Authority.' "

On October 2, 1967, Coffin, Goodman, Raskin, and Spock

* For the full text of the indictment, see the Appendix.

"held a press conference" at the New York Hilton Hotel.

On October 16, 1967, Michael Ferber and William Sloane Coffin, Jr., addressed a meeting in the Arlington Street Church in Boston, at which Coffin accepted draft cards turned in by Selective Service registrants.

On October 20, 1967, Coffin spoke at a demonstration outside the Justice Department, after which he, Raskin, Spock, and Goodman entered the Justice Department and together with other "co-conspirators abandoned a fabricoid briefcase" containing draft cards collected at various demonstrations throughout the United States.

How did these five wind up as accused conspirators? They hardly knew each other. Dr. Spock and Mr. Coffin had met glancingly on speakers' platforms, Michael Ferber had once exchanged a few words with Coffin in a church but had never spoken to any of the others. Four of them (Spock, Coffin, Raskin, and Goodman) had some months before participated in an eleven-man delegation to the Department of Justice; but in their busy lives this brief encounter hardly constituted acquaintance. When for the first time all five met together—after the indictment, in attorney Leonard Boudin's living room, to discuss their common plight—Boudin says the first thing he felt he could do for these conspirators was to introduce them to each other.

Because of the stellar quality of the defendants, the newspapers predicted a trial that would make social and legal history. Headlines gave it advance billing as a spectacular: SPOCK TRIAL MAY BE THRILLER (Washington *Post*), A LANDMARK CASE OF CONSCIENCE AND THE LAW (*Life* Magazine), CHALLENGE TO THE DRAFT (*The New York Times*). It would provide, the editorial writers said, the forum for a court challenge to the legality of the Vietnam war and hence of the draft, a crucial test case to explore and define the permissible limits of dissent guaranteed under the First Amendment. The eyes of the nation, indeed of the world, would be

on the Boston courtroom watching the outcome of a contest between the United States government and some of
its most distinguished critics.

The defendants themselves, some of whom had actively
sought prosecution for the purpose of testing the legality of
the war and of the draft, also anticipated a serious adjudica-
tion of these issues. "I'd be *delighted* if the government
would prosecute me!" Dr. Spock had said. Asked in the
course of the trial what he had in mind, he replied, "I meant
that if the government chose to prosecute me, I would be
glad to have this opportunity to prove that we were right."

But the government saw to it that he was not granted
this opportunity. Perhaps it was ingenuous of the defendants to believe that the government would permit them to
put its fundamental policies on trial; if so, this was a
naïveté shared by a sizable section of the press. For Dr.
Spock's day in court turned out to be entirely different
from what he had hoped for and what the press had predicted.

Benefits sometimes come disguised. If the trial did not
deal with the issues the defendants had tried to raise, it
did help to reveal some fundamental truths about the
nature of this kind of prosecution, and to dispel some illu-
sions about the efficacy of the courtroom as a forum for the
exposition of ideas.

2

Dr. Spock

Dr. Spock was already a dual legend. A young mother of my acquaintance was visited by an eighteen-year-old girl, a civil-disobedient who had marched with Spock-led militants since junior high school days. She spotted a copy of *Baby and Child Care* lying on the coffee table. "Oh—is that by THE Dr. Spock?" she asked. "Is he any good on baby care?"

In real life, he is as easy and straightforward as his famous book, as forthright as his platform speeches. There are no surprises in this large, kind-eyed man. Although his political outlook has veered all the way from support of Calvin Coolidge in 1924 to co-chairmanship of the National Conference for New Politics in 1967, one senses nothing contradictory or eccentric in his character. He still seems very much the product of his Protestant-Republican upbringing in the early part of the century, his present stand a logical development of the outsize New England conscience conferred upon him by his parents.

He and his wife, Jane, to whom he has been married for forty-one years, live in an attractive New York apartment furnished like an English country house. Everything about them is pleasantly old-fashioned; they have made no concessions in style of life either to the affluent society or to the young whose champion he has become. For example, they are beautfully dressed, he in conservative blue suit with gold watch chain across his waistcoat, she in very good New York clothes, her gray hair still fixed in the long, wavy bob of her youth. Their favorite relaxation is an expensive one— sailing in the Caribbean. Yet frugality is second nature; they never take taxis when a subway will do, and one of Dr. Spock's errands on the day the indictments were returned was cashing in the return stub of a $2.43 commuter's ticket at Penn Station. They contribute lavishly to the causes in which they believe. Their view of the proper uses of money, their "values" in this and other areas, seem to stem directly from their patrician New England forebears, to whom the virtues of economy, uprightness, and service to the community were simply habits of behavior to be cultivated throughout a lifetime.

Ben Spock grew up in a "devoted, puritanical family," oldest of two boys and four girls, ruled over by a "stern mother, a grave, awe-inspiring father." This recollection he ascribes to the Oedipus complex, for his sisters remember their father as "a darling person, always laughing." (He underwent five years of psychoanalysis as part of his psychiatric training, and bits of Freudian lore crop up frequently in his conversation.)

Ben Spock must have been an unusually satisfactory son, one of those first-rate boys who does everything expected of him and more, without the hint of a rebel about him. I begged him to tell about the very worst thing he ever did as a boy, and he really tried hard to conjure up the memory of some awful misdeed. "Well, I do remember one thing," he said finally. "When I was about twenty, my father lent me his car to go to a football game. I left the key in the ignition and the car was stolen by some joy-riders." "What did your father do?" "He just looked *very* grave," said Dr.

Spock, giving one of his explosive giggles. And his most severe conflict of conscience while he was at Yale came about as a result of being offered a particularly soft and well-paid summer job as tutor to a rich kid in Southampton. He longed to take it, but could not bear to face his mother's certain disapproval; instead he looked for the roughest and dirtiest job available, and spent the summer working ten hours a day on the Canadian Pacific Railroad.

The elder Spock was a corporation lawyer, general counsel for the New Haven Railroad and also for the Chase Brass Company in Waterbury, Connecticut. One day a labor organizer appeared in Waterbury, seeking to unionize the brass workers. The city officials became alarmed, so Mr. Spock advised the police chief to arrest the man as a trouble-maker, which he promptly did. The newly formed Yale Liberal Club called upon Mr. Spock in a delegation to protest this action. An explosion followed in which Mr. Spock berated his young visitors as "outrageous whipper-snappers." Ben, then in his senior year at Yale, watched from the sidelines. "I should never have *dreamed* of joining the Liberal Club. It would never have *occurred* to me to question my father's actions in this or in anything else." In fact, in his college days Ben took no interest whatsoever in politics except insofar as his father guided him. His first vote, when he was just twenty-one, was cast for Calvin Coolidge "because my father said he was the greatest president we've ever had."

In 1927, while he was still in medical school at Columbia University, Dr. Spock married Jane Davenport Cheney. They led a busy and blameless life, he pursuing his medical career and she raising their two sons, Michael and John, born in 1933 and 1944. The first public event that stirred them was the Spanish Civil War. While it did not occur to Dr. Spock to enlist in the International Brigade, the war filled him with anguish—each morning he would wake as though to a nightmare to read the steadily worsening news from the front. Jane raised funds for Spanish war relief. Like many of their generation, the Spocks watched with horror from afar as the fall of the Spanish republic was followed by the outbreak of World War II. They turned from the Republicanism of their early youth to become supporters of FDR and the New Deal, but the support did not go much beyond voting—"We weren't campaigners in those days."

Dr. Spock has never been a pacifist. "If another Hitler came along I would just as soon go to war and take the chance of being killed," he said. During World War II, from 1944 to 1946, he was a lieutenant commander in the U.S. Naval Reserve, serving as a psychiatrist in naval hospitals in New York and California. Never one to waste time, he spent the evenings writing *The Common Sense Book of Baby and Child Care.* Jane helped with the research and also as a listener; he read the manuscript out loud to her as he went along, perfecting the conversational, person-to-person style that two generations of parents have found so reassuring.

After the war, the Spocks lived in various places: Minnesota, Pittsburgh, Cleveland. His book was selling at the rate of a million a year (next to the Bible it is the biggest best seller in publishing history), he was on the staff of the Rochester Child Health Institute, the Mayo Clinic, Western Reserve University; he directed teaching programs in pediatrics and child psychiatry. In the evenings he wrote magazine articles on the problems of parents.

A magazine profile of Dr. Spock written in 1952, six years after his book was published, quotes one of his friends as saying that he was quite liberal during the twenties and thirties—subscribed to *The Nation, The New Republic,* and the like—but had become "increasingly conservative."

The fact is that Dr. Spock is something of a political

Rip Van Winkle. Totally immersed in his professional work during the whole long postwar, cold-war period, he virtually stood aside from politics—when he thought of world affairs at all, he uncritically accepted official American doctrine. Thus he saw the Korean conflict "as a necessary repelling of aggression under the aegis of the United Nations—at the time, it just seemed right. Here was a clear-cut invasion, you can't have *invasions* like this." Lately he has somewhat revised his opinions of Korea, and of the American role there as policeman. "It's turned sour, because, for one thing, North Korea is doing a lot better than South Korea." During the Eisenhower Administration, he did not dispute the President's view that domestic economies were needed in favor of more spending on armaments. "I *believed* in more arms at that time."

In 1960, Dr. Spock campaigned for Kennedy. He appeared on television with Jacqueline Kennedy, who murmured rapturously, "Dr. Spock is for my husband, and my husband is for Dr. Spock!" (Some newspapers treated his participation as a clever Kennedy gimmick to garner the "mother's vote.") A year after the election, in the fall of 1961, the Russians resumed the testing of nuclear bombs; and in March of 1962, Kennedy, while assuring the nation that America was far ahead in nuclear weaponry, announced that America would follow suit.

"I suddenly realized the whole *world* was in peril," said Dr. Spock, spreading his huge hands as though to ward off danger. "We've got to keep testing more, keep accumulating more nuclear arms—and of course Congress is always enthusiastic for more arms. In Cleveland, where we were living, business leaders were for more arms, the press was for more arms, labor was for more arms. It suddenly *struck* me—it was a *terrible* moment. After that, I was hooked for the peace movement."

Homer Jack, an executive of SANE, had written twice to

Dr. Spock asking him to join the organization. The first time Dr. Spock turned him down, fearful that to associate himself with the SANE message of the dangers of nuclear destruction would be unbearably upsetting to parents: "I told him I've spent my life *reassuring* parents, and wasn't about to start *alarming* them." But after the resumption of testing, he agreed to become a member of the national board of SANE, "and from then on, every step was logical."

His sudden decision to devote himself to the cause of world peace seems to have had the force of a religious conversion. The first job he undertook for SANE was to write the copy for a full-page advertisement scheduled to appear in *The New York Times* in April, 1962. The firm of Doyle Dane Bernbach said they would contribute the ad if Dr. Spock would prepare the text. This task caused him enormous anxiety, and in the course of it he forced himself to analyze and clarify his own stand on a multiplicity of complex foreign policy questions. "I had a fantasy of being queried by the press—'What's your position on Central Europe? Ghana? South America?' I *madly* wrote for a month, every free moment. Gradually this business of 'what's my position' got well settled in my mind." (One of the more tiresome criticisms leveled at Dr. Spock is that a baby doctor has no business mixing into foreign policy, which, say the critics, should be left to the experts.) The following year he became co-chairman of SANE.

The 1964 election appeared to Dr. Spock (as it did, indeed, to millions of others) as a clear-cut choice between the forces who would escalate the Vietnam conflict into a third world war, represented by Goldwater, and the will of the people for peace in Vietnam, expressed by the candidacy of LBJ. He threw his energies into the election campaign, made numerous speeches, appeared on television as the most dazzling star of the Doctors for Johnson Committee. To his amazement and gratification, two days after the election the President himself rang him up to thank him for his help. "He said in a voice of great humility, 'Dr. Spock, I hope I will be worthy of your trust.' And I answered, 'I'm sure you will.'"

Within three months Dr. Spock was peppering the White House with letters, "some harsh, some polite," denouncing the betrayal of Johnson's campaign promises. He sent the first letter to Jack Valenti, with instructions to give it to Mr. Johnson: "I said to him that I was not interested in a reply from an assistant, that as a campaigner for the President I felt I wanted to get through to him personally."

For those who have sought to convey their views on the war to the White House in hopes of getting a responsive answer, the Spock-Johnson correspondence will have a familiar ring. Thus when Dr. Spock wrote to urge a cessation of the bombing, saying he believed that further escalation "will cause worldwide alarm, intensifying division among our people," LBJ replied: "I will be grateful for everything that you can do for this same purpose of avoiding division among us." Most of Dr. Spock's letters were relegated for reply to McGeorge Bundy, Walter W. Rostow, and Donald W. Ropa, adepts all at appreciating views, welcoming further comments, assuring respectful consideration, continuing study, careful attention—and at regretting that the President's heavy schedule will not permit a personal discussion.

After that, Dr. Spock took to the streets. At first he hated marching, found it *"excruciatingly* embarrassing, like one of those bad dreams where suddenly you are downtown without any clothes on." It was not his style—at least not in the beginning, but his militancy grew with that of the peace movement around him.

Predictably, anguished cries of "Dr. Spock is being used!" and "Dr. Spock is using SANE!" reverberated through the national leadership of SANE. Founded in the early fifties by Norman Cousins as a politically pure, Communist-free organization, SANE had conducted many a security check within its own membership to purge those suspected of leftist leanings; and now their co-chairman was mixing and marching indiscriminately with anyone and everyone who was against the Vietnam war, be they New Left, Old Left, Quakers, Maoists, whether or not they had a clearance from the House Un-American Activities Committee or from SANE itself.

Because of his detachment from politics during the forties and fifties, Dr. Spock had escaped altogether that curiously unpleasant by-product of the cold war, the who-is-being-used-by-whom syndrome. The conflict that arose in SANE between the anti-Communists and the anti-anti-Communists (all Communists, real or imagined, having long since been eliminated from SANE's membership) seemed to him supremely irrelevant and self-defeating. "I was very strongly in favor of solidarity with all groups who want to end this terrible war, and *especially* the more militant ones, because you can count on them not to get scared out. I said the peace movement must hold together, must stop quibbling about who is eligible to belong to it. But some of these heresy hunters in SANE literally felt we should only consort with people who could be counted on to make a little speech denouncing Ho Chi Minh every time they criticized Lyndon Johnson."

The showdown came when SANE refused to support the Spring Mobilization of April, 1967, on the typically SANE ground that leaders of the march were expected to put all the blame for the war on the United States instead of placing equal responsibility on Hanoi. In the course of the infighting that followed, Dr. Spock resigned as co-chairman of SANE. In the autumn of 1967 he accepted co-chairmanship of the stormy and short-lived National Conference for New Politics, which he found a good deal more compatible.

Paradoxically, the Doctor's particular brand of undistilled old-fashioned New England morality seems to have brought

him into natural alliance with those of the younger generation who passionately reject the accommodations and com-
promises they associate with old-style party politics. "To me,
the impressive thing about kids nowadays is that they don't
worry much about ideology," he said. "They start out from
the premise, 'The world is rotten, the United States is rotten,
we've got to change it over.' Well, perhaps it's not *totally*
rotten, but I agree with them—why put up with *any* degree
of rottenness? They're not impressed with any of the values
they see around them. So they start at a more fundamental
level, they're willing to be a lot more *drastic,* to push much
harder. I think they're the only hope of the world, and
that's why I'm *delighted* to work with them."

Dr. Spock was due to retire from his post as professor of
child development at Western Reserve University in 1968,
when he would be sixty-five. "But I decided to retire in
June, 1967, one year early; I saw a complex year coming
along. I wanted to pursue my two *hobbies,* you might call
them, peace and sailing." His huge frame shook with silent
self-deprecating laughter at the idea of peace being a hobby.
His plan was marvelously, and characteristically, simple: he
would divide his time, spending alternate months sailing
off the Virgin Islands in his thirty-five-foot ketch and stump-
ing the country speaking against the war.

Future historians might find Dr. Spock's engagement book
a valuable guide to that complex year. Wherever the action
was, he was—on campuses, at huge open-air rallies, in audi-
toriums—he crossed the country a dozen times. "I *hate* to
turn down a request, especially from students."

One of his many appointments was with a couple of FBI
agents. "They had telephoned to ask to see me, and of course
I said I'd be *delighted,* that is, I should be very glad to tell
them what I was doing, and why. So we agreed on a time—
I invited them to come here to the apartment on a Friday
morning, December 5.

"But the day before the appointment, I happened to be down at Mayor Lindsay's office on a protest delegation. There had been a demonstration, and police had told the marchers they could go to a certain place; but when the marchers went there, they were arrested and thrown in paddy wagons. This seemed very *unfair*. There were some reporters covering our protest at the Mayor's office, and they said to me, 'Doctor, will you be there tomorrow morning at the Whitehall Street demonstration?' I answered, yes, of course I will—although actually up to that moment I had had no intention of going, because I had scheduled the appointment with the FBI.

"The Whitehall Street demonstration began at 6 a.m., so I asked Jane to telephone to the FBI first thing in the morning to say I was very sorry, I had been unavoidably detained, that I was down at Whitehall Street where I expected to be arrested and was therefore unable to keep our appointment. They said, 'Yes, we know all about that already'!" (More silent laughter.)

After these stops and starts, Dr. Spock and the FBI finally managed to find a mutually convenient time for the interview, which took place three days later on December 8.

"These two middle-aged citizens arrived. I greeted them, asked them to sit down, offered them a desk and writing materials in case they wanted to take notes. After I got them settled, they asked me how I got involved. I told them all about it, how I had supported LBJ in 1964, how LBJ had gone back on his word, how *desperately* important I thought it was to support the young men who are resisting the draft. The younger of the two was at my desk, writing busily. I warmed up to my denunciation of the war, in more detail, and he stopped writing! I said to him quite sternly, '*Put that down, please.*' He cringed!

"At the end of our discussion I told them that one thing that, to me, was horrifying was that FBI agents had gone round to the bus drivers who had contracted to drive demonstrators to Washington for the October demonstration, and had intimidated them, got them to go back on their promise. I said it was *outrageous*, totally *illegal*. The older man said, 'Doctor, if I thought there was any truth in this I'd resign from the FBI today.' "

Any page of Dr. Spock's engagement book, a dizzying hour-by-hour record of his antiwar activities, could have supplied the prosecutors with what they wanted to build their case against him. From the hundreds of entries they chose but two:

> October 2, 1967: 10 a.m., press conference, Beekman Room, Hilton Hotel
> October 16, 1967: To Washington—demonstration at Department of Justice

Together with his sponsorship of a declaration of support to the draft resisters, entitled "A Call to Resist Illegitimate Authority," these turned up in the indictment as Dr. Spock's "overt acts in furtherance of said conspiracy and to effect the objects thereof."

3

Michael Ferber

As we in the Resistance look out on a world that is
really a merry-go-round of blood and misery, a world of
widows and orphans and young men shipped home in
boxes and little children with their chins melted to their
chests, there is one very simple statement that has cogency
and meaning: *All men are brothers*. And the problem
that we have taken on ourselves is the problem of building that brotherhood into a social and political reality.
—David Harris, of the Palo Alto Resistance

Who aided and abetted whom?

Had the government chosen to do so, it could undoubt-
edly have made out a strong case against the draft resisters
for "counseling, aiding, and abetting" the four older defendants. In fact, Michael Ferber is more than a little irked
by the implication in the indictment that "somehow our
movement was spawned by an older generation, by a pediatrician, or a chaplain, or people who deal with youth in a
persuasive manner. Nothing could be further from the truth.
Dr. Spock would be the first to admit that if anyone has been
led astray it has been he, by his admiration for the young
men who have organized themselves into a national movement of noncooperation with the draft."

Ferber, who says he was brought up in the basement of

the Unitarian Church from the age of two, dates his involvement in New Left politics from the summer of 1960, when he was a fifteen-year-old high-school sophomore in Buffalo. "There was a picture on the front page of the morning paper of the San Francisco demonstration against the House Un-American Activities Committee, showing police hosing students down the steps of City Hall," he told me. "I wrote to some Berkeley students for literature, and got in trouble at school for making speeches against HUAC in the classroom." At Swarthmore, where as a scholarship student he majored first in mathematics, then in Greek, he joined one of the early chapters of Students for a Democratic Society in 1963. "Those were the good old days when the SDS was open to new ideas, experimentation, action. Our chapter won the first complete and total victory for the civil-rights movement in Chester, a town nearby. About one hundred of us Swarthmore students and two hundred blacks blockaded the elementary school, where conditions were vile. We shut it down, all the little kids went home. Some of us were arrested and spent the night in prison, but the next day the city government surrendered to all of our demands."

It seemed to Ferber that by 1967 the tone of SDS had changed. (He was now a Ph.D. candidate in the English department at Harvard.) "There were endless long, harsh wrangles over ideology, which led to factionalism and paralysis. The kids seemed to have exchanged one kind of suffocating stereotype—the one they learned from their parents and schools—for another, a sort of phony pseudo-working-class way of dressing and talking. And although SDS was on record as opposing student deferments, most of its members hung on to them." (Ferber himself is curly haired, clean shaven, and neat—he looks something like the Angel Gabriel in modern dress.)

His own decision to join the Resistance came after an unsuccessful application to his local draft board to change his student deferment status to that of conscientious objector. "I met with the five members of the board, and I tried to explain Unitarianism to them, but they couldn't understand the idea of a church without a creed. I tried to define for them the religious dimensions of man that can exist with or without a belief in God—Tillich's definition of religion as one's ultimate commitment or concern. At first I felt I was doing something noble, standing up for something I believed in; but after months of futile effort I realized that even if I won, the battle was far from noble. I got disgusted with the whole procedure, and when I decided to turn in my draft card on October 16, it was partly to regain my own sense of dignity, and independence from the whole rotten, absurd, illogical Selective Service system."

Although the Resistance was only one of the welter of newly spawned antiwar organizations (and a latecomer at that), it seems to have had an electric effect on the older generation. College professors and chaplains found themselves suddenly in the unaccustomed position of being *sought out* by students for advice. "Kids started coming round to discuss things," one told me. "They told their real anguish about the decisions confronting them, their sense of desperation."

The students' rallying cry, "from dissent to resistance," marked a dramatically new stage in the antiwar movement, paralleling, in the civil-rights movement, the transition from a stated policy of nonviolence to direct, forcible action. Their imaginations captured by the new rhetoric, thousands of clergymen, teachers, and other intellectuals were moved to action in support of the resisters. Despairing of the futility of antiwar marches and petitions, they took the long step further and signed "complicity pledges," in which they declared themselves ready to share with the resisters the dangers of prosecution for challenging the law.

Professor Nevitt Sanford of Stanford University put his

finger on the distinguishing characteristic of the Resistance kids in his testimony as a witness for David Harris, former president of the Stanford University student body, on trial for refusing induction: "As young people they haven't yet become committed to positions and roles in society which call for compromising. They are free to maintain their ideals and this may account for the annoying purity of so many of these young people. This may be the reason why the older generation becomes infuriated with the young; they are free to be good and the older ones are not. It is very unnerving for the older people to know they are corrupt and the younger ones are not."

The "annoying purity" is evidenced first of all by the fact that the majority of Resistance men are college students with 2-S deferments, safe for the moment from their draft boards, who have rejected their privileged position and publicly severed all connection with Selective Service, risking a five-year prison term. By the end of 1967 some two thousand had turned in their draft cards (and by the time of the Boston trial, four thousand)—a small number compared with the estimated twenty thousand draft-eligibles who had gone off to Canada, yet somehow far more "infuriating and unnerving" and threatening to the government.

Credit for the rapid growth of the Resistance from a scattering of individual draft refusers into a cohesive movement with its own distinct brand of uncompromising radicalism must go first of all to General Lewis B. Hershey. The Resistance kids say they love General Hershey and will miss him if he is replaced by some future administration, because, as Michael Ferber puts it, "Every time he opens his mouth he gets another couple of hundred draft cards."

Hershey inadvertently handed the Resistance a potent weapon against the draft, and a compelling argument for a policy of total noncooperation, in the shape of his "Memorandum on Channeling." The memorandum, issued by

Selective Service in 1965 as part of an "Orientation Kit," was intended for the eyes of the draft boards alone. But somehow it fell into the hands of Resistance organizers, who seized upon it as a prized captured enemy document and gleefully reprinted it in the hundreds of thousands as their basic recruiting leaflet. (As a result of this unscheduled distribution it was officially withdrawn by Selective Service and replaced by a bowdlerized version.) "It's one of the things that helped us to broaden our sense of what we were about and to define our real target," Ferber says.

"Memorandum on Channeling" reads like one of those clever parodies of government think-tank writing—*Report from Iron Mountain, The McLandress Dimension, The Patch Commission Report*—but it is nonetheless terribly real and dismally revealing.

It sets out with devastating clarity the hidden philosophy behind the draft law and shows point by point how the Selective Service system has been used to manipulate the lives of the entire eighteen- to thirty-six-year-old generation, whether they are subject to the draft or not: "Delivery of manpower for induction, the process of providing a few thousand men with transportation to a reception center, is not much of an administrative or financial challenge," says the memorandum. "It is in dealing with the *other* millions of registrants that the system is heavily occupied, developing more effective human beings in the national interest."

Channeling is defined in the memorandum as "the device of pressurized guidance," its purpose, "to control effectively the service of individuals who are not in the armed forces."

How is the control exercised? By "the club of induction," says the memorandum. In these days of nuclear and rocket warfare, it goes on to explain, the American public is becoming convinced that for "the mentally qualified man there is a special order of patriotism other than service in uniform. . . . It is in this atmosphere that the young man registers at age eighteen and pressure begins to force his choice. . . . The door is open for him as a student to qualify if capable in a skill needed by this nation. He has many choices and he is prodded to make a decision."

Selective Service gives not a hoot whether an individual registrant is a true-blue American patriot anxious to serve his country, or a self-centered type interested only in his own career, for channeling guarantees the same result will be achieved with each.

Having opted for a student deferment, the patriotic youth "can obtain a sense of well being and satisfaction that he is doing as a civilian what will help his country most. This process encourages him to put forth his best effort. . . . In the less patriotic and more selfish individual it engenders a sense of fear, uncertainty and dissatisfaction which motivates him, nevertheless, in the same direction. He complains of the uncertainty which he must endure; he would like to be able to do as he pleases; he would appreciate a certain future with no prospect of military service or civilian contribution, but he complies with the needs of the national health, safety or interest—or he is denied deferment."

The club of induction is poised over his head throughout his college days and beyond: "Throughout his career as a student, the pressure—the threat of loss of deferment—continues. It continues with equal intensity after graduation. His local board requires periodic reports to find out what he is up to. He is impelled to pursue his skill rather than embark upon some less important enterprise and is encouraged to apply his skill in an essential activity in the national interest. The loss of deferred status is the consequence for the individual who has acquired the skill and either does not use it, or uses it in a nonessential activity."

What of the enormous number of men rejected each year as physically unfit to serve and therefore placed beyond the reach of Selective Service? Outright rejection was once a problem because "the earlier this occurs in a young man's life, the sooner the beneficial effects at guidance by persuasion are futile. If he attempts to enlist at seventeen or eighteen and is rejected, then he receives virtually none of the impulsion the System is capable of giving him. If he makes no effort to enlist and as a result is not rejected until delivered for examination by the Selective Service System at about age twenty-three, he has felt some of the pressure but is thereafter a free agent." To prevent this undesirable situation, and to bring the unfit within the Selective Service fold, a new classification, 1-Y, was established: "registrant qualified for military service only in time of war or national emergency." The 1-Y registrant must report regularly to his draft board like everybody else. "That classification reminds the registrant of his ultimate qualification to serve and preserves some of the benefit of what we call channeling."

Summarizing the advantages of channeling, the memorandum says: "From the individual's viewpoint, he is standing in a room which has been made uncomfortably warm. Several doors are open, but they all lead to various forms of recognized, patriotic service to the Nation. Some accept the alternatives gladly—some with reluctance. The consequence is approximately the same."

For those who might feel that channeling is disquietingly close to totalitarian methods of controlling and manipulating the lives of the populace there are words of reassurance: "The psychology of granting wide choice under pressure to take action is the American or indirect way of achieving what is done by direction in foreign countries where choice is not allowed. . . . Selective Service processes do not compel people by edict as in foreign systems to enter pursuits having to do with essentiality and progress. They go because they know that by going they will be deferred."

The combustible mixture that set the young men of the Resistance aflame was compounded of the thoughts of General Hershey, the sickening revelations about the conduct of the Vietnam war—"the gray filth of the terrible news," as one put it—and in many cases their own fresh memories as SNCC volunteers in the South. They see the Resistance as "the nucleus, the germ, of what may in the future become a social movement which will help revitalize the spiritual charnel house that America has become."

Adherents of the Resistance, which did not exist with a capital R until the summer of 1967, conceive of it as a movement rather than an organization, although they sometimes speak of themselves as "non-card-carrying members."

Nobody quite knows exactly where it started. Bruce Nelson, a Resistance organizer in San Francisco, described it to me as a sort of brush-fire phenomenon in which small groups began to form spontaneously in a number of places in the winter of 1966 and spring of 1967. "A student at Cornell tore up his draft card in December, 1966, and with other Cornell students formed the Draft Resistance Union. The following April, more than 150 students burned their cards at a New York City burn-in. Coincidentally a Chicago group called Chicago Area Draft Resisters (CADRE) was organized; at first their orientation was neighborhood counseling, not resistance, but over the summer they turned to Resistance." (Bruce, who was a history instructor before he gave up an Oxford scholarship to work full-time for Resistance, has an excellent head for all these dates.) "In February, 1967, David Harris and three friends met in Berkeley to form the Resistance. Harris was always deeply involved with civil rights and peace, and by his example he was largely influential in starting the whole thing to begin open noncooperation and risk going to prison."

By the summer of 1967 there were Resistance groups, some with their own headquarters, printing presses, and full-time personnel, in a score of university towns across the country. The resisters are very strong for "a sense of community," and in some areas they have established communes where young people live together in an atmosphere of mutual sharing.

While all who are willing to risk severing connection with the draft are welcome, Resistance leaders are developing their own outlook distinct from that of other radical youth organizations. (They avoid the word "leader"; like the early SNCC workers, they are trying to escape from the leader-follower concept. Yet privately they will admit there are some whom the term accurately describes.)

The important currents in Resistance philosophy are described by Bruce Nelson as Gandhian, radical pacifism as a way of life: "Resistance appeals to the guy who has moved beyond liberalism, who can no longer accept liberal definitions of society. Many of us feel that electoral politics are irrelevant." What then lies ahead, and where is Resistance leading? "We're looking for direction toward a more systematic radical analysis of American society. But in the murky and fluid situation in which we find ourselves, blueprints are not helpful. The only way to build the future is to live it." Life style, brotherhood as a social and political reality—these are the concepts that dominate their thinking. Michael Ferber sees refusal to cooperate with Selective Service as only the beginning, "the first large, perhaps existentially crucial act—but only the first act in a whole way of life, in the construction of a whole movement that would be different from the other student and left movements that existed in America a few years ago."

The crucial difference between Resistance and other New Left groups, says Nelson, lies in the matter of "total noncooperation." He does not think much of the Stop the Draft Week activities of October, 1967, in which thousands demonstrated at induction centers and hundreds were arrested and jailed on misdemeanor and felony charges. "It had nothing to do with stopping the draft—it was a one-shot affair. Most of those involved still have their 2-S deferments—in relation to the ongoing work of draft resisting, it was rather inconsequential. In October, people were so caught up in discussion of tactics, the draft as an institution was never in focus. We see the draft as one expression of American militarism.

"The SDS position is that the way to organize resistance is to organize draft counseling, get deferments, keep out of the army and out of jail—which means going underground or going to Canada. The Marxist left say draft resistance is a middle-class kick—the Socialist Workers Party and Young Socialist Alliance say that. They say we should get into the army and organize there. That's the Progressive Labor line, too. The Resistance is more for Gandhian and Quaker types."

Among the tumult of voices that rose in protest against the war throughout 1967, that of the Resistance was often heard from the pulpit.

To Michael Ferber, brought up as a Unitarian (a denomination of which it is said that it addresses its prayers not to a deity but "to whom it may concern"), his church with its heritage of idealistic reform seemed the logical spot for a Resistance draft-card–turn-in ceremony.

The Resistance had set October 16 as the date for a mass surrender of draft cards throughout the country. In Boston, Ferber and his friends obtained permission to hold a "Service of Conscience and Acceptance" at the Arlington Street Church. "I inquired into the past history of that church and found that a draft-card–turn-in was nothing compared to what they used to do," he told me. "In slavery days they used to arm the congregation and conduct raids on the courthouse to free the slaves!"

Ferber described the service as a huge success: "Rev. Jack Mendelsohn, the minister of the church, officiated, and somebody had phoned Coffin, who came up from Yale to preach the sermon. In fact Coffin was a little jealous it was a Unitarian service, not Presbyterian! Although we warned people not to expect the Apocalypse, not to plunge thoughtlessly into this thing just because it looked like the morally right thing to do, more than twice as many as we expected joined the Resistance that evening. There were more than four thousand at the rally on the Common, and about two hundred and fifty guys turned over their draft cards to Coffin and the other ministers. At least fifty men burned their cards from William Ellery Channing's candlestick. It may have offended some Little Old Ladies, but on the whole the congregation was pleased to see their church packed for the first time in their memory."

It was against this background that Michael Ferber committed Overt Act #3 of the indictment: "On October 16, 1967, the defendant MICHAEL FERBER gave a speech entitled 'A Time To Say No.' "* The speech, which was the sole basis of the government's criminal conspiracy case against Ferber, went in part:

"We are gathered in this church today in order to do something very simple: to say No. We have come from many different places and backgrounds and we have many different ideas about ourselves and the world, but we have come here to show that we are united to do one thing: to say No. Each of our acts of returning our draft cards is our personal No; when we put them in a single container or set fire to them from a single candle we express the simple basis of our unity. . . .

"Let us make sure we are ready to work hard and long with each other in the months to come, working to make it difficult and politically dangerous for the government to prosecute us, working to help anyone and everyone to find ways of avoiding the draft, to help disrupt the workings of

* For the full text of Ferber's speech, see the Appendix.

the draft and the armed forces until the war is over. Let us make sure we can form a community. Let us make sure we can let others depend on us.

"If we can say Yes to these things, and to the religious tradition that stands with us today, and to the fact that today marks not the End but a Beginning, and to the long hard dirty job ahead of us—if we can say Yes to all this, then let us come forward together to say No to the United States Government.

"Then let our Yes be the loudest No our government ever heard."

4

Mitchell Goodman

During the trial, the prosecutor described Mitchell Goodman as the "detail man" of the conspiracy. The details of organizing support for draft resisters did indeed occupy most of his waking thoughts during the spring and summer of 1967, and an onerous task he found it to be. Mitchell Goodman is a driven man, a restless, emotional Prometheus forever struggling against the limitations inherent in organizing protest: the slowness of people to react, their unpredictability, their forgetfulness. He must have had an awful time with Norman Mailer, judging by Mailer's account in *Armies of the Night* of Goodman's efforts to get him moving, and he encountered similar difficulties with some of those who eventually wound up as his co-defendants.

He is a novelist and teacher, married since 1947 to the poet Denise Levertov. They date their activities in the peace movement from early 1965, the time of the first major escalation of the Vietnam war. He suffered over the Korean conflict—"I was anguished about it, tossing about at night wondering what to do," he told me, "but in those days Denise and I were completely apolitical, we weren't involved in anything, we were just two young and poor writers struggling to continue writing." Like so many who have remained outside the orbit of political action for all of their adult lives, Mitch and Denise were eventually led into it by the Pied Pipers of the Resistance. As Mitch put it, "The kids invented the Resistance movement, we came along behind."

At first their activities were tentative and sporadic. Goodman, who has a flair for the dramatic and newsworthy, organized a parade of World War II veterans down Fifth Avenue, "a solemn march in which we carried a coffin with a very simple sign on it that just said the number of casualties in the war. It was a very inventive kind of demonstration, it had a tremendous impact on the passers-by who saw it, and it got nationwide TV coverage." (Goodman himself had served as artillery lieutenant in World War II.) The same group gathered up all of their honorable discharges, citations for valor, and other army papers and went to the White House where they held a demonstration of veterans opposed to the war. When the President refused them audience, they took the papers back to New York and burned them in public in Union Square.

Goodman ran across the Resistance for the first time in May, 1967, when he was teaching at Stanford University. "I was deeply impressed by their courage and sincerity— people like David Harris, then president of the student body, who were willing to blithely throw up their safe 2-S deferments and risk prison for the sake of their principles. I decided to make an appeal to the Stanford faculty—I circulated a pledge of mass civil disobedience designed to stop the war. I was amazed when fifty faculty members signed the pledge, including eight full professors in the medical school, members of the campus ministry, and many of Stanford's most distinguished professors in the sciences and humanities. This was the first action of its kind anywhere in the country, it was the germ of the idea of adult support to the draft resisters."

Over the summer the Goodmans, encouraged by the response from the Stanford faculty, started peppering the East Coast intellectual community with mailings. "We sat down in our kitchen in Maine with Henry Braun, a poet and teacher who is a summer neighbor, and drafted 'A Call to Conscientious Resistance to the War.' We decided to stage something big in Washington at the Pentagon, to coincide with the plans we'd heard of from the Resistance for a nationwide draft-card–turn-in on October 16."

But all sorts of things began going wrong. The response to the Call was disappointing because so many people were away on vacation. Furthermore, Goodman learned that he had incurred the displeasure of the National Mobilization people, who already had elaborate plans of their own for a Pentagon demonstration on October 21. "They were very angry and upset, and they sent a representative up to Maine to see us about it. So at that point our plans were very much up in the air."

It was not until mid-September that Goodman learned about a group of adult supporters of the Resistance that included Noam Chomsky, professor of linguistics at MIT, and critic Dwight Macdonald. "Somebody told me they were working on a Call, too, so I went to see Chomsky at MIT. That's where I first saw a copy of the 'Call to Resist Illegitimate Authority,' in his office—I was amazed to see Denise's name and mine on the list of signers, because we'd never even heard of it. I liked the Call, although I thought the statement was an overwritten, overblown business."

Chomsky agreed that some sort of action by the adult group was needed to back up the Resistance plans for October 16—but what form should it take? "He thought the Pentagon idea was no good, especially since it would conflict with the National Mobilization demonstration. He suggested I should go and see Bill Coffin, whom I had never met but whom I knew, of course, by reputation. So I did. I had mailed Coffin a copy of my Call, but he had mislaid it.

We sat in his garden and chatted; suddenly Coffin said, 'Wow! I've got an idea. Suppose we get the draft cards that are turned in from all over the country, take them to the Department of Justice, and turn them over to the Attorney General?' "

And so it was settled. Coffin pointed out that somebody would have to do the work of organizing the project; Mitch agreed to be that man. "I went to New York and got tremendously involved, I worked about fourteen hours a day, seven days a week."

Organizing intellectuals, Mitch soon discovered, was uphill work. There were already half a dozen embryo organizations that had sprung up independently with identical aims: Support in Action, started by writers Grace Paley and Paul Goodman; Conscientious Resistance, those who had responded to Mitch's own Call sent out earlier that summer; Clergy and Laymen Concerned About the War in Vietnam, in which Coffin and Professor Seymour Melman of Columbia University were prime movers; and Resist, the Chomsky-Macdonald group of over-draft-age people, not to be confused with the draft-age Resistance (although Norman Mailer and others perversely insisted on doing so).

There were various Calls and Manifestoes, prized brain-children of literary prima donnas who didn't want a single word changed, that had to be consolidated into one document. At every turn there were obstinate and contrary individualists to be coped with. "Herschel Kaminsky of the National Mobilization was a drag, he didn't want anyone treading on his ground. He was preparing his own press conference at the Hilton Hotel but I finally got him to realize there should be *one* press conference to publicize all the antidraft activities, so that was set for October 2 at the Hilton. We had a meeting after the press conference in the Columbia Faculty Club, to set up a steering committee, but Coffin wouldn't come, nor would Spock. Raskin had been skeptical of the whole thing, he dragged his feet and so did

Arthur Waskow, Raskin's colleague at the Institute for
Policy Studies, although the night after the demonstration
Raskin said to me, 'I was wrong, it was terrific.' "

The difficulties that beset Mitchell Goodman will sound
all too familiar to the old organization hand who has been
through exactly this sort of thing time and again, but as
Goodman himself said, "We were rank amateurs." In their
efforts to bring the Resist message to the attention of the
nation, the rank amateurs may have exceeded their wildest
expectations.

That winter, Denise Levertov published an oddly pro-
phetic article in the *North American Review* in which she
took the media to task for their inadequate coverage of both
the October 2 press conference and the delegation to the
Attorney General's office. The newspapers, she complained,
had left out the names of most of the distinguished participants in the press conference, mentioning only William
Sloane Coffin, Jr., and Mitchell Goodman: "The speakers
whose names were left out were: Noam Chomsky, Dr. Benjamin Spock, Robert Lowell, Ashley Montagu, Paul Goodman, Dwight Macdonald, Mark Raskin, Arthur Waskow."
Moreover, "the delegation to the Attorney General's office
of clergy and professional people to declare their full support of the draft resisters, and to declare their intention
of continuing to counsel, aid and abet these young men, has
received relatively little publicity, but in its implications it
may turn out to be of considerable importance."

She need not have worried. Somebody was watching over
that press conference and taking down all the names, and
somebody decided that the implications of the delegation to
the Attorney General's office were of considerable importance.

Indeed, these two events became the core of the indictment handed down three months later by the federal Grand
Jury.

5

The Rev. William Sloane Coffin, Jr.

Walking through the streets of New Haven with William Sloane Coffin, Jr., is like being in a movie about a small-town folk hero. People come up to shake his hand, students run after him with urgent questions, old folks stop their cars to call out, "Good luck, Bill!" and "Howdy, Reverend!" Norman Mailer describes him as "one of those faces you expect to see on the cover of *Time* or *Fortune*, there as the candidate for Young Executive of the Year." (Actually he *was* chosen by *Life* in 1962 as one of the Hundred Young Men of the Year for his antisegregation efforts in the South.)

I had come to see Mr. Coffin in action at the Yale draft-card–turn-in, part of a nationwide demonstration called by the Resistance for April 3, three days after Lyndon Johnson's resignation speech. It was a kaleidoscopic day. Besides the main event, the law school held a mock Supreme Court session in which the Spock/Coffin case was disposed of (the "justices" regretfully upheld a lower-court conviction), there was a dinner in honor of the resisters who turned in their cards that day, a rally for Senator Eugene McCarthy. Through it, I caught glimpses of Coffin's wife, Eva (one of those faces you expect to see on the cover of Paris *Match* or *Elle*, there as the candidate for Ballet Dancer of the Year), in slimmest blue jeans, dashing about with her camera. She is the daughter of the pianist Artur Rubinstein. (I was told that when she became engaged to Coffin, in 1956, her father said, "I'm not sure I want a Billy Graham in my family," to which Coffin replied, "I'm not sure I want a Liberace in *my* family.") Although Eva Coffin has served time in jail as a civil-rights demonstrator and has participated in international peace meetings, she has preserved an acidulous European *sang-froid* about it all, in bracing contrast to the sometimes oppressive lovingness that characterizes some "movement" participants.

One incident that day afforded a fleeting preview of a dilemma that beset the defendants throughout the trial: the incompatibility of the exigencies of legal defense as seen by their lawyers, and the needs of the political movement as seen by themselves and their supporters.

Professor Abe Goldstein, who teaches criminal procedure at Yale Law School, met me before the demonstration and told me some of his views about defense strategy. He had been in the case from the beginning; Coffin had consulted him when he was first indicted, and they had associated James D. St. Clair, a Boston lawyer, as trial counsel. I asked whether Coffin, scheduled to speak at the draft-card–turn-in, would not in effect be repeating the alleged crime with which he was charged in the indictment. "Not quite," said Professor Goldstein. "In today's speech he will discuss the general political situation, and that's clearly protected by the First Amendment. He will be present at the occasion of the draft-card–turn-in, but the nature of his participation will be different. He won't actually handle the draft cards."

At Beineke Plaza, site of the Yale War Memorial, demon-strators were gathering, students for the most part with a sprinkling of townspeople. To my Berkeley-conditioned eyes, they seemed amazingly neat, nothing much longer than an English haircut, few beards and fewer beads, their attrac-tive young faces lit by the pale May sunshine. One of the monitors was patiently shouting instructions through a bull horn: "New resisters to the right. Old resisters to the left." Mock protest from a new resister at being forced to go to the right, and an answering protest from one of the faculty members: "What are we, the old pretenders?" It was a familiar atmosphere, compounded of surface jollity and an underlying sense of tragedy.

Coffin, last of several speakers, was given a standing ova-tion. "That's right, I guess you all needed a good stretch," he remarked, and then launched into his prepared speech, which (no doubt in deference to his lawyers) was a good deal milder than any of his speeches subsequently offered in evidence at the trial. For the defiant declarations that "I hereby counsel, aid, and abet draft refusal," the ringing demands to be arrested, was substituted: "Once again, I am pleased to be with these young men. I admire them and be-lieve theirs is the true voice of America, the vision that will prevail beyond the distortions of the moment."

Now came the ceremonial march of the young men to the platform, about thirty of them, each with his draft card in his hand. They were introduced by name from the micro-phone, some made brief statements, others simply handed their draft cards to one of the platform speakers. A dozen or more gave theirs to Coffin.

"But Mr. Goldstein said you weren't going to handle the cards," I said to him after the meeting. "Yes, I know Abe thought that, but what could I *do*? I mean these kids came up there to the platform and handed the cards to me—I couldn't very well put my hands behind my back. But I won't tell Abe, it would just upset him." I remarked that it might upset him even more if he learned about it for the first time at the trial from some FBI agent's testimony; a new thought to Coffin, who immediately phoned the Goldstein house and left a message with the maid: "Just tell Mr. Goldstein that I did take some of the draft cards after all."

The Coffins' house in New Haven is something like an English rectory run wild—dining room, sitting room, and kitchen are awash with copies of sermons, notes, speeches, letters, jottings. (Later, in the trial, testimony that a letter from Mitchell Goodman, regarded by the government as a key piece of evidence, was lost for several days amidst this clutter did not surprise me.) In a quiet moment between demonstrations we repaired thither, and talked about the path that had brought him, in these curious times, before the bar of justice as a prisoner accused of plotting against his government.

The accustomed progression that might have taken him from Phillips Exeter Academy through Yale into the family business (W & J Sloane) was interrupted by World War II. He went from Exeter into the paratroopers, where he served as captain until the end of the war. Unlike Dr. Spock, who abstained from politics during the postwar period, Coffin was very much a cold-war man. From 1945 to 1947, he served as liaison officer with the Russian army. "In those two years I watched the Iron Curtain descend," he said. "Stalin made Hitler look like a Boy Scout. I was very strongly anti-Soviet. In that frame of mind I watched the Korean war shape up. But I didn't follow it too closely, or question the causes. When I graduated from Yale in 1949, I was thinking of going into the CIA, but I went into the seminary instead. After a year at the Union Theological Seminary, when war with the Soviet Union seemed to be threatening, I quit to go with the CIA, hoping to be useful in the war effort. I was in the CIA from 1950 to 1953."

I asked him what he thought about the current revelations, in *Ramparts* and elsewhere, about the role of the CIA as subverter of student organizations, labor unions, cultural groups.

"I've a mixed set of feelings—knowing that during the Joe McCarthy period liberals in the CIA won a great victory, they were able to use the non-Communist left to beat the Communist left. The CIA financed the non-Communist left, they gave with minimal strings attached.

"In those days I had no quarrel with American policy— but in retrospect, I wouldn't be so innocent and smirchless. I used to be convinced that NATO was necessary. The question is, to what degree was there a threat of Stalin sending armies across Europe? My basic feeling was that we had a right to defend Europe against the Communist threat.

"But when SEATO adopted the same approach in Asia, I began to see the light. We were supporting counterrevolution in Vietnam, Africa, Latin America, supporting corrupt puppet governments—pouring money into these governments, supposedly to relieve starvation and get the economy on its feet, but the money goes straight down the drain, into the pockets of the Diems and so on."

The route that led Mr. Coffin to his present radical stand was carved out by his juniors, the college students of the early sixties who flocked South in the cause of Negro rights. "That was another big fat injustice that had to be fought," he said. In 1961, after his appointment as chaplain of Yale, he went to Montgomery with the Freedom Riders, was among those arrested and convicted for violating local Jim Crow laws, and was eventually cleared by the U.S. Supreme Court. Since then he had been in Southern jails a number of times —in Baltimore for protesting segregation in an amusement park, in St. Augustine, Florida, for joining another protest sit-in.

As the students moved toward "confrontation," so did

Coffin. He had taken strong issue with those who, like Staughton Lynd, a young history professor at Yale, maintained that the outcome of the 1964 election would make little difference. "But after the election it became clear who was right and who was wrong about that," he said. "I've been proved wrong time and again by people on the left in this way, and I have tended to move in their direction, toward their kind of radicalism."

By 1967, Mr. Coffin was deep in the antidraft activities that led to his indictment, preaching support for the draft resisters all over the East Coast.

Coffin shines as a raconteur. The eleventh, and final, overt act charged in the indictment is that on October 20, 1967, four of the defendants, Coffin, Goodman, Raskin, and Spock, entered the Justice Department with other co-conspirators and there "abandoned a fabricoid briefcase containing approximately one hundred eight-five (185) registration certificates and one hundred seventy-two (172) notices of classification together with other materials."

This event was described to me by many who were there (and we had it over and over again at the trial), but none infused it with the spirit of antic humor achieved by Coffin. He is a gifted mimic—he almost seemed to turn into the various participants as he described them—and he acted out the scene with a rhythm and timing that transformed Overt Act #11 into a kind of ballet of the absurd.

About five hundred Resistance members and supporters were gathered in the sunshine outside the Justice Department to hear brief speeches, turn in draft cards, and collect statements of support. "People say we're a Communist organization, but the fact is we're hopelessly unorganized," said Coffin. "We could use one or two good Communists. First everybody was sent to the wrong church, and then when the meeting finally got going on the steps of the Justice Department there wasn't even any lectern for the speakers, we had to send some students to fetch one."

Coffin's own speech from the Justice Department steps, Overt Act #6 of the indictment, went in part: "We admire the way these young men who could safely have hidden behind exemptions and deferments have elected instead to risk something big for something good. . . .

"We cannot shield them. We can only expose ourselves as they have done. The law of the land is clear. Section 12 of the National Selective Service Act declares that anyone 'who knowingly counsels, aids, or abets another to refuse or evade registration or service in the armed forces . . . shall be liable to imprisonment for not more than five years or a fine of ten thousand dollars or both.'

"We hereby publicly counsel these young men to continue in their refusal to serve in the armed forces as long as the war in Vietnam continues, and we pledge ourselves to aid and abet them in all the ways we can. This means that if they are now arrested for failing to comply with a law that violates their consciences, we too must be arrested, for in the sight of that law we are now as guilty as they."*

After the speeches, eleven selected spokesmen from the group moved forward to enter the huge bronze doors (opened but a crack by apprehensive Justice Department aides), among them, Dr. Spock, Mitchell Goodman, Professor Seymour Melman of Columbia, Professor R. W. B. Lewis of Yale, Marcus Raskin of the Institute for Policy Studies, "who was roped in at the last minute," his colleague Arthur Waskow, fellow of the Institute, and four young resisters, including Dickie Harris, a Negro from the West Coast.

"We were all dressed conservatively, looking very sober and solemn, thoroughly impressed with the seriousness of the occasion, except Harris. There was Harris, he had about three hundred sixty-five buttons pinned all over him, his pants so tight you couldn't get a match inside them, bushy African haircut. He was doing a sort of dance down the cor-

* For the full text of Coffin's speech, see the Appendix.

ridor . . ." (Here Coffin briefly turned into a jiving, derisive Dickie, lithely prancing and snapping his fingers in the air.) "On each side of this long corridor, office doors swung ajar as we passed—we saw the round, scared eyes of secretaries, all looking to see who had the bomb! Well, obviously, Dickie Harris! It was another world from the group outside on the lawn.

"The last door on the left was the conference room where we were to meet the Justice Department representative. It was a very impressive room, with a long, handsome mahogany table at one end; and there was Mr. McDonough, looking extremely tense." (Coffin suddenly became Mr. McDonough, looking extremely tense.) "Very stiffly and formally he asks us to please be seated, and says, 'Now, gentlemen, may I offer you some coffee?' Dickie Harris literally bounds into the air. 'Coffee! *Man!*' he shrieks, clapping his hands. McDonough was trembling so much he could hardly pour."

Coffee having been served all round, Assistant Deputy Attorney General John McDonough took down everybody's name and address, and Mr. Coffin led off with a brief statement for the group, a shorter version of the prepared speech he had given outside, repeating his intention to expose himself to arrest under the "counsel, aid, or abet" provisions of the draft law. Then the others spoke in turn, Dr. Spock expressing his annoyance that they had been received by an underling and not by the Attorney General himself. "Spock said it was insulting to the delegation, but I didn't think much of his point. I don't really believe in standing on one's own importance."

The older speakers were followed by draft-age resisters, each of whom expressed himself with suitable solemnity— and some with a measure of youthful pomposity—until Dickie Harris's turn came.

"He rounded on McDonough. 'Man, you gonna hear me?'

he demanded. 'Yes, I'm listening to you,' said McDonough nervously. 'I didn't say *listen,* man, I said *he-e-e-ar* me!' McDonough was looking most uncomfortable. Then Harris, with measured, contemptuous emphasis: *'Man . . . you . . . don't . . . exist.'* McDonough literally started checking himself out—patting himself up and down—and I thought, Watch out, McDonough! Here comes the West Wind! Harris was superb. Raw, good, strong black scorn."

All members of the delegation now having been heard, Coffin asked McDonough if he had anything to say in reply. "McDonough answered yes, he reached into his coat pocket and drew out a typed statement. Dickie Harris, with a great show of offended incredulity, said: 'Man, you ain't gonna *read* that?' McDonough affirmed that this was indeed his intention. 'Well I ain't gonna *listen.'* And exit Harris, hands on hips, leisurely pirouetting out of the conference room."

Mr. McDonough's prepared statement turned out to be a carefully phrased suggestion of the possibility that the delegation was in violation of the law. When he finished reading, Coffin stood up and moved to hand over the collection of draft cards.

Now, the last act of the ballet: as Coffin leans forward offering the briefcase, McDonough draws back. "He said, 'Am I being *tendered* something?' I answered, 'You are *tenderly* being *tendered* these draft cards and statements of support.' He pulled back again. I said, 'Now, shall we try it once more?' I handed them towards him, and he reared back. We did that once or twice—the group sat stunned. Arthur Waskow, a powerful stocky man with a wonderful rabbinical face, was watching this scene as though it were a Wimbledon tennis match, his head jerking back and forth following the action going on between McDonough and myself. I said, 'Well, suppose we try the table?' and I put the briefcase down in front of him. McDonough started back as though it were hot coals. Waskow stood there full of moral outrage. He said, 'Mr. McDonough, ever since I was a kid I've respected the law. As a representative of the Justice Department you are *required* to accept this evidence. You refuse to accept it? I demand a response!' McDonough was stunned, he was trembling visibly. He said, 'I have no response.' Well, Waskow told him it's now clear who is supporting and who is subverting the law. We said thanks for the coffee, and out we went."

6

Marcus Raskin

Marcus Raskin, intense, alert, and high-strung as a sparrow, was the only one of the five defendants to be acquitted by the jury. Yet history may credit him with having done more than any of the others to break ground for the academic community's rebellion against the Vietnam war. His book, *The Vietnam Reader*, written in collaboration with the French journalist and political scientist Bernard Fall, was the primary source material for the many study groups and teach-ins that sprang up on campuses across the country in 1965, which in turn gave rise to the full-fledged antiwar movement of 1967.

The Vietnam Reader is by no means a revolutionary tract, nor is Raskin a revolutionary man. It is a scholarly compilation of official documents and interpretative comment about the American involvement in Vietnam, and concludes with a proposal by the authors for a diplomatic solution to ending the war.

Although Raskin is only ten years older than Michael Ferber, they seem generations apart, each very much a product of his decade, separated by the great gulf that lies between the conformist college student of the Silent Fifties

and the campus activist of the sixties. At an age when
Michael Ferber was busily corresponding with the Berkeley
anti-HUAC demonstrators and organizing student protests
at his Buffalo high school, Raskin, at the New York High
School of Music and Art, took but a glancing and minimal
interest in politics and world affairs.

The Korean war started about a year before he graduated
from high school. He says that there was almost no talk
about the war among the students, either at high school or
later at the University of Chicago, where he attended college
and law school. "Some of my classmates were vaguely antiwar, but there was a pall on serious political discussions in
those days of the McCarthy repression for fear of some sort
of unnamed reprisal by the authorities. We shared the general liberal assumption that things were not really right in
the land, but our concern about national politics was not
great.

"Although there were 434,000 U.S. troops in Korea, almost as many as we have in Vietnam, there was little con-
sciousness of the war; people simply accepted it. There was
no serious or powerful sense of protest against it."

As an example of the level of college discussions in those
days, Raskin told of a prize competition, run by the University of Chicago faculty, for the best idea for ending the
Korean conflict. "One student proposed that instead of
dropping bombs, we should drop all our dirty laundry on
the Chinese in North Korea. They'd stop fighting at once
and start washing! Of course it was a terrible, sophomoric,
racist joke, but at the time we all thought it seemed very
clever and apt."

After finishing law school, Raskin married Barbara
Bellman, a college friend, and went to Europe for a year.
He returned in 1959, when he was twenty-four, to serve as
legislative assistant to a group of liberal congressmen, and
it is from this time that he dates his interest in politics,

international law, "defining political science as the operations of the state," and "the draft as a basic instrument in
those operations."

He made a comprehensive report on the draft law for his
liberal congressmen as prelude to their attack in Congress
on the automatic four-year extension of the draft. The effort
failed, but Raskin looks back on it as a highly educational
experience. "It was a very interesting moment for me, my
first big advisory political job. The argument we had to beat
was that if we don't have permanent conscription our worldwide commitments will become meaningless. This was my
first attempt to get at the issue. I began to see the draft as a
mechanism to perpetuate a permanent warrior-like men-
tality in this country. The 'channeling' notion has been
with us since World War II, but it flowered during the
Korean war. Channeling has turned America into a national
security state in which young people stay in school not because they are interested in learning, but because they're
subtly directed to serve a 'national interest' which is ex-
trinsic to their *real* and personally felt interests."

In the spring of 1961, on the day of American intervention in Cuba, Raskin joined the White House staff as disarmament adviser to President Kennedy, in which capacity
he drafted the basic legislation on disarmament. His relationship with the Kennedy Administration was short-lived.
Disillusionment with the New Frontier soon set in, partly
because of the Vietnam involvement. Raskin began to study
the Vietnam situation in 1961, long before the nation as
a whole became aware of what was going on there. "My
interest was on a policy level, Vietnam as an example of
the problem of the American national security state—the
consequences could only mean the distortion and debase-
ment of our hopes and plans for a Great Society. Our government was moving more and more in the direction of
Satrapism, the imperialist manipulation of small nations and

of power groups within those nations, the Diems and the Kys.

"A group of us in the Kennedy Administration, Richard Barnett, Arthur Waskow, and I, began seriously to think through the relationship of intellectuals to statecraft. We discussed leaving the government to establish our own institute, to be privately financed with no government strings attached. The Institute for Policy Studies grew out of this, and in the spring of 1963, I said good-bye to the government."

The Institute, of which Raskin and Richard Barnett are co-directors, has a staff of twenty-five which does work on education, foreign policy, economics, political theory. Barnett and Raskin co-authored *After Twenty Years,* a study of the cold war, and Waskow and Raskin collaborated on a book about the madness of nuclear strategy, entitled *Deterrence and Reality.*

The collaboration with Bernard Fall, who was later killed on a patrol in Vietnam, came about as a result of Raskin's growing concern over the emergent war. "In '61 and '62 I began to realize that American involvement in Vietnam would end up causing a great deal of trouble, that it was going to cause hell in American society. Fall's interest was very complex. He was an expert on Vietnam and on guerrilla warfare—a Hemingwayesque character, he viewed himself as beyond politics. But as the war grew uglier, he began to adopt my view of it, which served as the basis for our writing the book together.

"I thought it might be important just to lay out the facts and the policy issues involved," he said. "During that time every protest against the war was met by the government with the stock answer: You don't know anything about the background of the American commitment in Vietnam. And people *didn't* know much about it. Fall and I decided we should present the history of it in a reasonably dispassionate way, and show as best we could why and how America should get out."

The book was rejected by eleven publishers. "They said the war was a transitory episode that would soon be over, that the book would become irrelevant before it could be published." It was eventually published by Random House early in 1965.

The Vietnam Reader had an immediate and powerful impact in university circles. "We got a great number of letters from college students and professors. The book hardened up the lines, started people thinking about fundamental American policy," said Raskin. In the teach-ins and meetings that followed, Raskin debated Abe Fortas and his erstwhile colleague Walt Rostow on America's role in Vietnam. "Rostow attempted to justify the war in the context of the history of imperialism, that it is now America's turn to restore the balance of the world. Fortas said the purpose of the Vietnam intervention was to contain China, and that for this reason the Soviets really wanted us there. I argued that even if this is true it's not our task to do the Soviets' bidding, that the theory of 'great powers' politics is the last refuge of the scoundrel—cynically reducing these matters to abstractions while tens of thousands of Vietnamese were being napalmed."

Raskin credits Bernard Fall with having originally implanted the idea of "A Call to Resist Illegitimate Authority," the document that eventually became Overt Act #1 of the conspiracy indictment. "Fall became more and more committed, by 1966 it was clear where he stood. His greatest anger was directed against the American left, their failure to become aroused over the torture of Vietnamese prisoners of war and the use of napalm. There seemed to be no one to speak out against it, as the French did on Algeria. This turned me on to thinking about something similar to the 'Statement of the 121,' the French intellectuals' manifesto against the Algerian war. Arthur Waskow and myself wrote the 'Call to Resist Illegitimate Authority' in the spring of 1967—there were other drafts around the country, but ours was the final one that incorporated the others; it appeared in *The New York Review of Books* and was circulated throughout the antiwar movement."

The natural habitat of Marcus Raskin would appear to be the world of scholarship and letters. He is not by nature a street demonstrator. Was it not out of character for him to have joined the demonstration outside the Department of Justice on October 20 and to have accompanied the delegation to the Attorney General? And was he, perhaps, responding to the emotionalism of the moment when he turned in his own 4-F draft card that day? "I can't answer that," he said slowly. "Except to say that putting my card in with the others meant I was putting myself in jeopardy."

Part II

1

Games Prosecutors Play

There was much speculation in the antiwar movement about the genesis of the prosecution. Was it ordered, custom-made, by LBJ? Were there high-level, far-into-the-night deliberations involving flags on maps and Gallup polls? On what signal, from what source, do you indict Dr. Spock for conspiracy in an election year? Why and how were these five picked?

The tangled chain of events that led to the indictments originated in the flag-draped office of General Hershey.

On October 26, 1967, in the aftermath of Stop the Draft Week demonstrations, Hershey dashed off a letter to the 4,081 local draft boards recommending that the delinquency provisions of the Selective Service regulations be invoked against antiwar demonstrators. He advised the boards that "misguided registrants" who participate in "illegal demonstrations," who interfere with recruiting or otherwise violate provisions of the Selective Service Act should forthwith be declared delinquent, reclassified 1-A, and subjected to immediate induction. "Deferments are only given when they serve the National interest," he wrote. "It is obvious that any action that violates the Military Selective Service Act or the

Regulations, or the related processes cannot be in the National interest. It follows that those who violate them should be denied deferment in the National interest. It also follows that illegal activity which interferes with recruiting or causes refusal of duty in the military or naval forces could not by any stretch of the imagination be construed as being in support of the National interest." Twisting the knife, Hershey said that the delinquency procedure should be applied to *all* registrants up to thirty-five years of age, and that registrants in class 4-F or 1-Y found to be delinquent should "again be ordered to report for physical examination to ascertain whether they may be acceptable in the light of current circumstances."

The effect of Hershey's letter was to invest the local draft board with the powers of prosecutor, judge, and executioner over the registrants in their jurisdiction. If it decided that a registrant's activities were "illegal" or "not in the national interest," the board could then proceed to mete out swift punishment in the form of immediate induction into the armed forces. Some local boards went to work with a will: they reclassified to 1-A divinity students (who are specifically exempted from the draft by act of Congress), members of Students for a Democratic Society, an organization they deemed to be "not in the national interest," and in one case a totally disabled paraplegic, who appeared in a wheelchair at the Oakland induction center for his physical examination.

This use of the draft as a bludgeon to silence opposition to the war triggered the widest outcry that had yet been heard against Hershey's administration of the Selective Service system.

The letter was angrily denounced by *The New York Times,* the American Association of University Professors, the National Students Association, and Supreme Court Justice Abe Fortas, who said that General Hershey is "a law unto himself and responds only to his own conversation." The ACLU and the National Council of Churches filed suit on behalf of six war protesters who had been reclassified 1-A pursuant to the Hershey letter. Kingman Brewster, Jr., president of Yale University, called it "an absolutely outrageous usurpation of power," and several colleges and universities announced they would ban army recruiters from their campuses until the directive was revoked. General Hershey, now fighting a rear-guard action, said all this was "so much hocus-pocus," and told the *Times:* "The letter is only an opinion, because I don't have any power to direct local boards." He added plaintively, "Under the First Amendment, which they treasure so highly, I have just as much right as they do to state my opinion."

At this point the Justice Department moved in to pour oil on these troubled waters. On December 9, a highly publicized joint statement was released over the signatures of Attorney General Ramsey Clark and General Hershey announcing formation of a special unit in the Criminal Division, under the direction of John Van de Kamp, to speed up investigations and prosecutions of violations of the Selective Service Act and "related statutes" (for which read the Espionage Act of 1917) with special attention to violations of the "counsel, aid, or abet" provisions and the "obstruction of recruiting" provisions.

There is something for everybody in the memorandum. It upholds General Hershey's policy of declaring delinquent, reclassifying and subjecting to immediate induction registrants who fail to have their draft cards in their possession, fail to report for examination, or give false information. It promises to prosecute the reclassified registrant who refuses induction. It calls upon local law-enforcement officials throughout the country to "vigorously prosecute violations of local laws which may occur in demonstrations against the Selective Service System." And in a curiously ambiguous

paragraph it seeks to still the fears of college presidents and
editorial writers: "Lawful protest activities, whether directed to the draft or other national issues, do not subject
registrants to acceleration. . . . The lawful exercise of rights
of free expression and peaceful assembly have incurred and
will incur no penalty or other adverse action. These rights
are guaranteed by the Constitution. They are vital to the
preservation of free institutions, which our men in Vietnam
are fighting to protect."

Two days after this ringing affirmation of First Amendment rights was issued, John Van de Kamp and his colleagues went to work on the Spock case.

Why?

The answer given to me by John Van de Kamp was unexpectedly frank. He said: "The prosecution came about
as a result of our flap with Hershey about his October 26
letter to the draft boards. The prosecution of these five
was thought to be a good way out—it was done to provide a
graceful way out for General Hershey." The reason they
were singled out, said Mr. Van de Kamp, was that because
of "their names and personalities" the government managed
to subpoena a large amount of television newsreel footage
of these five. "We wouldn't have indicted them except for
the fact there was so much evidence available on film. They
made no great secret about what they were doing."

It all seemed so breathtakingly simple and matter-of-fact,
the way Mr. Van de Kamp told it. If one believed him literally, one would have to infer that Dr. Spock and the others
were offered up in unabashed response to political pressures,
as a sacrifice to assuage the feelings of an irascible old man
who had just been publicly rebuked by the Department
of Justice for overstepping his authority and becoming an
embarrassment to the Administration. And backing up General Hershey, that strange permanent fixture in the Washington scene, were his many friends in Congress demanding,

as did Representative Edward Hébert of Louisiana, "Let's forget the First Amendment. When is the Justice Department going to get hep and do something to eliminate this rat-infested area? At least the effort can be made." While appeasing these strident and bothersome voices of the far right, the prosecution would also serve as a pointed warning to the respectable dissenters who were beginning to be seen on television marching for peace, along with the long-hairs—all those suburban housewives pushing prams, those well-groomed executives in their thirties, those haunted, despairing parents of draft-age sons—to stay off the streets, away from meetings, and above all to keep out of range of the TV cameras.

John Van de Kamp, who was formerly U.S. attorney in Los Angeles, did not conform to my preconceived idea of a person engaged in this line of work. I suppose I was expecting a stone-faced, closed-minded bully of the Senator Joseph McCarthy stripe. In fact, he is mild-mannered and outgoing, a good public-relations man, concerned with the "image" of the Justice Department. He must have reached maturity about the time that word was appropriated by press agents to mean not so much a true likeness as a desirable representation. He let slip the fact that he reads *The New York Review of Books* (although later, after listening to the government's evidence in the trial, it occurred to me that this may be in the course of official duty). He told me that he is a bit too old, at thirty-five, to be a Spock-raised baby, and that being single he had never read *Baby and Child Care* before he became involved in the prosecution of Dr. Spock. He read it after the indictment was issued and thought it very good.

"The case came to the attention of the Justice Department when the delegation turned in the draft cards here on October 20," he said. "But the activities of the defendants were known of before; the FBI, as a general security precaution, had kept them under surveillance. October 20 was significant—the plans for that day had been announced before, in press conferences, then they appeared here, and a lot of that was on a film, too. My unit got the evidence together and commenced working on the case on December 11, and I worked all through the Christmas vacation on it."

He went on to explain that "draft activities have changed drastically in the past few months. We didn't have this situation in May, 1967. We're trying to get those who oppose the war to use legal political avenues to express themselves —for instance, they could support McCarthy, or Kennedy.* These five were justifying their activity on the basis they had no other recourse, which isn't so. The case was not brought up to buoy the hopes of servicemen in Vietnam, but to set guidelines for action within a legal framework."

Van de Kamp maintained that the White House had no part in the decision to prosecute the five, and was not even informed of it until the day the indictments were returned. The way he tells it, George Christian, White House press officer, called up the Department of Justice in a routine way that afternoon to inquire if there was "anything new," and was told, "Oh yes! We've just indicted Dr. Spock and four others for conspiracy." (An eminent and knowledgeable federal judge told me later that he thinks Mr. Van de Kamp must be either lying or misinformed about this, and he repeated the rude story about LBJ saying "I don't want nobody on my staff unless I got his pecker in my pocket." In Johnson's administration, said the judge, one would not indict Dr. Spock without first consulting the President.)

Mr. Van de Kamp, for one, does not want the government cast in a repressive image. I asked whether he anticipated a lot of additional prosecutions. "There are lots of cases under

* Pursuant to this philosophy, Van de Kamp ran for Congress in April, 1969, and was soundly beaten by Barry Goldwater, Jr.

investigation," he said, "and we're trying to get the Bureau [Justice Departmentese for the FBI] to get what we need. Counseling on the draft takes several forms. The Quakers are entirely legitimate, they basically provide a counseling service on the draft law. But other counseling services are proliferating, urging that draftees *resist* the law, whereas the Quakers are trying to operate within the *framework* of the law."

Mr. Ben Seaver, a leading Californian Quaker with whom I later discussed this, was most indignant to hear this milquetoast interpretation of their activities. "We have circulated far stronger 'aid and abet' statements than those sponsored by the defendants," he said. "We will support anyone who in conscience refuses to cooperate with Selective Service. But this isn't the first time the government has pushed the Friends aside when it comes to prosecuting, they just don't want to tangle with us."

What of public reaction to the prosecution? "I got a lot of letters from mothers protesting Spock's indictment—hundreds of them wrote. They said, 'How can you do this to this great man who has devoted his life to humanity?' " Van de Kamp's answer to the mothers' question was contained in a form letter that said in part: "It would not be proper for the Department of Justice to comment about a pending case. I can assure you that this Department is dedicated to the protection of the lawful exercise of rights of free expression and peaceable assembly . . ."

I asked about newspaper reaction, and mentioned that I had seen long and thoughtful articles in *Life, Look,* and *The New York Times Magazine* that had seemed to champion the defendants' cause, characterizing them as patriots and men of conscience rather than criminals, but Mr. Van de Kamp dismissed those as "puff pieces for Spock and Coffin." On the whole, he said, the press had welcomed the indictments: "Ninety-five per cent of the editorials say it's about time there was a confrontation. I was pleased, as I was very much concerned that this might be considered a repetition of the Palmer Raids of the 1920's" (in which many thousands were arbitrarily imprisoned or deported because of suspected radical beliefs).

Why were the defendants accused of conspiracy, I asked, instead of simply "counseling, aiding, and abetting"? "For good reasons, but I can't answer that," said Mr. Van de Kamp mysteriously. "It'll come clear to you at the trial."

2

Conspiracy

> It is a serious reflection on America that this worn-out
> piece of tyranny, this drag-net for compassing the im-
> prisonment and death of men whom the ruling class
> does not like, should find a home in our country.
>   —Clarence Darrow

The law of conspiracy is so irrational, its implications
so far removed from ordinary human experience or modes
of thought, that like the Theory of Relativity it escapes just
beyond the boundaries of the mind. One can dimly understand it while an expert is explaining it, but minutes later
it is not easy to tell it back.

This elusive quality of conspiracy as a legal concept con-
tributes to its deadliness as a prosecutor's tool and com-
pounds the difficulties of defending against it. It is hard to
find an antidote for the poison you cannot identify.

The experts themselves have trouble with it. Supreme
Court Justice Robert H. Jackson called conspiracy "that
elastic, sprawling and pervasive offense . . . so vague that it
almost defies definition." A legal text writer puts it less
elegantly: "In the long category of crimes there is none more
difficult to confine within the boundaries of definitive state-

ment than conspiracy." An English author remarks mournfully: "No intelligible definition of 'conspiracy' has yet been established." The lawmakers brazen it out by simply defining the crime in terms of itself. For example, the California Penal Code reads: "Conspiracy defined: If two or more persons conspire to commit any crime . . ."

A conspiracy, then, is a conspiracy.

The origin of the conspiracy doctrine is to be found in the murky past of English medieval history, in a series of statutes dating from the reign of Edward I. Ironically, these early statutes were intended to protect individual rights, specifically, to prevent false and malicious prosecutions. There was a built-in safeguard: people accused of bringing false accusations could be prosecuted for conspiracy only after the person wrongfully accused had been exonerated in a court of law.

Three centuries later, the notorious Court of the Star Chamber stood this idea on its head, where it remains today. In 1611 the Star Chamber declared that the essence of the crime of conspiracy lies in the *agreement*—not in a crime committed, but in the planning of a crime.

Thus conspiracy law relieves the prosecutor of the necessity of proving any actual wrongdoing by the defendant. As Clarence Darrow put it, if a boy steals candy, he has committed a misdemeanor. If two boys plan to steal candy but *don't do it,* they are guilty of conspiracy, a felony.

Because of this extraordinary feature, conspiracy has long been favored by prosecutors as a means to convict union organizers, radicals, political dissenters, opponents of governmental policies, and other troublesome individuals who could not otherwise be put behind bars.

In America, it was first used in 1806 against labor in the famous Philadelphia Cordwainers case, in which the court ruled that a strike (an agreement of journeymen shoemakers to "withhold their labor" from their masters) with the object of securing an increase in wages was a criminal conspiracy. The point is that for one man, or even several, to withhold their labor would not have been a crime. The crime lay in the *agreement* of a group to do so. (When, in 1821, a group of journeymen sought to turn the tables and convict the employers for combining to depress wages, the court held it was not criminal because the employers had combined to resist the oppression of the journeymen! "When the object to be attained is meritorious, combination is not conspiracy," the court explained.) Until concerted labor activities were legalized more than a century later during the New Deal, conspiracy was used again and again as a convenient and effective weapon for the suppression of labor unions.

Conspiracy had a great revival in the days of Senator Joseph McCarthy's ascendancy. In 1948, it was invoked against leaders of the Communist Party, who were charged under the Smith Act with "conspiring to advocate" the overthrow of the U.S. government by force and violence. Here we are two steps away from the crime itself. The defendants were not charged with committing acts of violence (except possibly against the English language, their use of which was called "Aesopian" by the prosecutor), or even advocating force and violence. A mild and peaceful lot, by today's standards, they were convicted, each and all, with monotonous regularity, by jury after jury, of *conspiring* to *advocate* the violent overthrow of the government at some unnamed time in the future. Eventually most of the convictions were reversed by courts of appeal or the U.S. Supreme Court, but the reversals were all based on technicalities; the basic conspiracy doctrine was left undisturbed by the Court's rulings.

The Rosenbergs went to their deaths, and Morton Sobell was sentenced to prison for thirty years, not, as is popularly supposed, for espionage, but for *conspiracy* to commit espionage, the government having no proof that they actually transmitted atomic secrets to the Russians. The record in the Rosenberg-Sobell case has never to this day been reviewed by the U.S. Supreme Court.

To the layman, the principal characteristics of conspiracy law seem wildly implausible, because they run counter to all ordinary definitions and all preconceived notions of how justice and due process are supposed to work.

In the first place, the government maintained that the conspiracy need not be secret, it may be carried out in full and open public view. The *Shorter Oxford Dictionary* defines conspire as "to combine privily," and quotes Lord Clarendon as saying, "In all conspiracies there must be great secrecy." But the law does not take account of the customary meanings of words. Although all of the acts charged against the Boston defendants were carried out in a blaze of publicity (and the government never suggested otherwise), the prosecutor argued and the judge ruled that this was no defense to the conspiracy charge.

The fact that the defendants were largely unacquainted with each other was, I was told, irrelevant. It is not necessary that the accused know each other, or know the names of unindicted members of the conspiracy, nor do they ever have to have corresponded or conferred to formulate their plans.

As Mr. Van de Kamp predicted, the reasons why the government found it highly advantageous to indict the five defendants for conspiracy, rather than for the "substantive acts" of "counseling, aiding, and abetting" the violation of the draft law, did become clear at the trial.

In the trial of a conspiracy case many of the procedural safeguards available to the defendant in an ordinary criminal case are suspended. From Van de Kamp and others, I learned about some of the exceptional rules that apply to conspiracy cases only, which make conspiracy such a handy charge to use in political cases:

Each member of a conspiracy becomes liable for the statements and actions of every other member, whether or not he has ever met the other members, whether or not he is aware of what they said and did. Only Ferber and Coffin were present at the Arlington Street Church ceremony at which draft cards were turned in, but the other three defendants were equally liable for everything that went on even though they were unaware of this rally until they read about it in the indictment.

Anybody who commits an act intentionally to further the objectives of the conspiracy becomes a member of the conspiracy. It is the position of the Department of Justice that this could include, for example, all 28,000 signers of the "Call to Resist Illegitimate Authority," all who voiced support at rallies where the defendants spoke, even newsmen who reported their speeches sympathetically. Furthermore, the hearsay statements of any one of these persons, whether or not he had been indicted as a conspirator, could be used as evidence against all of the others.

Accusations of crime are normally required to be specific as to time and place. In conspiracy cases, however, the prosecution is allowed extraordinary latitude. The sprawling indictment against the five, for example, gives the date of the crime as "From on or about August 1, 1967, and continuously thereafter up to and including the date of the return of this indictment," January 5, 1968. Yet August 1, it turned out, was an arbitrarily selected date, for all of the defendants had been engaged in the very activities for which they were later indicted for months or years before August. Nothing in their lives changed on that magic date. August *happened* to be the month when the "Call to Resist Illegitimate Authority" was first being circulated, and thereafter came the press conferences, rallies, and so on at which some of the defendants *happened* to be together.

Likewise as to place. The indictment, girdling the globe, alleges the crime to have been committed in "the District of

Massachusetts, the Southern District of New York, the District of Columbia *and elsewhere*" (emphasis added). And what of Outer Space?

This leads to another handy conspiracy exception that permits the government to pick the place of the trial. Ordinarily, under the Sixth Amendment, an accused has the right to be tried in the state and district where the crime was committed. But in a conspiracy case the prosecutor can choose the place for the trial from among any of the districts where he has alleged that "overt acts" occurred. The core of the government's case against Dr. Spock and the others was events that took place in New York and Washington: the October 2 press conference, the demonstration at the Department of Justice, the distribution of "A Call to Resist Illegitimate Authority." Yet the government found it expedient (for reasons that also became clear during the trial) to try the case in Boston, site of but one of the overt acts, the service in the Arlington Street Church in which only Coffin and Ferber had taken any part.

The overt acts cited in a conspiracy indictment may be entirely innocent (a telephone call, a chance encounter), and the evidence may be entirely circumstantial. All the government has to prove, as the prosecutor of the five said, is "an understanding, a meeting of the minds, implied or tacit." In the words of Justice Jackson, "a conspiracy often is proved by evidence that is admissible only upon assumption that conspiracy existed." Again, a conspiracy is a conspiracy. Little wonder that Judge Learned Hand called the conspiracy doctrine "the darling of the modern prosecutor's nursery."

Ordinary rules of evidence are changed. In nice, tidy crimes such as murder, or soliciting for immoral purposes, it is incumbent on the prosecutor to prove that the defendant actually did it. Had the government charged the Boston defendants with "counseling, aiding, and abetting" draft refusal, it would have had to produce some evidence that they had succeeded in persuading Selective Service registrants to violate the draft law. Presumably, the prosecution would have had to round up some young men to testify that they were influenced to turn in their draft cards because of something Dr. Spock said on television, or something William Sloane Coffin, Jr., said in a sermon, which would not have been an easy task. In a conspiracy case, the prosecutor has no such burden. It is not necessary for him to prove that the accused accomplished any of the objectives of the alleged agreement, for the crime is the agreement itself, and the case rests entirely on intent.

In this connection, General Hershey himself told me there had not been any increase in the incidence of draft refusal because of Dr. Spock's activities. He said, "None of these people have done more than irritate us in doing what we've got to do. We're dealing with an over-supply. In Oakland, for example, we ended up with everyone inducted—there was not a person who promised to come to Oakland for induction who failed to show up." (General Hershey was referring to demonstrations at the Army Induction Center in Oakland during Stop the Draft Week of October, 1967, in which some five or six thousand participated.) Then, are there no cases, I asked, where the demonstrations prevented anyone from being inducted, or from enlisting? Has anybody been prevented, stopped, or discouraged from going? "No, I don't think so," answered General Hershey. "They stopped them for some *minutes* in Oakland, that was all."

Furthermore, the Boston defendants were accused of *conspiring* to do something that, as a matter of explicit policy, the government does *not* consider an indictable crime. The joint memorandum issued by Hershey and the Justice Department specifies that Selective Service registrants who violate the regulations shall be reclassified 1-A.

I asked General Hershey what happens when draft cards

are turned in. He answered, "There's no disagreement between the Justice Department and us that a boy who turns
in his card can be reclassified rather than prosecuted. We
prefer to get him to perform his obligation. The effort
should be reformative rather than 'get-even.' " Van de Kamp
concurred in this: "The policy is to turn the draft cards over
to local boards, to give the registrants a grace period to re-
consider. If the registrant refuses to report for induction,
then he'll be prosecuted, but the strategy is to wait until
that time."

In the light of all these revelations about the workings
of the conspiracy doctrine as applied to the facts in the Boston case, the editorials which, as Van de Kamp told me,
"welcomed the indictment and said it was about time there
was a confrontation" make interesting reading. It turns out
that the welcome was based on a complete misunderstanding
of the nature of the case against the five.

The New York Times, in an editorial published shortly
after the indictment, baldly *misstates* the charge, saying the
five are accused of "counseling young men to violate the
draft." Nowhere, in seven paragraphs, does the editorial
mention conspiracy. Proceeding from this wrong premise,
the *Times* concludes: "The legal challenge to the draft and
the war which has been posed by the actions of Dr. Spock
and others belongs in the courts where it has been placed
by the Federal indictments. The moral questions raised by
the far-reaching acts of deeply troubled citizens are matters
of concern for every American."

James Reston, writing in the same vein, says, "The
United States Government has now brought the fundamental philosophical issue of the Vietnam war into the courts.
. . . Spock and Coffin, with the help of the Government's
indictment, have raised the basic question: Is the war not
only legally but morally right? Is it an offense to oppose
the war or to support it?"

Clayton Fritchey, in the New York *Post,* hoped that prosecution of these five might "prompt reassessment of the Vietnam war, especially the constitutional and moral aspects of it," in much the same way as prosecutions under the Volstead Act focused attention on the shortcomings of Prohibition. "There are certainly some pertinent questions about the present Selective Service System that could stand review, and it will surely be more helpful to thrash them out in the courts than in the streets. Since both the President and Congress have shied away from a formal declaration of war over Vietnam, it will be interesting to see what the courts may have to say about this as it affects the draft."

All three are dead wrong. The government never intended that there should be a "reassessment of the Vietnam war" or a "legal challenge to the draft and the war"; it took care to avoid bringing "the fundamental philosophical issue of the Vietnam war into the courts"; the indictment is specifically tailored to avoid "the basic question: Is the war not only legally but morally right?"

Had the government charged the defendants with "counseling, aiding, and abetting," there could have been a fighting chance of the confrontation sought by the defendants on the issue of the legality of the war and hence of the draft law. Instead, the government reached for the shabbiest weapon in the prosecutor's arsenal: the conspiracy charge.

How far could the government push its conspiracy theory? I showed John Van de Kamp a copy of *Dr. Spock on Vietnam,* an original paperback published by Dell three months after the indictments were handed down. In the foreword, Dr. Spock discusses "A Call to Resist Illegitimate Authority," which is Overt Act #1 of the indictment: "Older men were invited to sign the statement in order to give the resisters moral and financial support and to share with them the risk of five years in jail. I was one of those who made suggestions for the wording of the statement and was one of the original signers. I believed that draft resistance could become an even more powerful force than political action in compelling the Johnson administration to end its illegal war." And in the last chapter, "What the Citizen Can Do," Dr. Spock suggests that "if first 100,000, then 200,000, then 500,000 young American men refuse to be drafted—or, if they are already in the armed forces, refuse to go to Vietnam —they will make it difficult, if not impossible, for the Government to continue the war."

Now, I asked Mr. Van de Kamp, is that not a repetition of the overt acts charged, and could not Dell Publishers and the booksellers who handle the book be prosecuted as part of the conspiracy? He mulled this over for a while. "It's a question," he said finally—"I imagine Dell, *technically,* could be liable, conceivably they could be prosecuted." "And the booksellers?" "Yes, and the booksellers."

More disturbing glimpses into the vast potential scope of the conspiracy charge were afforded by John Wall, prosecutor of the Boston Five, during the arguments on the motions, a court hearing that preceded the trial.

The indictment charged that the defendants together with "diverse other persons, some known and others unknown to the Grand Jury," had conspired to violate the draft law. In the course of the arguments, defense counsel demanded to know the names of these diverse fellows. Mr. Wall explained for the government: The defense had already seen the faces of the co-conspirators in television newsreel films of various mass meetings, church services, press conferences. These films, which took a total of three hours to run, were in effect a preview of the government's evidence, said Mr. Wall. What more could the defense want? They have seen the co-conspirators in those movies—the participants in the press conference, the rallies, the demonstrations—the government doesn't know the names of all those people!

After court, I asked Mr. Wall about this. Did he mean

that anybody who happened into the range of the camera at these large gatherings is automatically considered to be a co-conspirator? He answered that the law is clear: that anybody who gives *encouragement,* who aids and abets the conspiracy, can be so considered. So, I asked, the man who claps and cheers like mad after Dr. Spock has spoken is a co-conspirator, but the man who sits glum, whose face betrays disapproval of Dr. Spock's remarks, is not? That is substantially correct, answered Mr. Wall.

The same sort of question came up again in these hearings in a slightly different form. This time, the defense lawyers wanted to know the names of the "diverse Selective Service registrants" who, according to the indictment, had been counseled, aided, and abetted by the defendants. Mr. Wall had a ready answer here, too. He referred the defense to the U.S. Census Bureau—because of the enormous amount of publicity given by the media to the statements and activities of Dr. Spock and others, he said, it could be safely inferred that every eligible draftee, every man between the ages of eighteen and thirty-six, had been counseled by the defendants to refuse the draft. John P. MacKenzie of the Washington *Post* followed up on this during the court recess, pretending grave concern for his own safety. He asked Wall: If the media are responsible for spreading the Spock message to the whole draft-age male population, is not a reporter who files a story about a demonstration, a television crew that films it, a news photographer who snaps it, part of the conspiracy? Mr. Wall, now rattled, avoided a direct answer. There is "no intention," he said, of indicting the media men.

Now the contours of a conspiracy to counsel, aid, and abet draft resistance begin to come clear. One can visualize a vast Brueghelesque canvas peopled with those who have in varying degrees aided and abetted the conspiracy. At the center are those who some years ago began to lift the corner of the rug and expose the nature of the war: I. F. Stone pounding out his weekly newsletter, Robert Scheer distributing his pamphlet *How We Got Involved in Vietnam,* professors and clergymen conducting teach-ins, the American Friends Service Committee, the Women's Strike for Peace. Surrounding them are all who have furnished eye-witness information about the American conduct of the war: Mary McCarthy with her account of corruption and cruelty in Saigon; Harrison Salisbury, whose revelations that the Administration was lying when it denied having bombed Hanoi were the first to be widely published in the U.S.; the editors of *Ramparts,* who published color photographs of napalmed babies; the news photographer who snapped the Saigon police chief in the act of murdering a prisoner of war; the TV crews who bring us nightly horror sequences of American planes strafing fleeing civilians; reporters who file accounts of acts of brutality committed by battle-hardened Marines. Nearby the Fulbright Committee is in session. While Walter Lippmann cheers him on, Senator Wayne Morse is on his feet blasting the Tonkin Bay resolution as a deliberate fraud on the Congress and the people. Eugene McCarthy in his courtly fashion is addressing his Children's Crusade. Somewhere up in the right-hand corner *New York Times* editorial writers are at their typewriters questioning the wisdom, morality, and legality of the U.S. involvement in Vietnam.

For surely it is the cumulative effect of these disclosures, and the unprecedented opposition to the war in high places, that first created and then nurtured the will to resist the draft.

3

A Pride of Lawyers

When Bertrand Russell was prosecuted during World War I for writing against the war and in support of draft resisters, George Bernard Shaw urged him to undertake his own defense: "I have an uneasy feeling that you will take legal advice on Wednesday," Shaw wrote, "and go into prison for six months for the sake of allowing your advocate to make a favorable impression on the bench by advancing some ingenious defence, long since worn out in the service of innumerable pickpockets, which they will be able to dismiss (with a compliment to the bar) with owl-like gravity.

"I see nothing for it but to make a scene by refusing indignantly to offer any defence at all of a statement that any man in a free country has the right to make, and declaring that you leave it to the good sense of the bench to save the reputation of the country from the folly of its discredited and panic stricken Government. Or words to that effect. You will gain nothing by being considerate, and (unlike a barrister) lose nothing by remembering that a cat may look at a king, and *a fortiori,* a philosopher at a judge." (Whether Russell took this advice or not is unclear; in any event the next letter in the collection, from Russell to his brother, bears the return address of Brixton Prison.)

This reads like a paradigm of the situation, and the dilemma, that fifty years later confronted the defendants in the Boston case.

The alternatives were these:

They could have pleaded guilty as charged and accepted immediate prison sentences; this was, in fact, the first, instinctive inclination of both Spock and Coffin. There were those in the antiwar movement who urged this course. The orthodox Gandhian civil-disobedients advanced the argument that Dr. Spock behind bars would prove to be an enormous, unbearable embarrassment to the government, and of commensurate value to the cause of peace. Others of more radical bent urged the defendants to refuse to dignify the bourgeois courts by standing trial since they would get no justice there. But the defendants were soon persuaded that the government had effectively deprived them of these options by charging them with "conspiracy" rather than straightforward violation of the draft law. They could not in conscience plead guilty to a crime of which they believed themselves innocent. To do so would be to invite the government to swarm down with similar indictments against dissenters across the country.

Having decided to plead not guilty, the defendants could have followed Shaw's advice and gone to trial without professional counsel. (The dramatic effect could have been dazzling: Spock in the dock quizzing the prosecution witnesses in his firm and fatherly way, Ferber calling all four thousand draft refusers as defense witnesses.) Again, they bowed to arguments against such a course. Since juries in political trials can generally be counted upon to return guilty verdicts, the best hope is for reversal of the conviction by the appellate courts. The chances are not good that a layman, "a philosopher looking at a judge," could sufficiently master the ins and outs of legal procedure, particularly in the swampland of conspiracy, to build an adequate record for appeal. To fail to defend as vigorously as possible, using the best available legal talent, could be construed as capitulation, some argued.

The third course, and the one the defendants chose, was to mount a full-scale legal defense, to employ what the newspapers called "a battery of top-notch lawyers."

Some weeks before the trial I was told "there are about twenty-nine lawyers in this case and they're all at each other's throats." An exaggeration, perhaps. Yet the possibility of a joint defense with a unified approach to the case was soon ruled out by events.

The American Civil Liberties Union was perhaps the only organization in the country that had the necessary resources, experience, and prestige to furnish such a defense and that would also have met with the unqualified approval of all the defendants. But the ACLU could not make up its collective mind, it reversed and re-reversed itself about entering the case, and at least one of its supporters ended up feeding lines to the U.S. prosecutor.*

In spite of the gyrations of the national office, the Civil Liberties Union of Massachusetts (one of the forty-three independent state affiliates of the ACLU, uneuphoniously known as CLUM) offered early on to furnish free legal defense to any of the Boston Five that so desired, and it stood firmly by this decision. Michael Ferber gratefully availed himself of the CLUM offer, and so eventually did Mitchell Goodman. The other defendants went about finding counsel each in his own characteristic way. Except for Raskin, who had been through law school, they were totally unversed in the ways of the courts and legal defense, and found themselves at sea in the matter of choice of counsel. (Real conspirators, such as Mafia types, would of course never be caught at this disadvantage. They are always

* For an account of ACLU's role in the case, see the Appendix.

"flanked by their mouthpieces" from the moment of the indictment.)

For a while lawyers were going in and out of the case as through a revolving door. Marcus Raskin had one set of counsel at the arraignment, another in between, and yet a third lot at the trial. Mitchell Goodman fired the lawyer who represented him at the arraignment and retained a CLUM volunteer. William Sloane Coffin, Jr., consulted his colleague Abe Goldstein of the Yale Law School faculty, who agreed to participate in his defense and line up trial counsel in Boston. Dr. Spock had heard of Leonard Boudin through Boudin's daughter Kathy, a young peace organizer in Cleveland who was a frequent visitor in the Spock home. When the indictment arrived, Boudin was the first name that came into his mind. Michael Ferber, not the sort to waste time worrying about lawyers, left his fate in the hands of CLUM and went about his business of organizing the Resistance.

None of the defendants was previously acquainted with his trial lawyer, and for the most part the lawyers themselves were unacquainted. The legal teams thus assembled were a very mixed bag indeed in terms of their political attitudes, types of legal experience, and hence approaches to courtroom strategy. The lawyers, from right to left:

James D. St. Clair, trial counsel for William Sloane Coffin, Jr., is a senior partner in the eminent Boston law firm of Hale and Dorr, highly rated by judges and fellow attorneys for his skill as a courtroom lawyer. He assisted the late Joseph Welch, also a member of the firm, as counsel for the Army in the Army-McCarthy hearings. St. Clair told me he does not regard himself as a civil-liberties lawyer. I asked him if he had previously been in many trials involving public issues. He answered that he had tried the case of the *Titicut Follies,* a documentary film about the shocking conditions in Massachusetts mental hospitals, and was now appealing an injunction against showing the film. On the other hand, he has been retained as special prosecutor for the Commonwealth of Massachusetts in a court test of the constitutionality of its marijuana laws. He is a professional in every sense of the word. As Coffin put it, "The trouble with St. Clair is that he is all case and no cause."

Professor Abe Goldstein, who sat with St. Clair as Coffin's chief counsel, was a partner in a Washington law firm, Donohue, Kaufmann and Shaw, before joining the Yale faculty. He is an authority on the conspiracy doctrine and has written legal articles on the subject. He told me that although he has "come to a position against the Vietnam war," unlike his client he does not partake of demonstrations and the like—he rather shuddered at the thought. But when Coffin was indicted, he sprang into action, and together with Professor Robert Lifton of the Yale psychology department collected the signatures of six hundred Yale faculty members on a petition of support for Coffin. "To whom was the petition addressed?" I asked. "To the whole world!" answered Abe Goldstein, with an expansive gesture.

Raskin's chief counsel, former Brigadier General Telford Taylor, has had a distinguished career in public law. He was U.S. chief prosecutor in the Nuremberg War Crimes tribunal, represented Harry Bridges in one of his several successful U.S. Supreme Court appeals, and the Mine, Mill and Smelter Workers Union in its successful defense against government charges of conspiracy to violate the Taft-Hartley Act. He is the author of a number of books and articles on political, legal, and military subjects and is currently a law professor at Columbia University. By a coincidence, a month or so before the five were indicted he had debated Leonard Boudin in a symposium at Columbia addressed to the question, "Does the Nuremberg war crimes doctrine apply to U.S. draft resisters and war protesters?" Boudin had argued the affirmative and Taylor the negative position.

Calvin P. Bartlett, retained by Taylor as trial counsel for Raskin, has practiced law in Boston for thirty-five years. His firm, Hill and Barlow, represented Sacco and Vanzetti in their last appeal, but that was a long time ago; Mr. Bartlett told me that he himself has not been much involved in civil-liberties cases. He has been Attorney General Edward Brooke's representative as prosecutor on the Massachusetts Crime Commission.

Edward Barshak, who took over for Mitchell Goodman after the arraignment, is a member of the advisory committee of CLUM—his interest in civil liberties, he says, goes "beyond the point where memory carries me back." He has had a great deal of experience as a trial lawyer, mostly in personal injury cases in which he represents both insurance companies and plaintiffs; he has tried very few criminal cases. He got into the Boston Five case almost by chance, having run into Jerry Berlin, head of CLUM, on a street corner one day and on impulse offered to help if needed.

William Homans, the CLUM volunteer who represents Mike Ferber, comes from an old Boston family with a strong civil-libertarian tradition; his aunt is that wonderful Mrs. Peabody, mother of a former governor of Massachusetts, who got herself arrested in a Southern civil-rights sit-in a few years ago. Homans has been involved in Resistance cases from the beginning. He told me that just before the mass draft-card–turn-in at the Arlington Street Church on October 16, he got a phone call from the minister of the church to ask if he would be willing to represent people who might be arrested as a consequence of their actions that evening. "I said, sure I would. Beginning about 2 a.m. my phone started ringing and never stopped! It turns out that each kid who turned in his card got a mimeographed sheet from the ministers with my name, office address, and home phone number. The police were out in force giving tickets to cars parked round the church, and all these phone calls were about traffic violations. Oh, what a headache," said Mr. Homans, clasping his head at the recollection. "It could be construed by the Bar Association as unethical advertising, but of course the ministers couldn't be expected to know that, they were just trying to help out."

In spite of the rather haphazard fashion in which he went about retaining counsel, Dr. Spock did well for himself.

The only non-Bostonian among the trial lawyers, Leonard Boudin, of the New York law firm of Rabinowitz, Boudin, and Standard, is a sort of Clarence Darrow of the appellate bar, very highly rated by fellow attorneys as an experienced champion of the rights of political dissidents. His thirty-odd years of law practice have included apprenticeship in the office of his famous uncle, the late constitutional lawyer Louis Boudin, counsel for a number of militant trade unions in the CIO organizing days; innumerable battles on behalf of unfortunates dragged before Senator Joseph McCarthy's committee in the late forties and unlamented early fifties; representation of persons subpoenaed by the House Un-American Activities Committee, both at the hearings and in subsequent appeals from convictions for contempt of Congress. As the leading practitioner in the country on passport law, Mr. Boudin won the "right to travel" cases in the U.S. Supreme Court, involving the State Department's refusal to issue passports to those suspected of leftward leanings. He successfully appealed the case of Julian Bond, black legislator deprived of his seat in the Georgia House of Representatives because of his criticism of American policy in Vietnam. Mr. Boudin's law firm represents, among other clients, the Cuban government in all legal disputes between the Cubans and the United States. But with all this, his experience in jury trials is minimal. "How

many jury cases have you tried?" I asked Mr. Boudin. "Well
—possibly half a dozen, before the Spock case," he replied.

In this *galère*, it was clear that nobody was going to surrender an inch of leadership to anyone else—there would
be no chief counsel or top committee to direct courtroom
strategy. Lawyers are by training supremely self-assured,
competitive, individualistic souls, accustomed to running
their own show in their own way and taking advice from
nobody, least of all other lawyers. Differences over tactics
arose at once and waxed and waned throughout the trial.

Leonard Boudin proposed as a minimum step toward
lawyerly cooperation that each client should write out a
statement of facts—details of his own participation in the
overt acts, his recollection of the events—to be made available to all counsel as an aid in preparing the case. St. Clair
refused on behalf of Coffin, and the suggestion was tabled.

There was very brief preliminary consultation among
the five legal teams about peremptory challenges of jurors
but open disagreement amongst them at the time the
challenges were made.

There was no discussion among the lawyers of the content of testimony to be presented through their clients and
other defense witnesses, no consultation about the cross-
examination of prosecution witnesses, or even about cross-
examination by defense counsel of each other's clients.

As of the time the prosecution rested its case, no lawyer
was telling the others whether or not his client would testify in his own defense. According to Mr. Boudin, it is
probable that none of the other lawyers would have permitted their clients to testify had not Dr. Spock insisted
on doing so. "I told them it was inconceivable that my client
could go through this kind of case without testifying, that
he had a larger interest in giving a true picture of what happened. Even though there was a good chance the government didn't have a *prima facie* case, both Spock and I felt
he couldn't *not* take the stand."

As the trial staggered on, and as the lawyers got better acquainted and (albeit grudgingly) more appreciative of each other, hurried consultations did develop among some of them. But Raskin's lawyers spoke only to God, and remained aloof from the others throughout.

Differences of approach to the defense spilled over from the courtroom into the area of lawyer-client relationships. To what degree should the defendants be restrained from persisting in their life of crime (advocating draft resistance, associating with others who did so) at least until after the trial was over?

James St. Clair and Raskin's lawyers thought the defendants should lie low and say nothing about the case and draft resistance. Homans took something of a middle ground: "I advised Ferber that much as I'd like to see him keep silent, I've no right to restrict his freedom of speech, although I'd appreciate it if he would refrain from discussing the facts of *this* particular case," he told me. "I think all the lawyers except Boudin, who's used to this sort of client, would prefer the defendants to remain silent." (Homans looked more than a little apprehensive when I mentioned that I had just seen an article by Ferber in the latest *New York Review of Books,* entitled "On Being Indicted." Such is the cross that lawyers of the likes of Ferber's must bear.) Leonard Boudin made no effort to muzzle Dr. Spock: "As I saw it, that was what the case was all about, his right to speak his mind." Boudin added as an afterthought, "Although I think I will suggest that he refrain from using the word 'we' until after the trial."

Before and during the trial, the exigencies of a conventional defense against the conspiracy charge often seemed on a direct collision course with the needs of the antiwar movement.

There was a move afoot by some of the defendants and their supporters to form a defense committee that would raise funds, disseminate literature about the case, organize protest meetings and picket lines. Boudin supported this idea, but it was vetoed by some of the other counsel on the ground that such a defense committee could be construed as a broader and bigger conspiracy.

As Mitch Goodman tells it, the sense of united purpose among the defendants engendered by the indictments—"the collective sense of the trial"—dissipated soon after the arraignment because of the intervention of some of the lawyers. "The evening of February 5, after the arraignment, Spock, Coffin, Ferber, and myself held a Service of Rededication at the Arlington Street Church, where we re-enacted the conspiracy. Five men, including ministers and a rabbi, conducted the service—they stood in for the conspirators—and received twenty-nine draft cards from young men in the audience.

"But some of the lawyers objected to this sort of thing—the lawyers had a terrible effect on us. They began to separate us. The five of us never even saw each other after that until the pretrial hearings, when we just met in the courtroom. The lawyers prevented us from taking our case to the people, into the streets, holding demonstrations and picket lines, or from any sort of public collaboration with the Resist groups."

The often divergent approaches of the lawyers to defense strategy were indicated in their pretrial briefs, or "motions," submitted to the court months before the trial. While there were many points in common (all attacked the indictment from every conceivable angle, all said the alleged actions of the defendants were protected by the First Amendment), there were revealing differences in emphasis.

Leonard Boudin's brief on behalf of Dr. Spock was accorded the widest newspaper coverage as pinpointing the fundamental issues in the case: Can it be a crime to oppose the war and conscription if the war itself is illegal, if the war violates the U.N. Charter and international law, if crimes against humanity and war crimes are being committed in the course of the war? Moreover, our government agrees that it is bound by the principle it established in the War Crimes Trials at Nuremberg, that individuals are criminally responsible for their participation in war crimes and in the planning and waging of an illegal war. Is it not then manifestly unjust to compel a citizen to choose between violating a federal law and participating in an international crime?

This is the so-called Nuremberg defense, and here was a historic occasion for putting it to a test. Through the testimony of twenty-five experts on the origins and conduct of the Vietnam conflict, Boudin proposed to establish the factual groundwork:

The U.S. presence in Vietnam, far from bringing stability and democracy, has brought political and economic chaos and a deterioration of human values; the present South Vietnamese government is working against, rather than for, freedom and democracy; the U.S. conduct of the war, in violation of international conventions, has been marked by bombings of noncombatants, wanton destruction of civilian dwellings, the use of torture in interrogation of prisoners.

The government in its answering brief contended that "defendants in the present case have no standing to raise the 'legality' of the Vietnam conflict" and that "the doctrines enunciated by the Nuremberg War Crimes Trials . . . do not bear in any way on the criminal conduct with which defendants are charged. The short answer to the attempt to raise a 'Nuremberg defense' in the present proceedings is that a registrant could not be held criminally liable merely for cooperating with the administration of the Universal Military Training and Service Act during the pendency of a war and that he has no legal justification for refusing to do so. One who conspires to counsel, aid, and abet such refusal is in no better position."

Raskin's and Coffin's lawyers submitted briefs asking for severance of their clients' cases—that is, separate trials. Abe Goldstein explained the reasons for this move to me: "There's an inherently prejudicial impact on the jury in a joint conspiracy trial. The defendants *look* like co-conspirators, sitting together in court." The contrary view was held by other defendants and their counsel: in a political case in which such issues as the legality of the war and the right to dissent were being raised, it is desirable for the defendants to take the offensive and to demonstrate maximum unity to the jury by their joint presence. (However, in retrospect, Boudin says, "Had I known how *little* we'd be together I might also have moved for severance. In reality there was so little togetherness, we might as well have each run our own trials.")

One of the wilder flights of legal sophistry was achieved in the (unsuccessful) motion for transfer of Raskin's case to Washington, D.C. The argument is based on "prejudicial newspaper publicity" in the Greater Boston area. To substantiate it, Raskin's lawyers cited a story in the Boston *Globe* which "fixes the five defendants with the sobriquet, 'The Boston Five.'" No matter that this "sobriquet" was adopted early on by the Resist movement and by the defendants themselves; no matter that the Boston *Globe* was consistently well-disposed to the defendants' cause from the beginning and gave their views generous coverage.

The brief goes on to quote some statements of Dr. Spock as reported in the *Globe:* "*We* gave the young men moral and financial support to end this illegal war . . . *we're* not going to anoint ourselves with guilt, *we're* going to plead innocent . . . *we're* trying to save the country . . ." And Coffin: "*We* believe the Selective Service law has to be tested." "In contradistinction [says the brief], Mr. Raskin is quoted in the *Globe* as saying: '*I* don't believe there has been a conspiracy. That's why *I* pleaded innocent' (emphasis supplied)." This was my first introduction to the abstruse subject of Okay and Taboo Words, on which we all became experts during the trial itself.

Part III

1

Going
Through the Motions

My first opportunity to see the lawyers in action came in April, about a month before the trial, when they appeared to present oral arguments on the pretrial motions before Judge Francis J. W. Ford, one of Boston's six federal district judges.

Judge Ford's courtroom on the twelfth floor of the Boston Post Office Building eventually became a home away from home for those of us who attended the trial. It is a small and incommodious place that seems to have been designed with a deliberate eye for maximum airlessness, discomfort, and bad acoustics. The London *Times* described it as "vaguely lavatorial"; yet it is a cut above that with its institution-buff-colored walls, flattened cornices picked out in gilt, and varnished wooden seats. As backdrop to the bench is a map of America with a scroll bearing the names of illustrious jurists of the past, and the legend: "Justice is the Guarantee of Liberty."

Most of the dramatis personae of the case were assembled for the hearings as for a dress rehearsal: judge, counsel, defendants and wives, the press—an unusual turnout for arguments on the motions, for although this initial courtroom encounter is of great importance in the trial drama, it is the lawyers' day alone.

They will be arguing questions of law, and their clients, if present, are there only as bemused spectators. In the parry and thrust of argument, the lawyers, inheritors of the tradition of trial by combat, have their first opportunity to sort out the strengths and weaknesses of opposing counsel, and, in the case of these defense lawyers, of each other. Personal idiosyncrasies are noted. Is the deputy U.S. attorney easily moved to anger? Can this be used to advantage later, before the jury?

Above all the judge is watched for every clue to his personality and his possible biases. Is he neutral? No one is, completely. Whom will he be neutral against? He pulls his ear. Is this a sign of irritation? Sympathetic interest? Boredom?

The Boston court opens in formal fashion, there is little change in procedure from the Crown Court for Massachusetts Bay Colony that sat here two hundred years ago. The clerk raps with his gavel, we all rise and stand at attention. He is followed by the crier, who utters ritual words from far away and long ago, and on this cue Judge Ford shuffles in from right stage.

Judge Ford is eighty-five years old, sometime U.S. attorney in Boston. His tenure in that office is lost in antiquity; even James St. Clair, who has practiced law in Boston for twenty years, does not remember that far back. There has been much speculation among the defendants about the judge. The words "fair-minded," "tough," "alert despite his age" have been hopefully bandied about by knowledgeable Bostonians. It is at once apparent that he runs a very tight ship indeed, a Charles Laughton commanding his *Bounty*.

Before we are well settled in our seats again, he has announced in rapid order the ground rules for this hearing:

The "Nuremberg defense" contentions are "not justiciable." Dr. Spock's motions to challenge the legality of the Vietnam war and to take depositions abroad are denied. The legality of the war and the draft is not a relevant issue in this case and there will be no argument on it by any of the parties. (It is apparently almost unheard of for a judge to refuse to allow counsel to speak on their motions; but Judge Ford has his own way of doing things.)

What had seemed to some the central core of the case has been excised in two brief sentences. Ours not to reason why, at least at this stage, for the judge's word is absolutely final so long as the case is before him. Only after the trial, months or possibly years hence, might this issue be resuscitated in the course of an appeal.

The rest of the first day is anticlimactic. The lawyers behave with the circumspect and wary formality of strange dogs preparing for a fight. Defense counsel rise in turn to hammer away, carve away, chisel away (depending upon individual style) at the indictment, which document is variously described as "seriously vague," "overbroad" (a good Scrabble word), "a remarkable instrument," "fatally imperfect," and "a big, empty, open-ended bag."

A lawyer's motion is quite literally a *move,* as in a chess game. By his motion he seeks to persuade, or "move," the judge to rule on some preliminary matter. This day motions were made by each of the defense lawyers for dismissal of the indictment. The judge was unmoved.

Did they seriously expect the judge to dismiss the indictment, we ask them during the recess. No, of course not. This is all part of the advocate's testing and probing, laying the proper legal basis for a later appeal.

Legal discourse tends to lull the brain, interspersed as it is with strings of case citations and traditional clichés of the profession: "incompetent, irrelevant, and immaterial," "chilling effect on freedom of speech" (which evokes visions of a protest demonstration caught in a snowstorm), "cruel and unusual punishment." In the special language of the law every word must be hedged with all its known synonyms so that the effect is sometimes that of listening to a thesaurus being read out loud: "together and with each other," "rules, regulations, and directions," "neglect, fail, refuse, and evade." Yet in the course of the day the main thrust of defense objections to the indictment becomes clear enough:

The act of surrendering the draft cards at the Department of Justice was a form of symbolic speech, intended as a dramatic act of protest against the war, and is therefore protected by the First Amendment.

The language of the statute, which makes it unlawful to hinder administration of the draft law "by force and violence *or otherwise*," is too vague because how can anyone know what "or otherwise" means? Compounding the vagueness, the indictment charges the defendants with hindering "*by any means* [emphasis added]," with sponsoring "a *nation-wide* program of resistance [emphasis added]" to the draft. Does this mean they are held responsible for whatever is done anywhere in the country, in all fifty states, against the draft?

All of the acts charged took place in public—the widest possible participation and maximum publicity were actively sought by the defendants, who were speaking openly on public issues. Where then is the conspiracy?

The defendants engaged in these acts on the basis of their belief that the Selective Service law is invalid when enforced against those who conscientiously object to the Vietnam war.

Failure to possess a draft card is not a crime, the defense asserts, it is merely a violation of administrative procedures established for the convenience of draft boards.

The Selective Service Act provides for delinquency proceedings against those who fail to register, or who turn in their draft cards—they may be reclassified 1-A, and become subject to immediate induction. Therefore (reasoned Mr. St. Clair), the induction process for those whose draft cards the defendants turned in to the Department of Justice was in fact speeded up—so that the defendants, far from *hindering* the administration of the draft law, *facilitated* it because the violators are immediately identified, reclassified 1-A, and "go to the head of the class." The defendants look askance at this interpretation of their actions.

Arguments follow on the motions for a "bill of particulars" and "discovery," an effort to obtain from the government information about its evidence needed to prepare the defense and avoid unfair surprise. Defense counsel demand to examine the Grand Jury minutes, also any photographs, films, statements by defendants, books, papers, documents that may be offered as evidence. They want the names and addresses of the "diverse other persons" with whom the defendants are accused of conspiring, also the names of the "diverse Selective Service registrants" whom they are accused of counseling.

During these arguments on discovery there was a revelatory moment. At one point, as a routine matter, all defense counsel joined in a motion to require the government to state whether or not it had obtained any evidence against the defendants through wiretapping. The reason for the motion: because wiretapping is illegal, evidence thus obtained is deemed to contaminate the whole prosecution case, for even though the wiretapped conversation may itself be entirely innocuous and have no direct bearing on the case, it may have furnished police or FBI with important leads to other evidence against the accused.

This matter was taken up in chambers, out of the presence of the press. Later, we learned from the lawyers what had happened. The prosecutor admitted that he had indeed obtained a little something along these lines—wiretapped conversation between one of the defendants and a non-defendant—but, said he, it would not be a part of his case since it was irrelevant to the issues. He handed over a sealed affidavit, containing the wiretapped evidence, to the judge, who, after examining it, ruled that it had nothing to do with the conspiracy case. Defense counsel did not press a demand to see the affidavit; they never even learned which of the defendants was involved, or whether more than one had been the subject of governmental eavesdropping.

Why did they not insist that the government divulge the content of the wiretapped conversation so that they could determine for themselves how it might affect their clients' case, and whether it could be used as a point on appeal in case of a conviction? Presumably, because they feared the consequence of a public disclosure that one or more of the defendants was on telephoning terms with politically suspect characters subject to having their phones tapped.

The incident does point up the persistence of habits of thought that stem directly from the era of the McCarthy prosecutions: an inhibiting fear, to which even lawyers of the stature of these are not immune, of being sucked into guilt by association. Months after the trial, at least one defense lawyer had second thoughts about the wisdom of this exercise in lawyerly caution. Leonard Boudin told me, "We may have moved too quickly into an aura of respectability. I wouldn't do it again; I think we were wrong to have conceded that point."

In response to defense discovery motions, government acceded to an advance showing of their three-hour-long movie—television newsreel films of the New York press conference, the Arlington Street Church meeting, the demonstration outside the Department of Justice—and court is adjourned while they do so. To the annoyance of the press, only defendants and counsel are admitted to the private showing. John P. MacKenzie of the Washington *Post* makes a fuss about this, he storms up to the clerk of the court protesting that freedom of the press is being abridged. "Tell it to the judge." So he does; and soon returns, considerably subdued. "What did the judge say?" "He said, 'No.' "

Assistant U.S. Attorney John Wall rises to argue for the prosecution. The right of free speech is not absolute (predictably, Mr. Wall here recalls the man falsely shouting "Fire!" in a crowded theater). No court has ever held that counseling others to commit a crime is protected by the First Amendment—does the defense suggest that counseling somebody to commit murder is so protected? (Mr. Coffin, puzzled, whispers to his neighbor, "But we were counseling people *not* to commit murder.")

It has been suggested, says Mr. Wall, that the defendants had no recourse other than the one they chose to express their opposition to the war. Not true! They could have run for office on an antiwar platform or supported a peace candidate. The defendants knew the law, knew what they were *not* supposed to do, but they went ahead and did it deliberately. Their belief that the law is unjust is no excuse. Defense counsel maintain that the defendants' actions were only a form of "symbolic speech" protected by the First Amendment. On the contrary, the indictment charges them with counseling others to break the law.

And so it goes for two days, by the end of which the judge has denied most of the defense motions. We go our separate ways to wait for the beginning of the trial.

2

The Case for
the Prosecution

1.

Long before court time on the first day of the trial, a large crowd of three easily distinguishable groups began to assemble in the corridors: supporters of the defendants, that familiar mélange of carefully dressed older liberals ("always wear your best clothes to the picket line") together with students and maybe students in all manner of dress and length of hair, wearing a dazzling assortment of peace buttons in which the omega, symbol of the New England Resistance, predominated; the press, marked by a slight aloofness from the others; and the prospective jurors, already a race apart, well brushed, apprehensive, bewildered, summonses in hand. Inside the courtroom, men were setting up equipment, and we got glimpses of a movie projector, screen, and masking tape being applied to windows. A Justice Department official staggered by, loaded down with reels of film. "Is that the *corpus delicti?*" said a newsman, and Daniel Lang, there to do a piece for *The New Yorker,* remarked: "Say, I didn't know the *movie* rights had been sold already!"

The prevailing atmosphere was that of pleasurable anticipation of some sort of entertainment, particularly after the defendants and their families began to arrive and there were introductions and bows all round: smiling, courtly Dr. Spock with pretty Jane; Mike Ferber, his arm round his girl friend's waist; magnificent Mrs. Sloane Coffin, Sr., who may not have been best pleased when her son was indicted as a felon but who turned out to be the most steadfast and supportive trial fan of them all; the Goodmans with their handsome draft-aged son in tow; the Raskins surrounded by well-wishers from the intellectual community—all seemed relieved that after the long months of waiting the trial was at last to begin, and they radiated confidence in the justness of their cause.

Before the trial proper got under way, there was an important preliminary skirmish. Leonard Boudin had spotted the fact that there were hardly any women amongst the potential jurors—the hand that rocks the cradle and turns the pages of *Baby and Child Care* was notably absent. He rose to challenge the whole array on the ground that it was not representative of the community, and in doing so immediately fell afoul of Judge Ford.

Boudin explained that defense counsel had only just seen the list of the venire shortly before court opened, that his concern arose from the fact that of eighty-eight names there were only five women—but the judge interrupted: "My understanding is that women don't have to serve unless they wish. No further colloquy from you, please." (It turned out the judge was wrong about this, he was confusing Massachusetts state courts, where women are not obliged to serve, with federal courts, in which there is no such rule.) Boudin stood his ground, announced that he intended to challenge the venire and wished to question Russell Peck, chief clerk of the court charged with assembling the jury, about his methods of selection.

This was finally allowed. Russell Peck proved to be a surprisingly urbane witness. He was formerly assistant dean of Harvard Law School, and, in keeping with a certain academic tradition, rides a bicycle to work. He testified that he sent out summonses to appear for jury duty to names on the "police list," which is a street list of residents something like a city directory.

His intention, Mr. Peck said in response to questioning, was to send the notices to men and women alike. But as a practical matter, Boudin pointed out, the statistics indicated that notices were sent to many fewer women than men. "It makes me look like a misogynist," answered Peck unhappily (whispered conferences among the local evening-paper reporters: "What was that?" "How do you spell it?").

Boudin produced one of the police lists and asked Mr. Peck to show just how he chose the names to which notices were to be sent. Did he use some mathematical way of getting a random selection, taking every third, fourth, or ninth name? No, he just looked up in the air and put his finger down on the list—wherever his finger landed, he put a mark next to the name and that was the name to receive the notice. "Is there a reason why you don't use the method of taking every third, fourth, or ninth name instead of sort of looking in the air and putting your finger on the book?" asked Boudin. "I would suppose there isn't enough time and help to make the mathematical computations necessary . . ."

A Harvard math major in the audience is frowning in deep concentration over a notebook, busily filling its pages with spidery hieroglyphics, figures, and symbols. He comes up with the answer and passes it to the press: had the selection been truly random, the probability of this proportion of women to men in the array would be about one in a trillion, which he writes out as a decimal point followed by twelve zeros.

Mr. St. Clair got closest to the knuckle. He elicited that women who show up for jury duty, particularly housewives, are more likely to be excused than men, and this makes for more paperwork. Mr. Peck has said he is short-handed; is it possible that if he sees the word "housewife" next to a name, he slides his finger down a notch to the next male name? "It could happen." "In the drawing of the array for this case, *did* it happen?" "I couldn't tell . . . it's possible." "Is it *probable?*" But the judge won't have it. "You don't have to answer that question. Strike it out." Boudin's motion is disposed of in short order (denied), and the process of picking the jury goes forward.

Defense lawyers were by no means displeased with the outcome because the clear-cut discrimination against women could make an excellent point on appeal. At least one client, Mr. Coffin, saw it differently. "To think we should go through all this effort to challenge the entire framework of our country's foreign policy—and may win our case because an overqualified man, bored with his job, took a few short cuts in selecting the jury!"

The clerk twirls a wheel, twelve names are drawn, twelve men file into the jury box. Defense counsel, informed by Judge Ford that they would not be permitted to interrogate prospective jurors, had submitted a list of proposed questions designed to reveal probable prejudice against the accused. These are ignored by Judge Ford, who merely asks of each juror called whether he knows any of the counsel in the case or has done business with them, whether there is any reason he cannot render a fair verdict in this case, whether he has formed any opinion as to the guilt or innocence of the accused. No, no, no, they answer. "This juror stands indifferent," the judge announces, and then come the peremptory challenges. These are assigned, fifteen to the defendants and ten to the government, to permit counsel to reject jurors without having to give any reason.

The defense is here at a disadvantage; they know nothing

whatsoever about the potential jurors except their names and occupations, whereas the prosecution, as I later learned from John Wall, had availed itself of the facilities of the FBI to learn what it could. Two women find their way into the jury box (for the wheel of fortune is more impartial in this regard than Mr. Peck's trick finger) and one Negro; they are at once bounced by the government. It is hard to discern any real pattern in the challenges on the defense side and indeed there is open disagreement among the five legal teams over several jurors. The government is more predictable. A young man carrying a book is excused, and another, wearing side-burns and carrying an extraordinary psychedelic umbrella, has barely warmed his seat before he is off and out. ("I wanted to shout 'Drop the umbrella, kid!' " says Mr. Coffin.) Those who are challenged stalk off with half-sheepish, half-angry expressions; during the recess one of the women excused by the government complains bitterly to the press. "I'd have voted for the prosecution anyway!" she says.

By the day's end, the all-white, all-male jury and three alternates are seated. Before adjournment, the judge announces to the jurors that they will be sequestered until the end of the trial in the custody of U.S. marshals, who will find places for them to stay, care for their every need, and provide "suitable entertainment"! Some of the defense lawyers object to this, but the judge overrules them. The marshals, suddenly transformed into nightmare Cook's tour leaders, herd their charges out to waiting cars in which they will proceed to the jurors' homes to fetch toothbrushes and pajamas.

2.

Nature copying art as it does, the older lawyers turn into Daumier or Spy cartoons before one's very eyes. They are ordinary human beings in the corridors, but up there at counsel table, or prancing toward the bench, every pout, smile, frown, or gesture takes on the slightly distorted dimension of caricature. Leonard Boudin, unruly wisps of silver hair atop a twinkling face, bobs about the courtroom in an elegant sort of waltz step like an untidy Christmas-tree ornament loose from its mooring. He seems to have about four pairs of spectacles, which he keeps changing like a conjurer with rabbits in a hat. Iron-gray James St. Clair, severely formal in real life, has a seraphic courtroom smile, which he alternates with a brooding stare through his mod half-glasses (another stage prop?). Calvin P. Bartlett, slow and funereal in his demeanor, does the most extraordinary things with his mouth, pursing it up like a goldfish about to snap at a morsel of food. William Homans ambles about like a kindly bear, a large rugged man, shock of black hair, New England granite face. Edward Barshak is the only straight-man in this cast, trim, soft-spoken, matter-of-fact in appearance and style.

Judge Ford, in flapping robes, his face grown large and spready with the years, uses his castered swivel chair to propel himself from side to side of the bench—a very old, very cross toddler maneuvering about in his stroller. John Wall, at thirty-seven easily the youngest lawyer in the case, has not quite got there yet. But one can already see traces of the cartoon-Wall-to-be, given a few more years: retroussé nose, pale belligerent eyes under which bags are just beginning to form, a soft, embryonic jowl.

The first several trial days are all his, for it is customary in the Boston federal courts for the government to present its entire case, give its opening statement and put on all its witnesses, before the defense lawyers address the jury.

Just before Mr. Wall starts, the judge calls a brief bench conference. Later, we get the sad news that the wife of one of the jurors had run off with another man the minute she heard they were to be sequestered! ("I can see her, rushing to the dictionary to look up 'sequester,' " said the Old Trial Hand.) The juror is excused to go home to look after his children and is replaced by Alternate Number One.

Mr. Wall first reads through the indictment, then pauses to explain: "You see, members of the jury, that the indictment charges essentially four things: a) charges the defendants with counseling, aiding, and abetting Selective Service registrants to refuse and evade service in the armed forces, and all other duties required of registrants; b) charges them again with counseling, aiding, and abetting . . ."

His colleague moves warily forward to pull his coat as a forest of defense lawyers rise to object. What has gone wrong, we all wonder? Oops! Mr. Wall has forgotten to say the Magic Word "conspiring," but this is soon corrected; and Judge Ford explains: "Members of the jury, a conspiracy may be defined as a breathing together, a plan, an agreeing together." (The whole courtroom visibly holds its breath at this definition.)

That being settled, Mr. Wall proceeds to outline the government's case in minutest detail. It takes several hours. At times it is very difficult to keep in mind that what he is describing is criminal activity.

The prosecutor's opening statement to the jury in a criminal case customarily consists of a narrative outline of the evidence he intends to introduce, so that as each witness appears the jury will readily recognize how his testimony fits in as a link in the chain of evidence against the accused: ". . . the evidence will show that on the afternoon of December 12 the defendant purchased a .45 Colt automatic at the Friendly Gun and Sporting Goods Store . . . Mr. F. Friendly, proprietor, will testify that the defendant entered his store that day and he will produce a sales record as evidence of the transaction, $42.50 plus sales tax . . . police officers called to the scene will testify that the small enclosed kitchen where the victim met her death measures approximately eight feet

ten inches by twelve feet one inch . . . testimony of two fire-
arms experts will establish that markings on the fatal bullet
are consistent with the gun being fired point-blank at close
range . . ." and so on.

Mr. Wall conscientiously follows this general pattern, with
disconcerting effect. As his case turns entirely on the spoken
and written word, he devotes most of his opening to reading
the speeches and publications of the defendants. The first
witness, Mr. Wall tells us, will be a special agent from the
Federal Bureau of Investigation who will testify that he attended a press conference at the New York Hilton Hotel on
October 2, 1967; this press conference is Overt Act #2 of the
indictment. ("An FBI agent at a *press conference?*" whispers
my seatmate. "That seems a bit wasteful of taxpayers'
money.")

Mr. Wall presses on to describe the scene of the crime:
"The evidence will show that the physical layout of the
room was about seventy feet by fifty feet; that there was one
entrance that was being used at the time; and that adjacent
to that entrance in full view was a table; that within the
room, at one end of the room was a speakers' platform or a
raised table or raised tables, and in the center of those tables
was a podium or rostrum; that facing the head table, raised
table, were a number of chairs and that occupying those
chairs were, for the most part, newspaper reporters, cameramen, sound men, the evidence will indicate about forty in
number."

Mr. Wall's accent is Bostonian, but his delivery is that of
a BBC announcer reading the news, giving each item the
same ponderously enunciated dramatic emphasis with no
change of pace— (". . . headless corpse found today in the
Left Luggage at Paddington Station, showers, with bright
intervals, throughout Britain . . .")—so that he has us all
agog with the one entrance, the raised table or tables, the
podium or rostrum. What can he be leading up to? The

denouement is a letdown, for who else would one expect to be occupying chairs at a press conference but reporters and cameramen?

Among the speakers at the press conference (Mr. Wall continues) were four of the defendants: William Sloane Coffin, Jr., Dr. Spock, Mitchell Goodman, and Marcus Raskin. "Also Paul Goodman, identified as a writer. Paul Goodman is not a defendant in this case. Also introduced was Noam Chomsky, a professor of linguistics at the Massachusetts Institute of Technology. He is not here today, to my knowledge."

Leonard Boudin rises to say that Noam Chomsky is in fact here in the courtroom, to which Wall rejoins: "At least, he is not sitting here at the bar as a defendant" (impressive pause) "*today!*" A subdued murmur of indignation runs through the spectators—"Ohrrrn," like the sound a French movie audience makes when the film breaks down, and a giggle or two is heard from the section where Chomsky is sitting. Boudin is up again: "May I ask the Court for a ruling on that last remark?" Judge Ford: "No further colloquy, please. Go forward."

"The evidence will show that Agent Miller when he entered the room was not challenged in any way and of course the evidence will show he did not volunteer that he was an FBI agent," continues Mr. Wall. Agent Miller, it appears, gathered up mimeographed hand-outs at the press conference, pamphlets, statements by Mitchell Goodman and others. Mr. Wall now proceeds to read some of them out, first a speech by Coffin, then an appeal letter for support and funds signed by Chomsky, Coffin, Spock, and Dwight Macdonald. "Below the signatures are perforated lines, and below that it reads as follows: 'Clip and send to Resist, Room 510, 166 Fifth Avenue, New York, New York, and the zip.'" ("But what *is* the zip? Haven't we a right to know? What's he trying to conceal?" hisses restless Dan Lang.) "And underneath that, preceded by four dots: 'I wish to sign "A Call to Resist Illegitimate Authority." ' And the next line, which is preceded by four dots, says, 'I enclose a contribution.' And then there are four more dots, and it reads, 'I am interested in joining a group in my community.' " The perforated lines and dots begin to sound like a sinister code—the Triangle System used in the Battle of Algiers?

Mr. Wall now reads out loud the "Call to Resist Illegitimate Authority," Overt Act #1 of the indictment. It is a long, well-reasoned manifesto, and he reads it in tones tremulous with some unfathomable emotion—indignation, perhaps? That is, indignation at the lawlessness, the temerity of the authors? Yet the authors' own indignation comes through in a curiously vivid kind of way, like those TV programs of artworks in which the original colors are glaringly heightened by the reproduction process:*

" 'To the young men of America, to the whole of the American people and to all men of good will everywhere:

" '1. An evergrowing number of young American men are finding that the American war in Vietnam so outrages their deepest moral and religious sense that they cannot contribute to it in any way. We share their moral outrage.

" '2. We further believe that the war is unconstitutional and illegal. Congress has not declared a war as required by the Constitution. Moreover, under the Constitution, treaties signed by the President and ratified by the Senate have the same force as the Constitution itself. . . .

" '3. Moreover, this war violates international agreements, treaties and principles of law which the United States Government has solemnly endorsed. The combat role of the United States troops in Vietnam violates the Geneva Accords of 1954 which our government pledged to support but has since subverted. The destruction of rice, crops and livestock;

---

* For the full text of "A Call to Resist Illegitimate Authority," see the Appendix.

the burning and bulldozing of entire villages consisting exclusively of civilian structures; the interning of civilian non-
combatants in concentration camps; the summary executions
of civilians in captured villages who could not produce
satisfactory evidence of their loyalties or did not wish to be
removed to concentration camps; the slaughter of peasants
who dared to stand up in their fields and shake their fists
at American helicopters—these are all actions of the kind
which the United States and the other victorious powers of
World War II declared to be crimes against humanity for
which individuals were to be held personally responsible
even when acting under the orders of their governments and
for which Germans were sentenced at Nuremberg to long
prison terms and death. . . .' "

The "Call" goes on to say that "every free man has a legal
right and a moral duty to exert every effort to end this war,"
and enumerates some of the forms of resistance against illegitimate authority by young men in the armed forces and those
threatened with the draft. "Many of us believe that open
resistance to the war and the draft is the course of action
most likely to strengthen the moral resolve with which all of
us can oppose the war and most likely to bring an end to
the war. . . . We call upon all men of good will to join us
in this confrontation with immoral authority. Especially we
call upon the universities to fulfill their mission of enlightenment and religious organizations to honor their heritage of
brotherhood. Now is the time to resist." Mr. Wall ends with
a flourish. " 'For further information contact Resist, 166
Fifth Avenue, New York City,' and the zip code."

During the recess we reporters wonder *why* Mr. Wall is
reading all this stirring stuff to the jury. "You'd think it
would make the *jurors* want to sign the 'Call to Resist.' "
"Perhaps that's why he wouldn't tell the zip code?" "And
the exact dimensions of that room where they had the press
conference—what was that all about?" "That's just because

he's a prosecutor, doing his thing. He didn't think it would be right just to say they had a press conference in the Beekman Room."

There are more documents: a long one by Mitchell Goodman, calling for adult support for the young draft resisters and outlining plans for forthcoming activities: on October 16, "hundreds, perhaps thousands, of young men will meet in cities all over the U.S. to return their draft cards and refuse all further cooperation with the war policy" . . . during the same week there will be acts of civil disobedience at induction centers, including an attempt to interrupt the functioning of the Oakland Induction Center . . . on October 20, a demonstration outside the Justice Department, culminating in the presentation of turned-in draft cards to the Attorney General. " 'We will, in a clear, simple ceremony make concrete our affirmation of support for these young men who are the spearhead of direct resistance to the war and all its machinery,' " intones Wall/Goodman. " 'The draft law commands that we shall not aid, abet, or counsel men to refuse the draft. But as a group of the clergy have recently said, when young men refuse to allow their conscience to be violated by an unjust law and a criminal war, then it is necessary for their elders—their teachers, ministers, friends —to make clear their commitment, in conscience, to aid, abet, and counsel them against conscription. Most of us have already done this privately. Now publicly we will demonstrate, side by side with these young men, our determination to continue to do so . . .' "

Now Mr. Wall moves on to Overt Acts #3 through 5, the Arlington Street Church rally at which Michael Ferber, Mr. Coffin, and a number of other ministers made speeches and at which Coffin and others accepted draft cards. Wall/Coffin preaches the sermon to the jury: " 'I am afraid that the government is afraid of a moral confrontation of those who today and this week are determined to counsel, aid, and abet those of you who are in the Resistance. The government will back off, I am afraid, from this small confrontation and thereby prove its own convictions that it hasn't enough morality on its own side to carry through and win such a confrontation. Well, if that is the case, then let the last word go to those of you who are engaging today in a solemn act of civil disobedience, which for some of you reflects religious obedience.' "

The evidence will further show, says Mr. Wall, that Mitchell Goodman and his wife, Denise Levertov, sent a registered letter to the Attorney General saying there would be a large meeting outside the Justice Department on October 20, and asking for an appointment on that day for a delegation to present the draft cards. And an FBI handwriting expert will attest that those are indeed their signatures on the letter! Mr. Wall reads aloud this letter.

The Goodman letter is precursor to the government's *pièce de résistance*, Overt Acts #6 through 11, the confrontation at the Justice Department on the afternoon of October 20. Mr. Wall outlines for the jury what took place there.

First there were speeches outside the building by the defendant Coffin and others. Then a number of young men from various Resistance groups throughout the country (Michael Ferber among them) came up to the microphone and deposited into a pouch "objects which they identified as draft cards and other documents." A group of eleven (including all the defendants but Ferber) entered the Department of Justice and met in the Andretta Room with Assistant Deputy Attorney General John McDonough, with whom they conferred for about an hour. They offered him the briefcase containing "among other things charred remains of what were purported to be burned draft cards," various mimeographed copies of draft cards, and "a large number of valid Selective Service notices of classification"— McDonough refused to accept the briefcase so they left it on the table. When they emerged, Mr. Coffin reported on the conference to the demonstrators outside and John Wall reads out what he said:

" '. . . Let me simply sum up my own deep feeling, one which I have had now for some time. We've come here today in as dignified and as solemn a manner as possible for a moral, legal confrontation with the proper agency of our government. If this government cannot accept this type of confrontation, then it surely says something about its own convictions that it does not have enough morality on its side to carry through with such a moral confrontation. Furthermore, I want to say very clearly that in my own mind, at least, if the government refuses to confront us in a solemn, dignified, nonviolent fashion, then it must bear the onus for some of the less nonviolent, the less dignified, the less respectable demonstrations which may now begin to occur throughout the country . . .' "

There is more, and it begins to sound like one of those Calendars of Coming Events sent around in the peace movement: "Don't miss these important dates! Your chance to meet and hear . . ." Dr. Spock in Philadelphia at a Women's Strike for Peace meeting; another press conference in New York to announce the Whitehall Street demonstration; the Whitehall Street demonstration in which Spock and Goodman were arrested; more press conferences, newspaper interviews, protest rallies. (In the end, it turned out a lot of this was thrown in for effect, because much of it never was introduced in evidence.)

Mr. Wall winds up: "At the conclusion of all the evidence in this case, the physical evidence and the testimony from the stand, I shall again talk with you and consider with you at that time the significance of this evidence, the significance of the physical evidence, and the significance of the statements that were made, after which I shall ask you to return an appropriate verdict."

3.

The first witness, an FBI man named Lawrence E. Miller (addressed as "Agent Miller" by the lawyers), unexpectedly provided a welcome bit of comic relief. He is the agent who attended the press conference at the Beekman Room on October 2; but it soon develops he can hardly remember anything that went on there. We go through all the dimensions of the Beekman Room again and learn the additional information that the entrance is a *double* door leading off the lobby, that the room can be partitioned into *three* sections; and that it is adorned by a mural "like a row of buildings and a garden, a regular mural," behind the speakers' table; but after that, Agent Miller dries up. He remembers that several people were seated on the platform —among them Mr. Coffin. Judge Ford asks, "Can you point him out?" Agent Miller looks desperately round the courtroom—the judge rescues him by saying, "Stand up, Mr. Coffin." Coffin does so, to a burst of laughter from the spectators. Dr. Spock was also on the platform (kindhearted Dr. Spock, smiling broadly, stands up to save the witness from further embarrassment), Paul Goodman, Noam Chomsky, Ashley Montagu, Marcus Raskin, Dwight Macdonald, Robert Lowell . . .

Wall tries to get Agent Miller to tell the jury what was said at the press conference. Well, Dr. Spock said the war was militarily unwinnable, and that LBJ was trying to save face. And Goodman read a statement, he said legal authority is not . . . here Agent Miller stops short, and is allowed to have a look at his notes. Oh yes, he said legal authority is not fixed . . . Up jumps Leonard Boudin to say the witness doesn't seem to remember *anything*. Gales of laughter.

Somewhere along in there Dwight Macdonald said he was ashamed to be an American, Raskin said the government

must be called on to halt the war, Coffin called on the clergy
to provide churches as a refuge for draft resisters, and
Mitchell Goodman announced draft resistance plans for the
week of October 16–21, including plans to demonstrate at
the Oakland Induction Center.

At this point the judge wants to know which Goodman is
which—Paul? Mitchell? And Noam Chomsky has been variously pronounced Neil Comsky, Noel Kimsky, Norman
Comstock . . . The witness refers to "Howard Waskow, a
friend of Raskin's" (meaning Arthur Waskow, Raskin's colleague at the Institute for Policy Studies), and quotes him as
saying, "If it were no crime to participate in this war it was
no crime to *refuse* to participate in this war."

Each time the witness drops the name of an unindicted
person, defense counsel object, but the judge barks them
down: "Excluded! Go forward! No more colloquy!" Sometimes he leans toward the jury to tell them they must not
consider the statement of such a person until they have found
there is evidence he was a member of this conspiracy, or that
they may only consider his statement when they have found
he is part of the conspiracy—a phrasing that calls forth re-
newed objections and a stream of counsel toward the bench
for one of their innumerable huddles out of earshot of
the jury.

Cross-examination is in alphabetical order of defendant,
so that St. Clair for Coffin goes first and Boudin for Spock is
last. The wild part is that they know, we know, everybody
except the jury knows, that soon we shall be shown a film of
that press conference—and that defense counsel have been
furnished with a transcript of the sound track. They also
have copies of Agent Miller's handwritten notes and his
typed memorandum.

St. Clair has put aside his flashing smile for the moment
in favor of his stern glare. He elicits the fact that there was
nothing secretive about the press conference, nor was there

any violence there; that there were 373 names on the "Call to Resist Illegitimate Authority"; that Mr. Coffin did not have anything to say about plans for the Oakland demonstration. (There is more, but it is all repetitive of what we have already learned of Mr. Coffin's views in the government's opening statement.)

Mr. Homans, for Michael Ferber, wants to know if Michael Ferber was there. He was not. And is his signature among the 373 names on "A Call to Resist Illegitimate Authority"? The witness cannot recall, but Mr. Wall jumps up to stipulate that Ferber's name is not on that document. Was the meeting in the Arlington Street Church discussed? The witness doesn't recall. Was Ferber mentioned at all at the press conference? No.

Did Ashley Montagu say "Lyndon Johnson is drunk with power"? continues Mr. Homans. Or did he use the words "frightening power-drunk politics"? Agent Miller stares into the middle distance, trying to recall. And what about the words "clique—power-happy" that occur in the handwritten notes, whereas the typed report records "drunk with power"? Were the words "drunk with power" used at the meeting or not? Agent Miller thinks the inference was made, but he does not recall the exact words used. Are there other instances in which the handwritten notes reflect the inference rather than what was actually said? Perhaps . . . "the notes are not verbatim . . . handwriting is not the best."

Mr. Barshak in his methodical way tries to put a few things to rights about what his client, Mitchell Goodman, said at the press conference. How many times did he refer to the Oakland Induction Center? The witness doesn't know. Did Goodman discuss the findings of some AID mission people just returned from Vietnam? Somebody discussed that, but the witness isn't sure who, he can't remember if it was Goodman. Did Goodman say anything about a conscientious commitment to support the young men of the

Resistance? The witness can't recall, he didn't take everything down . . .

Calvin Bartlett draws a bead on the handwritten notes. "Did you write 'Marcus Raskin, little man'? And 'Clique in power—power-happy—bandits, thieves'?" Yes, says Agent Miller, he did. And his notes on Raskin read: "President does not have private information sources, as he should know as he was an advisor, JFK, and he sat in on National Security Council meetings." "And 'baloney'? Why did you write 'baloney' after Mr. Raskin's statement?" But the judge won't have it: "Strike it out." "I pray your Honor's judgment," says Bartlett. "Strike it out! That is English. Strike it out. Next question."

Bartlett, hands behind back, immeasurably slow of gesture, presses on: "What follows the word 'baloney'?" "Those are just doodles." "Dooooodles?" repeats Mr. Bartlett mournfully. "That is what I call them." The audience roars.

The notes are in fact rather full of doodles, scribbles, and question marks. What do all those question marks mean? Mr. Bartlett finally drags it out of balky Agent Miller: three question marks after a sentence is his own private way of reminding himself that this was a major sentence; one question mark means a question; and two question marks, after the word "Coffin," mean that Mr. Coffin had suggested a question-and-answer period to follow the speeches. ("That's a hard code to crack," cracks Dan Lang.) But those of us who are taking notes at the trial are all too painfully aware of what question marks really mean: they mean a failure to grasp what is being said.

Leonard Boudin patiently goes through Dr. Spock's remarks at the press conference, sentence by sentence, and after each sentence he asks Agent Miller if he recalls Dr. Spock saying that, and if it is in his memorandum to his superiors in the FBI. Didn't Dr. Spock say he is opposed to the war because it is morally wrong, it is destroying the good name and leadership of the United States? asks Boudin. In substance he did, answers Agent Miller. But that doesn't appear in your memorandum? No, it doesn't.

Agent Miller's memory is now receding to the vanishing point. Among the things he does not remember Dr. Spock saying are: If we succeed in bombing Vietnam to rubble we will be up against the Chinese . . . The young men are not only justified in resisting the draft but they deserve our thanks for refusing to take part . . . Spock and millions of others voted for LBJ because LBJ specifically promised he was against escalation of the war. I don't recall, says Agent Miller, it isn't in my memorandum, it isn't in my notes . . .

Boudin assumes a more-in-sorrow-than-in-anger expression; he is a teacher trying to get a recalcitrant kindergartner to recite his ABC's. He puts several pairs of glasses on and off in rapid succession, does a waltz step or two, and ruefully pouting, consults his notes.

"Now, Agent Miller, did Dr. Spock say, 'We have been engaged in political action'?" (Miller, in despair, is shuffling some papers on his lap.) Boudin rounds on him: "ARE YOU LOOKING AT YOUR NOTES?" Miller, unhappy, says he is not. "Have you recalled *anything* without notes in the past two days?" demands the exasperated kindergarten teacher. "Did you look at your notes before you testified here in court?" Miller says he did. But not, it seems, to good advantage. He cannot recall Dr. Spock saying that for the first time the majority of the American people oppose further escalation, nor anything else along those lines . . . there is nothing like that in his notes. Soon Boudin, with a courtly and beaming "No further questions, your Honor," returns to his seat.

It is almost over. St. Clair asks a few more questions, and Mr. Wall tries once more to clear up the Paul and Mitchell Goodman mixup ("Would it be contempt of court to send him Norman Mailer's book, Paul and Mitchell Goodman-wise?"), and soon Agent Miller thankfully steps down.

Fade out Agent Miller and fade in the real thing, the television newsreel film of the press conference, in which we find out what actually did go on there.

Dr. Spock, somewhat larger than life in glorious technicolor, is excessively photogenic—in the film he is everybody's favorite uncle, direct, no-nonsense, speaking from the depth of conviction. "I don't *want* to be arrested, but I'll do anything to help the opposition to the war. Thousands of young men are dying to save face for Lyndon Johnson. Therefore, I believe young men are justified in not taking part in this *outrageous* war."

A reporter asks Dr. Spock whether he has considered encouraging Americans to express their convictions at the polls (and now we come to the Spock statement that Leonard Boudin was unsuccessfully trying to get Agent Miller to remember).

"I think that we've been very active," says Dr. Spock in his rumbling, confident voice, "and I would like to draw your attention to the fact that in the 1964 election I and millions of Americans went to the polls to vote for Lyndon Johnson and the Democratic Party, because Lyndon Johnson very specifically promised that he was against escalation of the war in Vietnam. We did that, and Lyndon Johnson and the Democratic Party has *betrayed* us. This has not kept us from political action since. We've been engaged in writing letters, writing telegrams to the President and our representatives. We are partly satisfied to realize that now, for the first time this fall, a majority of the American people, according to the polls, are *opposed* to further escalation and believe in either de-escalation or withdrawal."

Mr. Coffin speaks of the historic role of the church as sanctuary, and suggests that the synagogues and churches should today offer asylum to those young men who cannot in conscience agree to be inducted: "If these young men should be arrested in the churches, we who have given them aid and comfort should also be arrested, because if they are guilty of violating a law which violates their conscience, we are no less guilty of violating that same law, for if you read Section 12 of the National Selective Service Act, it states very clearly that anybody who knowingly counsels, aids, and abets another in refusing induction into the army will be guilty up to ten thousand dollars fine and five years in prison."

The confusing "Goodmen," Paul and Mitchell, are both on hand, just as Agent Miller said they would be, and Mitchell Goodman does tell about some AID mission people who "resigned because they could no longer tolerate the position they were put in in Vietnam—it was they who called this war an overwhelming atrocity, and they have seen it for years at first hand." He reads a long document and announces plans for draft resistance activities around the country, all of which we have already heard in Mr. Wall's opening statement. Marcus Raskin, up there at the speakers' table with the others, is seen and not heard.

4.

For those of us who attended the trial every day, the courtroom was an enclosed world with a life of its own, not unlike life aboard a cruise ship; time seemed to slow down and then speed up in the most unaccountable way. The first three days seemed like an eternity, the fellow passengers in the press section already old friends or enemies. There were about thirty press people in all; a large contingent from the Boston papers, some out-of-town and wire-service reporters, a few magazine writers. Occasionally somebody showed from the foreign press, and there was one mini-mini-skirted young lady with credentials from the London *Times* to whose legs Michael Ferber had already written an ode, already confiscated by Mr. Coffin for safekeeping (or further research) until the end of the trial.

The main press pals in my corner were Anson Smith of the Boston *Morning Globe* (an editorial writer by nature, assigned to cover the trial because of his special knowledge of the case); Carol Liston, a lovely dark-haired eager girl-reporter who did the "color" for the *Globe*, which means interviews with the defendants' wives, corridor gossip, the trial scene in general; Sandy Levinson of *Ramparts*, trial sweetheart, who vowed to make every one of those jurors smile at her before it was all over (and she so nearly succeeded that at one point the judge sent his clerk over to tell her to stop distracting the jury); Jack MacKenzie of the Washington *Post*, true reporter and defender of free press; David Lyle from *Esquire*; Joseph Sax, a young law professor covering the trial for the Michigan *Daily* and the *Yale Review*; and Dan Lang of *The New Yorker*. Dan has a low threshold of boredom, and he mercifully enlivened each day with his restive *sotto voce* comments: "Jessica, would you ask the bailiff to close the door? I'm afraid if *I* ask him he'll think I'm trying to avoid the draft."

The enemies were seated at some distance (for we had long since chosen sides), they were mainly troglodyte types from the local evening papers who specialized in making nasty comments about the defendants. There was a little tiff between one of these and Michael Ferber. Ferber had asked him to stop talking so loud, he couldn't hear the testimony. The Boston Evening troglodyte shot back, "Why don't you cut your hair and get it out of your ears, if you can't hear?" Michael, having none of that, briskly offered to have the judge cite him for contempt of court.

Outside our snug world a storm was blowing up. Across the Common, just a short walk from the courthouse, is the Arlington Street Church, and there two young war resisters, offered sanctuary by the minister, had been holding out against the authorities for some days. They were Robert Talmanson, a twenty-one-year-old Bostonian whose appeal from a three-year prison sentence for refusing induction had just been turned down by the U.S. Supreme Court, and William Chase, a nineteen-year-old deserter from the army. There had been rumors that the marshals were going to come and get Talmanson (they were leaving Chase for the army to deal with), and Dan Lang left the trial to observe this scene. He arrived back considerably shaken. It had been a muddy, bloody, sickeningly unequal battle in pelting rain. It had started off peacefully enough: the marshals went into the church, Talmanson read a statement and offered no resistance, he was carried out limp. About three hundred young people massed outside the church were prepared to block the way and prevent the marshals from taking Talmanson off. At first the atmosphere was almost jolly; Talmanson, flanked by marshals, sat on the sidewalk reading aloud from a book of Chinese poetry, while his supporters shouted encouragement. Soon police reinforcements arrived and the battle was on. "Incredible—really frightful," Dan kept saying, shaking his head. He had seen girls dragged by the hair, boys beaten into unconsciousness, heard the urgent screams of the wounded. "The Boston Civil Liberties Union says it is the worst case of police brutality here in fifteen years."

On the screen facing the jury box, while the bloody battle of the sanctuary rages outside, Mr. Coffin is saying: "If there are going to be arrests, then let these arrests be made in the churches and synagogues." Overt Acts #3 and 4 are unfolding: the speeches of Michael Ferber and Coffin at the draft-card–turn-in ceremony on October 16 in the same Arlington Street Church. There are two short films of this, one in color. The color film is rather beautiful: the church decorated with bunches of leaves and berries like an English country church at Harvest Festival time, the solemn young men coming up in turn, holding their draft cards to the bright candle flame, the black ashes put in a silver bowl all among the Harvest Festival leaves. We only hear a fraction of the speeches, but we know what has been said because Mr. Wall has read them out loud in his vibrant tones. ("Reads with expression. Not for nothing on the school debating team," comments Dan Lang.)

The movies themselves take just a few minutes, but they are preceded and followed by interminable cross-examination of the hapless TV photographers who chanced to be assigned by their studios to take these particular films on that particular day. All five teams of defense lawyers take their turn. The point of the cross-examination is to establish that the film shows only a tiny, selected portion of the total proceedings at the church, that this portion was chosen by the photographer for filming because of its drama or newsworthiness, and that those defendants who weren't there weren't there. It seems to take forever to establish these self-evident facts.

After the movies some still photographs of the same scene are offered in evidence, and this time there is reprieve from cross-examination: a welcome stipulation by the defense lawyers, who are all agreed, apparently, that these things are real photographs, taken by a real photographer, of a real scene at the Arlington Street Church.

5.

The prosecution case is sometimes reminiscent of one of those old vaudeville gags in which a man is revving up a huge car. He works away at a dozen knobs, pumps furiously at the gas pedal, fills the air with hideous noises and billows of smoke. Just as the audience thinks the machine is about to career over the footlights and into the orchestra, it emits a little squeak and gives up.

Thus William H. Monagan, who, after being sworn as the government's next witness, states that he is the Assistant

Records Administration Officer for the Department of Justice. Mr. Wall shows him Government Exhibit 2-A, which was pretrial Exhibit 4, and we all know what that is: it is Mitchell Goodman's letter to the Justice Department in which he asks for an appointment with the Attorney General for October 20. Next, Mr. Wall elicits from Mr. Monagan that his duties are to receive and process the mail and distribute it to the different offices within the divisions of the department. Mr. Monagan has brought some records with him at Mr. Wall's request. What are they? They are called post office manifests. When registered mail arrives at the Department of Justice, it is delivered in the pouch, a receipt is given for the pouch by number, and in the pouch is a manifest which lists the registered mail, and this is a manifest kept daily. As well as the manifest there is a record card. This is a record of an individual piece of mail, it tells when the mail was received and who it is from.

Mr. Wall now brings out that the record card contains further information; it identifies the registered piece of mail, gives the number that ties the registered piece of mail in with the sender, and contains the name of the signer. These are daily records kept in the regular course of business. Mr. Monagan is the custodian of those records. The soporific effect of all this information begins to take its toll of the jurors, several of whom are nodding off.

The judge, waking up with a start: "Are they records of the Department of Justice?" The witness: "Yes, sir." The judge: "All right, go ahead."

The witness does so. He produces Exhibit 2-A (Mitch's letter), and under questioning testifies that he is the custodian of it, that it is in the regular course of business to keep such records, that any entries made therein by the Department of Justice are made at or about the time reflected therein. There is a Department of Justice date stamp on the document, and the date indicated is October 17, 1967.

And now, referring to that part of the exhibit which is an envelope, there is a postmark on it, and the postmark date and place are New Haven, Connecticut, October 16, 1967.

Audible yawns are heard in the press section, and a subliminal hiss of "Stipulate!," directed at Mitch Goodman's lawyer, who perhaps was dozing off himself. Mr. Wall continues: "Is there a registered mail number on that document, on the portion of it that is the envelope, that is?" "Yes, there is." "What is that registered mail number?" "It is 20019." "And I hand back to you Government's A-2 for identification and do you see that registered mail number 20019 reflected there in that document?" "Yes, sir." "What do you call that document again?" "This is a post office manifest." Et cetera. Finally, "No further questions." And, mercifully, no cross-examination.

But this is not yet the end. The next witness is a U.S. marshal also bearing documents. We know, from Mr. Wall's opening address to the jury, that there is at least a handwriting expert lurking in the wings to testify that this is indeed Mitchell Goodman's signature, and—who knows? —he is probably flanked by writing-paper experts who will testify that the letter is written on a piece of 8½ x 11 grade-B typewriting paper with self-seal envelope, U.S. Patent Pending. Kind Mr. Barshak at last comes to our rescue and utters the merciful words, "I will stipulate that the letter sent to the Attorney General was written by Mr. Mitchell Goodman."

The judge calls on Mr. Wall to accept. Mr. Wall: "Yes, I will stipulate that the letter which is headed 'From: Conscientious Resistance, 451 Wellesley Road, Philadelphia, Pennsylvania,' dated October 7, 1967, date-stamped at the Justice Department October 17, 1967, together with attachments, one, 'A Call to Resist Illegitimate Authority'; two, 'Civil Disobedience Against the War'; and three, an envelope containing all the aforementioned documents, postmarked

October 16, 1967, New Haven, Connecticut, with a return address, Yale University, 258 Yale Station, New Haven, Connecticut, with a registered mail No. 20019 was signed by Mitchell Goodman, the defendant in this case."

It is of course the same old letter that Mr. Wall read in his opening statement, a request for an appointment with the Attorney General. But he does not spare us, he reads the whole thing again. We wish that Mitchell Goodman had not stuffed those enclosures into the letter, because Mr. Wall reads those out again too, all the way to their climactic end, which turns out to be "printed by volunteer labor," in spite of the fact that we have heard them in their entirety in his opening. The effect is that of being trapped for the second time round in a continuous movie. Lunch comes and goes, and he is still reading.

By about the fourth day the inner rhythm of the trial, of what is going on beyond the barrier that separates participants from observers, is emerging.

The opening words of the clerk, Austin W. Jones, Jr., and the crier are no longer an obscure jumble, we know them by heart. Mr. Jones, a handsome, decisive Negro, standing erect and tall, stares off into the distance like a military man and intones: "Mr. Crier, open *this* session of the District Court." The crier, one feels, must have been chosen for his looks; he has a wondrous old bird's face, all beak, sharply sloping forehead, tiny, hooded eyes. He says his lines in a soft but fervent monotone: "All persons having anything to do before the Honorable, the Judge of the United States District Court now holden at Boston within and for the District of Massachusetts, draw near and give their attendance and they shall be heard. God save the United States of America and this honorable Court." (As far as we can make out, this is the total extent of the crier's duties; although on one occasion, when there was laughter in the courtroom, he did call out "Quiet there." "I wonder if he'll get time and a half for that?" mused Dan Lang.)

Generally the proceedings open with a bench huddle. It is just out of earshot, we can only hear a few tantalizing snatches; but after court the lawyers sometimes let us see the daily transcript, and, feeling like guilty eavesdroppers, we see what it was all about. This sort of thing: Boudin: "I now move for a mistrial on the ground that on five occasions the instructions to the jury implied or assumed the existence of a conspiracy. Your Honor said, '*Until* there is some evidence that the defendant Ferber was a member of *this* conspiracy.' I suggest to your Honor that the words 'this conspiracy' means to the jury that there *is* a conspiracy." The judge: "Motion for a mistrial is denied. Let's get on with the case."

We have begun to sense the likes and dislikes developing beyond the barrier. The judge is fond and fatherly toward the jury, he leans over to them beaming, and sometimes we can tell from the clatter of masculine ha-ha-ha's that he has made a joke or two as he greets them in the morning. His manner toward Mr. Wall is hard to determine; we don't think he actually *likes* Mr. Wall, rather he seems to steer him as elder to novice. Often, he does not wait for Mr. Wall to object to a defense question, he anticipates him. "Strike it out! Go forward." His voice, deeper than gravel-toned, has the timbre of a truck shifting gears on a hill.

Among defense counsel, James St. Clair is the fair-haired boy. In chambers (we learn), the judge kids around a lot with St. Clair. "Fiddlesticks, Jim! Oh, cut that out," but that, alas, is the extent of it. He seldom rules in St. Clair's favor. Leonard Boudin is the un-favorite. At one of the bench conferences the judge, in a voice loud enough for the press to hear, threatened him with the fate of "the Dennis lawyers," meaning defense counsel for Communist leaders in the first Smith Act trial, who drew long jail sentences for contempt of court.

6.

The solid center of the prosecution case was the series of events at the Department of Justice on October 20: the demonstration of some five hundred outside the building at which draft cards were turned in from all over the country, the eleven-man delegation, including four of the defendants, that sought to tweak the beard of government by demanding a "legal confrontation."

As these unfold on the screen and in the testimony of John P. McDonough, the Justice Department aide who, with John Van de Kamp, received the delegation, the difference between the kind of confrontation they were demanding and the one set up for them by the government is glaringly illuminated. Coffin is there right enough in the movie, inviting prosecution, practically saying, "Come and get me!" and "I double-dare you!" And here he is in the courtroom, defendant at the bar, in a case in which all of the issues he was bent on raising have long since been stripped away. The single point for the jury to consider as they watch the movie is: Did Mr. Coffin *conspire* with the other four? Or with any of them? Or with persons known and unknown to the Grand Jury?

On the screen, Mr. Coffin is addressing several hundred young demonstrators gathered in the sunshine outside the Department of Justice. "It is not we who are demoralizing our boys in Vietnam, but the government by asking them to do immoral things. As the war to us is immoral, so also is the draft." Dr. Spock is up there applauding, and we see the top of Marcus Raskin's head somewhere in the crowd.

Now the young men come up one by one; "John Sanna, Buffalo Resistance—I only got my own card, I'll add it to New York." "Lenny Heller, California Resistance, 298 cards." "Michael Ferber, from Boston Resistance. I bring from the Arlington Street Church 237 cards." "Paul O'Brien, Chicago Resistance. I've got 45 cards and a few assorted words of welcome for federal marshals and the like."

The next reel shows Coffin reporting back to the crowd outside on the meeting just held with John P. McDonough, the Attorney General's representative. Again it is a familiar text to us, one of those read by Wall in his opening, but Coffin's sense of outrage is better than the ersatz editions: "We tried to make it very clear to him that we were faced with a moral issue at the point of the war itself. We reminded him of the 1949 Geneva Agreement that the United States had solemnly signed regarding the conduct of war. We told him of our determination to stand solidly with the young men who felt in conscience that they could no longer cooperate with the armed services as long as the war continues, and we offered him these cards.

"He then refused to accept them. An incredible thing when you stop to think of it: one of the highest officers of the law in the United States was really derelict in his duty to accept evidence of an alleged crime—he simply refused to accept the cards which we put on the table. He also refused to discuss any of the laws upon which we are prepared to base our case. He made lots of comments about Section 462. He made no comments whatsoever about the Geneva Agreement that the United States solemnly signed. . . ."

The events within the Department of Justice are now related by John P. McDonough, who turns out to be easily the best of the government witnesses. He is fluent, well organized, there are no hesitations, few little confusions, none of the diversions provided by Agent Miller. He is a gentleman and a scholar, sometime acting dean of Stanford Law School. He testifies that he and John Van de Kamp shook hands all round, offered coffee, and asked everyone to sit down. (Van de Kamp, present throughout the discussion, was apparently a silent spectator. He was never called to testify.)

As usual we start right at the beginning, with the dimensions of the Andretta Room and the dimensions of the conference table therein. Joseph Cella, a member of Van de Kamp's unit, who is conducting this portion of the government case, asks, "For whom was the Andretta Room named?" "For a former Assistant Attorney General for Administration, Sol Andretta," answers the witness. Judge Ford perks up: "He had charge of narcotics enforcement at one time?" Mr. McDonough: "Your Honor, my knowledge about Mr. Andretta doesn't go that far back." "Mine does. Next question," says his Honor genially, to a burst of okay laughter. (We have long since discovered that the courtroom is never admonished not to laugh when the judge gets off one of his sallies.)

Mr. McDonough's account of the meeting in the Andretta Room, although long and detailed, does not differ substantially from that of Mr. Coffin. There are one or two small slip-ups: he got Arthur Waskow's name down as Harold in his original notes and at one point in his testimony refers to him as Andrew Koskow. Then he confuses Waskow and Raskin, attributing to Raskin Waskow's statement that "the draft cards which the briefcase contained were evidence of a violation of federal law and that it was my duty as a member of the Department of Justice to receive that evidence."

After everybody had spoken, and Dickie Harris had stormed out of the meeting, things seem to have fallen a little flat. Mr. McDonough, kindly schoolmaster, testifies that he told the group they had presented their views articulately and moderately, and that he would convey them to the Attorney General, who is a just and concerned man who would listen even though he might not agree. Follows the tendering of the briefcase full of draft cards, McDonough's refusal to accept them, and after a few more exchanges the delegation's departure leaving the briefcase on the table.

St. Clair cross-examines, this time with his glittering equal-to-equal smile. He tries to get Mr. McDonough to concede that the visitors were seeking a challenge of what they regard as an unconstitutional law for purposes of making a test case, but Mr. McDonough is too slippery for him. In response to questions he says they did not mention the "just-war doctrine" and that he is not familiar with that term, he doesn't remember the phrase "legal and moral confrontation" being used.

> Q. (St. Clair): You read the act to them and they said, sir, "We are violating the law, here is the evidence," and they insisted that you take it?
> A. That is true.
> Q. And you recognized that they were doing that in order that there be a prosecution so that they could test these laws; you recognized that, didn't you?
> A. No, sir.
> Q. You didn't?
> A. No, sir.
> Q. Don't you know that what they were seeking was a test case regarding the legality of the war?
> A. No, sir.

Mr. St. Clair tries another tack:

> Q. In the course of your preparation for this conference, sir, did you come across the words "symbolic speech"?
> A. No, sir.
> Q. As an acting dean of the Stanford Law School—

Mr. Cella, Wall's colleague at counsel table, rises, but the judge does not wait for him to speak up: "Strike out that line of questioning completely, about symbolic speech. Strike it out!"

Mr. St. Clair asks for a bench conference on this. His point is that the decision rendered by the First Circuit Court in the O'Brien draft-card-burning case makes it clear that turning in a draft card is symbolic speech, because the Court held that burning a draft card was symbolic.*

Judge Ford: I am not going to allow you to ask this witness questions about symbolic speech and get out into left field or right field or center field.

St. Clair (not afraid to play around): Center field is more appropriate. It is right on the target.

Judge Ford: You are not going to be there! Excluded. Let's get on.

St. Clair does so, and now he turns to another point:

Q. In the course of your preparation, sir, did you learn that a violation of the regulations requiring possession of a draft card at all times would result in the reclassification of the registrant?

Judge Ford: Strike the question out. Excluded.

St. Clair: Would your Honor note my exception?

Judge Ford: Yes.

Q. Did you learn, sir, that the lack of possession would subject an individual to prompt induction?

Mr. Cella is on his feet; again, before he can say anything, the judge raps out, "Excluded on objection of the government." "I didn't hear an objection," objects St. Clair. Judge Ford: "Mr. Cella rose. That was a *symbolic* objection." Laughter in the courtroom; the judge looks pleased with himself.

St. Clair wants to know whether anything was said about each speaker stating his *individual* views. Mr. McDonough answers that Mr. Coffin said each would speak for himself, they were not there as representatives of organizations.

The U.S. Supreme Court later reversed this decision.

St. Clair (bearing down): So you understood that opinions of each were the independent views of each speaker?

McDonough: No.

Q. You were told that?

A. No. He said they were not speaking as the representatives of any groups.

Q. Was the word "individual" used?

A. I don't recall.

Q. There's no reference to "individual views" in your report?

A. No.

Mr. St. Clair's point, of course, is to slip across to the jury the idea that these eleven people were there as individuals and not as conspirators. Mr. McDonough's role is to give an account of the meeting that will be close enough to the truth not to invite demolishment when the defendants testify, yet not to yield an inch on the conspiracy. So he concedes that they were not there as representatives of anything, but balks at the words "individual views" and "independent views." The jurors may or may not be grasping these fine points.

This particular bone having been thoroughly worried, St. Clair sits down and the other defense lawyers get along.

Homans simply asks whether Mike Ferber was there. No, he wasn't, as everybody knew by now.

Ed Barshak carefully and methodically takes the witness through the steps by which the various drafts of his report to the Attorney General were prepared, starting with the rough draft made by McDonough and Van de Kamp immediately after the guests had departed; "Does the word 'rough' imply you were not giving the precise language?" Yes, that is what the word "rough" implies, it develops after a good bit of lawyerly exchange. And what about the FBI men outside the door of the Andretta Room? Mr. Wall objects to this. Judge Ford: "Oh, let him answer, the FBI's always outside doors." (This got such a burst of laughter that the judge pulled it again, later. The question of FBI agents listening once more came up, and the government objected. Judge Ford: "There's nothing wrong with FBI agents outside doors." He paused for a moment, glared menacingly, then added, "They're needed outside *some* doors.")

Nonrecollection now sets in, but Mr. McDonough's failure to recall comes over a good deal more smoothly than Agent Miller's. In response to Ed Barshak's questions, he does not remember what Waskow said to substantiate his view that the draft law is unconstitutional, nor any discussion that the draft law violates freedom of religion because of the treatment of nonreligious objectors (which was one of Coffin's main points), nor anybody protesting against the escalation of the Vietnam war.

There is a fuzzy exchange in which Calvin Bartlett goes into the seating order of the meeting and tries to dislodge his client Raskin from the chair in which somebody spoke of "dereliction of duty." Leonard Boudin, playing his game of Tom Tiddler's Ground with Judge Ford, tries to establish the eminence of persons who support the Resistance ("Did you know that Melman and Waskow are professors? Do you recognize names of Stanford professors on the 'Call to Resist Illegitimate Authority'?") and he soon gets shouted down by the judge. His next ploy is to establish that although Mr. McDonough knew full well that his visitors were about to commit a crime in his presence, he gave them no warning. He slips in:

> Q. You allowed them to come in and served them coffee and then you indicted them?
> Judge Ford: Strike it out!
> Q. After the conference ended, were any others present at the conference indicted except for these five defendants?
> Judge Ford: Strike it out!

Q. When you were at law school did *you* ever sign anything similar to the "Call to Resist Illegitimate Authority"?

Judge Ford (making a run at Boudin in his swivel chair): STRIKE IT OUT!

After McDonough's testimony Mr. Wall told the press that his case would take at least another ten days to present —another two full trial weeks. This seemed impossible, for what else was there to say? Nothing much, it turned out. Evidently Mr. Wall was simply trying to put defense counsel off their stride with a surprise resting of the government's case.

The prosecution's case does in fact sputter on fitfully for two more days, for the most part the same familiar potpourri of films, still photographs, and FBI agents, to wit: another TV film of Coffin outside the Justice Department (the press now knows his speech by heart and some quietly chant it out in unison with the sound track); two FBI photographers bearing still pictures of the same scene (to defense objections of repetitiveness, Wall answers they are not repetitive, one shows "Raskin smiling faintly," upon which Raskin, sitting in defendants' row, smiles faintly); the FBI agent who made an inventory of the contents of the fabrikoid briefcase, which included registration certificates, notices of classification, and an envelope containing "past remains" of draft cards; the two FBI agents who visited Dr. Spock in his home, by appointment.

Agent Webb of the FBI laboratory in Washington, a highly qualified chemist and physicist whose credentials alone take some minutes to recite, gives a demonstration of some of the more esoteric uses to which modern technology can be put. He testifies that he analyzed the cremated remains of draft cards turned in at the Justice Department, and has preserved them by mounting them in glass. He shows the slides, which are rather decorative and look something like pressed autumn leaves. Next he shows some immensely enlarged photographs of the remains which look something like Rorschach tests. These are passed round amongst the bemused jurors.

The next three witnesses spell toil and trouble not so much for these defendants as for unknown young men in Ohio, New Jersey, and Massachusetts. They are executive secretaries of local draft boards of these states, the only women that have thus far appeared in this masculine trial, and counsel keep addressing them as "sir," out of habit.

Their role is to identify the partly burned draft cards as belonging to registrants in their jurisdiction, and this they do with relish. The draft-card remains, and the preserving of them under glass by the scholarly FBI laboratory expert, were good for a few derisive comments in the press section. But suddenly it all turns sordid and depressing, jerked out of the fantasy world of FBI technicians into the real world where the owners of these cards will soon be in custody facing several years in prison.

One of these unfortunates is outside the courtroom under government subpoena. Mr. Wall proposes to bring him in to be identified. Bench huddle. Boudin objects: "I consider it pure drama and prejudicial. I don't know whether or not he has long hair." Judge Ford. "I *hope* he has long hair. We will have no further colloquy. Bring him in." Enter and exit the resister, hair medium, in short order.

We are almost at the end. A student newspaper reporter, David Dickerman, testifies about a press conference in New Haven at which Mr. Coffin said that those over draft age should be concerned about students in the Resistance, and should act as conduits in aiding and abetting them. There is a long and confusing cross-examination in which Mr. St. Clair tries to establish that Mr. Coffin never said he was a *leader* of the Resistance. This is like an obstacle race:

> The witness: I don't recall at any point that he called himself a leader of the Resistance.

The Court: We know that. That is admitted.

The witness: I don't recall that.

Mr. Wall: It is *not* admitted, your Honor. That is *not* admitted. That is in.

The Court: The very expression "leader"?

Mr. Wall: Leader.

The Court: You have the article. Read what Dr. Coffin said about being a leader.

The witness: I don't have him quoted as saying anything in that regard.

More of this cross-fire, then St. Clair: So then can't we agree that he was not a member of or the leader of this movement you have described?

Mr. Wall: Objection. That calls for a conclusion.

The Court: Strike it out.

Mr. St. Clair: Let me withdraw it. Rev. Coffin did not say in any form of words he was a *leader* of the Resistance, did he?

The Court: Let the jury decide that. He has already testified as to what he was a leader of.

(Joseph Heller, thou shouldst be with us in this hour. "I always didn't say you couldn't punish me, sir.")

The final act is a bit of slapstick: a one-and-a-half-minute clip from a TV film of Dr. Spock sitting-in at Whitehall Street. He is sitting in awkward posture in the middle of a phalanx of policemen; there is a close-up of his large, kindly face peering out between their legs and he is saying: "Oh, I think that the police have been very decent, shown a lot of self-control. I have no complaints. The point of this demonstration is to bring home particularly to the American people the fact that we think that the war is disastrous to our country. We're also demonstrating here to show our solidarity with the young men who are resisting the draft." In answer to a reporter's question he says: "The police were like a very good football line in closing up every gap. When

I tried to go over the top of the barricade they cheerfully strong-armed me back."

The film whirrs off the reel, the lights go up, and Mr. Wall, looking pleased as a cat in cream, says: "The government rests."

So that is the government's case.

What does it all add up to? A miscellany of public utterances, public appearances, sermons, press conferences, printed declarations of beliefs, overlaid with the trappings of criminal detection—the G-men, the registered-mail custodian from the Department of Justice, the carefully preserved cremated-draft-cards-sous-cloche. It is not hard to guess at the workings of the prosecutorial minds that assembled all this evidence, or at the effect it is supposed to have on the jury: is not the very presence of the FBI at a press conference, or in the home of Dr. Spock, proof enough that the defendants were doing something they shouldn't?

Strangely, the conspiracy seemed to have got lost in the shuffle. We strained to hear evidence of conspiracy in all the days of testimony but none emerged. In fact, from at least one source one could infer that the conspiracy charge was very much of an afterthought. The two FBI agents who spent several hours interviewing Dr. Spock in his apartment on December 8, nearly three weeks after the Andretta Room conference, were clearly not investigating a conspiracy. They asked no questions about Dr. Spock's contacts with the other four accused—perhaps they were privy to secret information that he had no relationship with them?

3

The Case for the Defense

1.

The front benches in the spectator section of the courtroom were reserved for the relations of the defendants. The Family Pew, we called these seats; and, in fact, Mr. Coffin's sister, Margot Lindsay, with an instinct for elegance and the ability to take charge, had furnished them with long foam-rubber pew cushions borrowed from her local church to ease the agony of all-day sitting.

As the defense case opened there was an atmosphere of near-euphoria in Defendants' Row and the Family Pew, for at last (it seemed) each of the five would have his day in court, the free and full opportunity to speak his own mind about the circumstances that brought him to his present predicament. The wives were out in force, and we sighed for *Women's Wear Daily* to record their outfits: Mrs. Spock and Mrs. Raskin in competing lacy white stockings and mod outfits; Eva Coffin in light-blue raincoat, accompanied by her two pretty, pale little children; Denise Levertov *en écossais* with sensible English walking shoes. Mr. Coffin's mother, in veily hat and white gloves, had invited many a niece and nephew, handsome prep-school boys in Brooks

Brothers jackets, elegant debs in Italian knits, to come and hear Uncle Bill testify. Before court opened, she went round greeting them: "My dear, how lovely to see you. *Isn't* this *nice.*" One could hear Spode teacups clinking in the background as at some family gathering for a rite of passage.

Yet the courtroom proved to be a woefully inappropriate forum for the elucidation of philosophical and political beliefs. It seemed to divide into two incompatible spheres: the world of the defendants, conscience-driven, haunted by the spectre of the Good, Obedient German, determined to do absolutely everything in their power to stop what they regarded as acts of comparable bestiality on the part of their government; and the fettered world of the law court with its creaky procedures, its irrational rules of evidence, everyone with half an eye on the appeals court to come.

In an ordinary criminal trial, it is the job of the defense lawyer to prove that his client didn't do it—or, if he did do it, there were extenuating circumstances: he acted in self-defense, he was provoked, he had not meant any harm, he was not aware that his action was illegal, he is a hard-working person of good character who would not be likely to commit a crime. Even if the prosecution clearly has the goods on the defendant, there are still a hundred tricks in the defense lawyer's bag. So direct examination is designed to elicit such responses as: "I saw her coming at me with the kitchen knife . . ." "She had refused to wash the dishes that evening . . . I only meant to scare her . . ." "I didn't know it was loaded . . ." Then the boss comes on to testify that the defendant has never missed a day's work, is liked and respected by his fellow workers; and the mother, to say he was always a good boy, never gave her a moment's trouble. The purpose of the exercise is to scatter seeds of reasonable doubt in the hopes that at least one or two will take root and flower during the jury's deliberations.

The prosecutor's job on cross-examination is to demolish this line of reasoning and get the jury's mind back to the criminality, wiliness, lack of credibility of the accused which he has established in his part of the case. "Isn't it a fact that you took out a thirty-thousand-dollar life insurance policy on her just the week before? . . ." "The fact is you lay in wait behind the broom closet and stalked her with a loaded gun? . . ." "You say you remember seeing the time on the kitchen clock, yet you *don't* remember the date?" And so on.

This is what is known as the adversary process. "The truth, the whole truth, and nothing but the truth"—which witnesses are sworn to tell—is in fact one of the most empty and mendacious clichés of all time. If the truth becomes hopelessly obscured in the course of the trial, this is of little consequence to the defense lawyer, whose concern is the acquittal of his client, or to the prosecutor, who is bent on chalking up another conviction.

The techniques of the adversary process, grafted on to a trial of political ideas and actions, produced some grotesque results in this case. Although there were some very high points indeed during the testimony of the defendants— their explanation of how they had arrived at their beliefs and what prompted them to the course of action they had followed—there were also some very low points when, prodded by their lawyers and chivvied by judge and prosecutor, some of the defendants seemed first to waver about the meaning of what they had done, and then to retreat in disarray.

Here is William Sloane Coffin, Jr., at his best, persuasive and sincere, testifying in his own defense on direct examination about his reasons for participating in the October 20 demonstration at the Department of Justice:

> Mr. Coffin: I had essentially three purposes.
> The first was to provide moral support for these men who had already turned in their draft cards.

Secondly, my purpose was to try to force the government to prosecute us for apparent violation of Section 12 of the National Selective Service Act. My reason for doing this was to have a court case where the questions could be posed: Is the war legal or illegal? Are the provisions of the draft law that relate to conscientious objection constitutional or unconstitutional?

Thirdly, my purpose was to make the best of this occasion, that is the assemblage of distinguished personages, like Dr. Spock and Robert Lowell, to help these young men reach the country with their message, to try to get the country to understand they were, in fact, conscientious, that they were, in turning in their draft cards, coming out from behind their deferments, and, in the case of seminarians, coming out from behind exemptions, because seminarians are totally exempt from the draft. Therefore, in turning in their draft cards, they were turning in the very dodge the draft system provided them as students and, hence, far from being cowardly, they were being very courageous, as well as, in my opinion, very conscientious.

My intention was to try to win the minds and search the consciences of the American government, the Congress, and the people.

But often bits of legalistic trickery, dear to the heart of the courtroom strategist, produced the most deplorable absurdities. Here is Coffin at his worst, a noble lion forced to jump through his trainer's hoops, answering the very next set of questions put to him by Mr. St. Clair:

Q. Now, sir, did you at that time believe that the delivery of the draft cards to the Attorney General would hinder or impede the function of the draft?
A. Certainly not.

Q. Why not?

A. Because turning in a draft card speeded up a man's induction and in no way impeded his induction.

Q. How did you believe it speeded his induction?

A. I knew a man lost his 2-S deferment and became a 1-A delinquent if the government chose to use this occasion to change his classification.

Too clever by half. Is the jury really supposed to think that Mr. Coffin's purpose in handing over the draft cards was to clear the way for inducting the registrants into the armed forces? This was the very point made by Mr. St. Clair in the arguments on the motions. It was bad enough then. To cause the defendant to repeat it on the witness stand seemed an affront to everything the defendants stood for.

Cross-examination is like a particularly devilish sort of guessing game in which the player must watch out for charged and sinister hidden meanings of words or suffer a demerit.

Mr. Coffin, answering Mr. Wall's questions about his conversation with Mitch Goodman in New Haven, inadvertently lets slip the word "agree":

"He [Goodman] said that he was concerned for these young men, wanted to provide moral support. He mentioned what he had heard about the plans for a demonstration in front of the Pentagon; that he was not certain that this represented the kind of best support we could give them. I agreed with him . . ."

Mr. Wall pounces on it: ". . . it was your idea to collect the cards and turn them in at the Justice Department?" "That's right." "And you *agreed* to do that with Mr. Goodman? He *agreed* with you at the time to do that?" (Now Mr. Coffin sees that he is in trouble): "No—he said he would check out the idea with a few other people, and if it seemed good we might go ahead with it." (But Mr. Wall chases him back to "agree"): "And he did check it out and he called you later and said that the people he had talked to about it liked it?" "That's correct." "And he *agreed* to go ahead with you and do that?" (No way out now): "Yes."

Later on there is more of this. Together, Mr. Wall and the judge maneuver the witness into "agreeing" with Michael Ferber:

Q. You agreed with Mr. Ferber at the Arlington Street Church, did you not, that you were going to meet in Washington and these and other cards would be turned in?

Mr. Homans: Object to the word "agreed."

The Court (overruling the objection to the question): No. It may be put and answered.

A. That's what the invitation called for, to which a variety of people were responding in their individual ways.

Q. And you agreed with Mr. Ferber, isn't that correct?

A. I agreed with those to accept the invitation and meet at the Justice Department.

Q. So that's at least Goodman and Ferber with whom you had agreed to go to the Justice Department on that date, isn't that correct?

(Homans objects, is overruled.)

A. No, that's not correct.

Q. (in tones of incredulous indignation): You *didn't* agree?

A. No.

(Now the judge takes over): But it was understood between the three of you that you would, is that right?

A. It was understood—

Judge Ford: Well, that's the same thing.

On the charge of counseling, the thrust of St. Clair's direct examination was to prove that in no instance did

Mr. Coffin counsel the uncommitted among the young to turn in their draft cards; he merely intended to offer support to those who had already decided to do so.

Asked by Mr. St. Clair what he meant by his speech at the Justice Department in which he pledged to "counsel, aid, and abet young men of conscience," Mr. Coffin replies, "I intended two things: one, to support those who had *already* in conscience decided not to serve in the armed forces as long as the war in Vietnam continues, and that is why the wording says, 'We hereby publicly counsel those to *continue* in their refusal,' as they had already made up their minds, and, secondly, as I said, I intended to precipitate a test case by deliberately taking the language of Section 12 of the National Selective Service Act and using it to see then in the courts whether, in fact, we had violated any law or not."

On cross-examination, this denial of counseling the uncommitted became an easy mark. First, Mr. Wall sets the stage at Arlington Street Church: "You were dressed in clergy's robes? . . . You conceived of it as a religious ceremony? . . . Of course there were other skilled and experienced speakers? . . . We might even say moving speakers?" to all of which Mr. Coffin assents.

Q. And did it occur to you that in those circumstances and that house of worship [he pronounces it "warship"], in clerical garb, you and others, particularly you, might move some of those that had less iron in their spine than others to act on their convictions and turn in their draft cards?

A. No, it did not.

Q. Did not?

A. It did not.

Q. It was not your intention to convince anybody at all to turn in his draft card there, is that correct?

A. That is absolutely correct.

Q. And you didn't feel that the circumstances were such that some persons might be convinced to make up their minds, had they been on the fence, to turn in those cards to you, all of you in a group, with a large crowd, with the moral support of the clergy; that didn't occur to you, did it?

We squirm in sympathy for Coffin. He answers that there was always an outside chance that something like that might happen but that it was not his intention, nor his understanding of the purpose of the service.

Q. How about that outside chance, didn't you approve of that outside chance?
A. No.
Q. As a man that felt that strongly about the injustice and the immorality of the war, you wouldn't seek to get converts to your view?
A. The turning in of the draft card is an eminently personal decision.

Here, the judge, always ready to lend a helping hand, takes over from Mr. Wall: "Put the question again, and answer the question." The question is read back—a tiny breathing space, a moment to think, but Mr. Coffin doggedly stays with his position.

A. No, I would not seek to get converts to my view, in that sense.

The word game goes on, and now we discover why Mr. Wall worked in the phrase "on the fence" just a while ago. He proceeds to read back some testimony in which Mr. Coffin had explained on direct examination why he favored the idea of taking the draft cards to the Justice Department rather than to the Pentagon: ". . . it seemed to me better we should have a solemn, dignified, nonviolent-at-all-cost type of demonstration in order to be heard more clearly

by people who were *ON THE FENCE* as regards the war
and who would be put off by a more way-out kind of
demonstration." Mr. Wall fairly bristles and throbs with
indignation as he pursues this:

Q. So whatever your intention was at Arlington Street
Church, certainly at the Department of Justice your intention was to reach the *uncommitted;* is that a fair statement of this?

A. I was thinking primarily, when I said that on
Wednesday, of the "over-age" group.

Q. You didn't *say* that, though, did you?

A. No, I did not say that but I recall now very clearly—

Judge Ford: No, you have answered. You didn't say
it.

Q. You weren't thinking of that young group who
might turn in their cards and sever all relations with the
Selective Service system?

A. No, I was not.

Q. (withering sarcasm): You were not. You weren't
trying to influence them, you were just trying to influence the over-age group to commit itself?

There was no opportunity here for Mr. Coffin to explain
what had really been in his mind. It seems most likely that
his main purpose in going to the Justice Department *was*
to reach the over-age group; as every newspaper reader
knows, the younger group were out the next day in tens
of thousands, in head-on conflict with the authorities at
the Pentagon. And Coffin had rejected this demonstration
in favor of one that he thought would be more effective
with the respectables in the peace movement.

It seems, too, that the self-evident purpose of these big
public ceremonies is to establish a climate of opinion, a
level of protest against the war, in which ever greater numbers of the young *will* resist the draft and ever greater num-

bers of older people *will* support them. Surely those who publicly express dissenting opinions do so for the purpose of persuading their audience to their viewpoint. As Coffin had testified on direct examination, "My intention was to win the minds and search the consciences of the American government, the Congress, and the people." To this extent, there is no discernible difference between public speaking and "counseling."

However, we would have believed Coffin if he had said he never tried to put any pressure, direct or subtle, on any registrant or group of registrants to violate the law and refuse the draft. This would have been out of character not only for Coffin himself but for the Resist movement generally.

The courtroom is no place to explore these fine distinctions, for in the straitjacketed confines of cross-examination the prosecutor has the sole maneuvering power and can predetermine by his questions what shall and shall not emerge of the defendant's philosophy.

However, even prosecutors sometimes slip up. A brief, random ray of light was shed when Mr. Wall, recalling the film of Coffin smiling and shaking hands with the young men at Arlington Street Church who came to give him their draft cards, asks what words he said to each—"Were they words of encouragement?" With measured emphasis, Mr. Coffin replies: "The words were, '*Are you sure you know what you are doing?*' In one case I gave the card back to a person because he was a law student and I remember saying, 'You're out of your mind.'" Needless to say, Mr. Wall quickly backs off from this line of questioning.

2.

The newspapers described Mike Ferber variously as "angel-cheeked," "disheveled 23-year-old cherub," "baby-faced graduate student," "child of the New Left." In any event, he belongs to the tell-it-like-it-is generation. For two full days before he was scheduled to testify, Bill Homans had put him through the cross-examination drill, a time-honored device in which the defense lawyer plays the role of prosecutor, throwing every sort of curvy question at his client to prepare him for the real thing. "At the end, I told him, 'You'll be all right if you just stick to the truth,' " said Homans. "But then I saw the whole session had been rather a waste of time—he's incapable of *not* telling the truth."

Ferber proved to be an unflappable witness. He does not suffer from the wearying self-righteousness of some of his *compères*, he is tough, able, and at times very funny. In spite of the obstacle course set up by the prosecution, he managed to clarify his own concept of "counseling" draft resistance.

Judge Ford evinced the esteem in which he held the cherubic lad by reading, shuffling papers, and whispering to his clerk throughout the testimony.

On direct examination, Ferber described the planning meetings that preceded the Arlington Street Church rally on October 16. In these meetings, which were attended by ministers and draft resisters, the main policy discussion centered on how to avoid a situation in which young men who hadn't made up their minds to turn in their cards might be moved to do so by the emotionalism of the moment. Precautions were taken against this; speakers were instructed on no account to exhort the audience to turn in cards, to say nothing that might propel them into making an on-the-spot decision.

Furthermore, an announcement was made at the church rally that all turned-in cards would be kept available for several days so that those who changed their mind after the meeting could recover their cards; in fact, five or six men did come to Ferber later to ask for their cards back.

One of these testified as a witness for Ferber (he had had

second thoughts about turning in his card after talking with his wife and his lawyer). And Ferber's roommate of two years, a graduate student at MIT, testified that he still has his draft card intact, that "Mike is very hesitant to pressure anyone to turn his card in, never suggested I should turn mine in." On cross-examination, Wall (now pleased with this phrase) asks the MIT student, "So *you're still on the fence?*"

The position of Mike Ferber and his colleagues in the Resistance emerges clearly from all this: they do not favor spur-of-the-moment decisions to sever connections with Selective Service by people who have not thought it through, have not weighed all the very considerable consequences.

Mr. Wall tries to shoot it full of holes with heavy sarcasm: "You're another preacher not trying to make converts? . . . you didn't intend anyone to act? . . . to attract the uncommitted? . . . to convince people on the fence?" Ferber, imperturbable, waits for an opening, which soon comes.

Q. Mr. Ferber, when you said toward the end of your speech on October 16, 1967, at Arlington Street Church: "Let us make sure we are ready to work hard and long with each other in the months to come, working to make it difficult and politically dangerous for the government to prosecute us," what did you mean by that?

A. One of the things I had in mind when I said that was political campaigning to end the war, that our example was a kind of petition to Congress to act, and that it might encourage candidates to run for office and might outrage the sensibilities of Americans that we felt we had to come to this action, and so on.

Q. Is that all you had in mind?

A. Yes, to the best of my recollection.

Q. And you are a great adherent of staying within the political system, using the ballot box, to change things, are you?

A. Among other things, yes.

Q. Among what other things?

A. Among demonstrations and protests.

Q. Including civil disobedience?

A. On occasion, yes.

Q. "Working to help anyone and everyone to find ways of avoiding the draft," what did you mean by that?

A. I meant that we, who are now in the Resistance, who are not *avoiding* the draft, would help other people find legal ways to do so.

Q. Did you say "we who are not avoiding the draft"?

A. We in the Resistance were not avoiding the draft.

Q. You were not avoiding the draft?

A. No.

Q. You are not avoiding the draft, you are rejecting it completely, is that right?

A. I am resisting it.

Q. In any event, you are not going in the armed forces, are you, come hell or high water?

There are objections to "hell or high water," and Wall substitutes: "In any event, you in the Resistance are not going in the army, are you?" More objections, and the judge says: "Well, he isn't in, yet; that is all I know. He is in 1-A now, isn't he?" This starts a small row, with Boudin objecting that Ferber's draft status is completely irrelevant. Finally we are back on course.

Q. "To help disrupt the workings of the draft and the armed forces until the war is over," what did you mean by that?

A. I meant that individuals would refuse on their own to cooperate with the draft system and the armed forces, that is by conscientiously refusing to take part in it until the war was over.

Q. Individuals would refuse on their own?

A. Yes, naturally.

Q. Without any attempt to convert them by you?

A. To what position?

Q. To refusing to go into the service?

A. No, we have not been *converting* people to do that.

Q. Did that include sit-ins at induction centers for the disruption of the draft?

A. I never advocated sit-ins at induction centers.

Q. You don't subscribe to that as a method of stopping the war, stopping the administration of the draft?

A. Do I now or did I then?

Q. Did you then or do you now? We will start with: Did you then?

A. Did I then? I think not then.

Q. You think not; you don't know?

A. Well, it had never come up. I was aware that another group was doing so on the West Coast. I wanted to see how that went.

Q. "Let us make sure we can form a community," what did you mean by that?

A. A number of things: I meant in particular that we should find ways to—well, to get to know one another better; to make sure that what we had done was not just an isolated act of protest, but that our own personal lives would be improved; and that we would help, help really comfort each other in the trials that might come.

Mr. Wall is not doing too well with this witness, and now he turns to the publication of Ferber's speech, "A Time to Say No"—Did Ferber know it was going to be published? No. Didn't it occur to him that it *might* be published? Yes.

Q. But your intention would not be to influence any reader later who happened to see it to your view on the draft?

A. *Yes, to my view on the draft.*

Q. Now, you maintain that you were not trying to

make converts in the church when you were making that speech, is that correct?

A. That's correct.

Q. Well, what effect were you trying to have on persons who had made the resolve to turn in their draft cards and to disassociate themselves from the Selective Service system?

A. To help deepen their understanding of what they were about to do.

Q. And their commitment?

A. Yes, and their commitment . . .

It has been rather like watching a far-off swimmer fighting his way against the current through buffeting waves. There is satisfaction on the whole among the courtroom spectators, they feel their man reached shore.

3.

Mitchell Goodman's main contributions were twofold. First, he caused Mr. Wall—who has a short fuse at the best of times—to flip completely. At one point, during a bench conference, Wall denounced Goodman as "a fraud and a liar" in such thunderous tones that it was picked up by the sharp-eared press.

Second, Goodman made such hay of the alleged conspiracy, made it seem so hopelessly and risibly inefficient, that puckish Mike Ferber was moved to draw up his own Motion for Severance:

"The defendant Ferber makes a Motion for Severance on the ground of incompetence on the part of his co-conspirators who, the testimony has shown, were unable, despite their best efforts, to conspire, combine, confederate, or agree to do anything, and in general could not organize their way out of a paper bag."

On direct examination Mr. Barshak got Goodman to describe his antiwar activities at Stanford, with the veterans' group in New York and Washington, and his efforts to organize East Coast professional people during the time of the alleged conspiracy.

A frustrating time seems to have been had by all. After his visit to Coffin, Goodman testified, he wrote the now-famous letter, subject of expert pouch-and-manifest evidence, asking for an appointment with the Attorney General. "I mailed the letter off to Coffin, asking him to sign it and send it on. My hope was that he would get others at Yale to sign it, because I was afraid we weren't going to get any response to the letter."

Q. You called Rev. Coffin at some time after having sent him that letter?

A. Right, about four or five days later.

Q. What was the gist of that telephone conversation?

A. Well, I said to him that the person in Washington who was helping us to make arrangements had called the Justice Department, and they had no letter. I said to the Reverend Coffin, "What in the world happened to the letter? It is getting late. We have to get that letter to them if we are going to get any appointment."

Q. What did he say?

A. He said, in effect, "Oh, my God, I forgot it." And I said, "Please put it in the mail immediately."

The Whitehall Street demonstration, as described by Goodman, was also beset with mortifying stumbling blocks arising out of the vagaries and unpredictability of organizers, rank-and-file demonstrators, newsmen, and policemen.

Q. Tell us everything that happened.

A. I arrived early in the morning, about quarter of six, it was dark and somewhat confusing and I didn't know where I was. People were milling around. Everyone seemed to be looking for a center, that is, someone to tell them what to do.

I noticed there were a great many police.

Then someone indicated to me that there was a platform and a man standing on it with a microphone. . . . I moved over toward the platform, where I met a number of people I knew in New York who were down there as well, and then I realized it was David McReynolds on the platform and I knew that he was the organizer.

Q. Did he give some directions or something at that point?

A. Yes. He was talking about what would happen to try to orient people, and after a few minutes he said, ". . . Those who want to commit civil disobedience form on this side and those who want simply to be in a legal picket line form on that side."

I moved over to the right side; I knew I was going to be in the civil disobedience part of it.

We got together in a very rough formation and I found Dr. Spock there, . . . I was pleased and surprised to see him . . . people were being pushed right and left by news photographers and television men who were creating a terrible scramble. It was hard to keep organized. . . . Finally we conferred with the police officer and a lieutenant. . . . It was so dark and so confused. . . . There was a large number of police officers massed on the steps of the building. . . . We came up to the barrier.

Q. What happened there?

A. *Nothing* seemed to happen. We just stood there.

Q. Who is "we" at this point?

A. I was standing next to Dr. Spock, and Dr. Spock was so thoroughly surrounded by newspapermen and television people we were isolated from everybody else.

Q. What happened at that point?

A. We stood there for a few moments and Dr. Spock said to me, "What are we supposed to do?"

And I said to him, "Well, I don't really know but we are supposed to get through here to that place on the sidewalk. The only one who *really* knows is David McReynolds."

At that point I shouted to some people behind us, "Where's David McReynolds?"

Nobody knew.

And so Dr. Spock heard this and he was terribly busy with these television people and then he said to me, "Well, we can't just *stand* here. This is foolish."

And so the next thing he did was to get down on his hands and knees to try to get under the barrier.

Q. And did you?

A. I got under there with him; right.

Q. What happened then?

A. We stayed there thinking the police would let us through in a few moments and they didn't. So we got up, we stood there a few moments longer and I thought, well—

Q. You can't tell us what you thought. Just what happened.

A. I started to call for Inspector [Sanford] Garelik, the Chief Inspector of the New York City police force. . . . I shouted over the barrier, hoping to reach him.

Q. Then what happened?

A. There was no response and Dr. Spock said again, "Well, this is foolish, just standing here. I thought that arrangements had been made for us to go through."

I said, "Yes, arrangements, I thought, had been made, but *where* is David McReynolds? Because he is the spokesman."

Q. Then what happened?

A. Dr. Spock put his leg up on the barrier and tried to get up on it and the police officers behind the barrier put their arms up, they were obviously intent on not hurting him. Then I called for Inspector Garelik.

Q. Did Inspector Garelik show up at this point?

A. At that point, he emerged from a group of police officers near the steps.

Q. Did Inspector Garelik come over to where you and Dr. Spock were?

A. He approached me, as I was calling for him.

Q. Did he tell you what to do?

At this dramatic moment, Dr. Spock in the act of breaching the barricades, Goodman shouting for Garelik, a sudden and unexpected squall blew up in the courtroom. Wall objected to what Garelik said as hearsay, but the judge overruled him: "Let him say what he said. Let's get it over with." The overruling of an objection by the prosecution was such a startling switch that one or two spectators gave the judge a little hand. But the judge was far from pleased at this acclaim: "Did I hear applause down there? All right, everybody out of here but the press. Come on please, I am ordering them out, every one of them, all but the press. Stop these demonstrations!" he roared. Everybody filed out, some waving surreptitious good-byes to the thunderstruck press, the defendants' wives moving like proud and angry swans. The wives were let back in after a while, on one of Leonard Boudin's few successful motions in this court.

Meanwhile, back at the barricades, it developed that after a few more stops and starts everybody got arrested who wanted to.

Q. And was it an orderly procedure, people getting up and leaving with the police officers who were arresting them?

A. Oh, yes, certainly orderly. . . .

Q. And you were charged with violating the city ordinance? . . .

Q. And that is the end of Whitehall, is that it?

A. That is the end of it as far as I know anything about it, yes.

4.

Everyone becomes an amateur lawyer. Mitchell Goodman, on cross-examination, says that he had phoned a student in Palo Alto to alert him about the Justice Department demonstration: "I told him he'd learn more details through the network, through the grapevine." The trial fans exchange anxious glances, and during the recess there is much criticism of Goodman. "Tsk, tsk! He should *never* have said 'network' and 'grapevine.'" "What an unfortunate choice of words!" "Yes, he really slipped up there, played right into the prosecutor's hands."

On the other hand, why *shouldn't* he have said "network"? Is there a network of people, and particularly students, in this country who oppose the war and exchange information on all manner of antiwar activities? Of course there is, just as there is a network of conservationists, or philatelists, or amateur-radio hams. But the spectators have been sensitized by all that has gone before to the danger lurking within any word connoting mutuality: we—our—agree—concerted effort—network, and the like.

The temptation of witnesses to try to outfox the lawyers at their own game was great and at times disastrous. The performance on cross-examination of Professor Seymour Melman, who testified as a witness for Marcus Raskin, could serve as a model of how *not* to comport oneself on the witness stand.

Melman is professor of industrial enginering at Columbia University, author of several books on sociological subjects, and director of research for *In the Name of America*, an impressive compilation of news reports about war crimes in Vietnam published by Clergy and Laymen Concerned About Vietnam. In a word, he is a distinguished personage in the intellectual community.

Professor Melman was one of the eleven-man delegation that entered the Justice Department. His testimony was important to Raskin's case, because he established that Raskin was invited by Coffin to join the group only at the very last minute as an afterthought, and also that it was Waskow, not Raskin, who accused Mr. McDonough of dereliction of duty in refusing to accept the draft cards.

In cross-examination Mr. Wall made no effort whatsoever to shake this testimony, in fact he never even referred to it. Instead, he went after the witness and demolished him, which proved all too easy to do:

In Round 1, Wall tries to pin down that Professor Melman went into the Justice Department for the purpose of turning in the briefcase with draft cards to the Attorney General, but Professor Melman, a shade too jaunty and self-assured, says, "I did not *possess* a briefcase with draft cards."

Wall (light jab to the right): You had no intention to go in there and turn in those draft cards to the Attorney General as a purported violation of the Selective Service law?

The witness (looking anxiously for an escape hatch): Answer that question, your Honor?

Judge Ford: Sure, answer it if you can.

The witness (trying to dance out of reach): I think I responded to the same question before.

Judge Ford (with asperity): Well, do it again.

The witness: I said that I was not in possession of draft cards.

Judge Ford: Did you know there were draft cards in that briefcase?

The witness: It was said there were draft cards.

Judge Ford: Do you know that they were?

The witness: No sir, I did not with my own eyes see a draft card. I don't know how to recognize one.

Judge Ford (now furious): Wait a minute! Were you told that there were draft cards in the briefcase?

The witness: There may have been.

Judge Ford: WELL, WERE YOU *told* THERE WERE?

The witness: Yes, sir.

The witness has been badly pummeled, but it gets worse. In Round 2, Wall asks if he saw some men putting their draft cards in the briefcase. "They may have," says the reluctant witness. The judge orders him to answer whether or not he saw it, and the witness still insists he saw no draft cards, he wouldn't know how to recognize one. He adds rather prissily, "It's my duty, sir, to speak with exact knowledge for what I know *exactly* . . . ," which is exactly the sort of thing the judge won't tolerate. "Stop that and answer the question!" he orders. "No speeches. Put the question." The question is reread.

Judge Ford: And the answer is?

Professor Melman: Some persons said they were putting their draft cards in. Other persons put in other pieces of paper.

Round 3 deals with Marcus Raskin's draft card, which Mr. Wall now produces and shows to the witness, who says he does not recognize it as a draft card.

Judge Ford: Do you know what that paper was, that document that was shown to you? Do you know what it was?

The witness (on the ropes): It doesn't say "draft card" on it, no sir.

Judge Ford: DO YOU KNOW?

The witness: No, sir. I read the print. It does not say "draft card."

Judge Ford (fit to be tied): No more talk, please!

The end is not long in coming. In Round 4, Wall moves on to read back McDonough's testimony about what Professor Melman said at the conference in the Andretta Room, and asks if that *is* what he said. "Not in the way just stated."

Judge Ford: DID YOU SAY IT IN SUBSTANCE?
The witness: I don't know what the word "substance" means.

A clear-cut K.O. Or rather, Melman, swinging wildly, has managed to knock himself out. "No further questions," says Mr. Wall. "Step down," says the judge, and with that Professor Melman is unceremoniously dropped back into the shadows.

5.

Marcus Raskin took the stand on the day RFK died. The Boston *Herald Traveler*, in an editorial on the assassination, noted that "in this nation and abroad people are saying what has become virtually a cliché: 'America is a violent and sick society,' " and then went on to top that with a cliché of its own: "Nor is it only the oppressed, the desperate, the irrational who defy the law. Americans of the stature of Dr. Benjamin Spock and the Rev. William Sloane Coffin stand charged with an anti-draft conspiracy. . . ."
As court opened Judge Ford announced: "All rise and remain silent for two minutes in respect for the memory of Robert F. Kennedy." We did so, and a pervasive, empty sort of gloom filled the courtroom. In this atmosphere Raskin testified on direct examination about the roots of violence:

In the period immediately at the end of the summer of 1967 I debated Senator McCarthy on the problem of the Vietnam war and the crisis in American cities, and I said that nothing would be able to be done about violence in American society unless the Vietnam war was stopped, that the state itself was now the spearhead of using violence, and that people, individuals, were taking their cue from the state itself as to the use of violence.

Raskin, who is one of the foremost experts in the United States on the Vietnam war, did his best to give the jury a short course on the subject:

I found out, for example, that as the result of American bombing policy in South Vietnam, specifically, that as many as two million refugees existed in 1966 in South Vietnam; that by 1967, the projection was that of being three million refugees.

I learned—and let me continue that part of it, if I may: It meant that an entire culture was being uprooted; that the young were taken away from their parents and that the old, in effect, were left to die in many cases. They were resettled in some cases in large settlement camps which to a very great extent, according to first-hand reports which I received from Bernard Fall and other people, were very similar in their judgment to concentration camps.

I also learned that there was a continued pattern of the use of napalm in South Vietnam for the purpose of hunting supposed members of the National Liberation Front. So that the use of such a weapon was that in attempting to find one or two guerrillas, what we would do is destroy whole villages.

And this was, as I understood it, under the Geneva Conventions of 1949 an illegal act.

I further learned that the United States had very greatly increased the use of defoliants in South Vietnam which was for the purpose of attempting to find guerrillas in the jungles or guerrillas in rice paddies.

The problem was that this also was destroying the land and it was destroying, as well, many people beside the land.

Furthermore, the amount of defoliants used has increased over the past four years by a factor of about five.

I further learned that by the late summer of 19—

The Court: You were informed.

The witness: I was informed.

The Court: Strike out the word "learned." You were informed, go ahead.

The witness: I was informed that by the summer of 1967, forty per cent of those serving in Vietnam were people who were drafted into the armed services.

Furthermore, I had also learned—

The Court: No, been informed.

The witness: Excuse me.

I had been informed that the Gulf of Tonkin Resolution, which was predicated on an attack, supposed attack by the North Vietnamese PT boats on American warships, was basically incorrect. That, therefore, the Gulf of Tonkin Resolution, as it was presented to the Congress, was not a true and accurate picture of the events which occurred in the Gulf of Tonkin at that time. . . .

I was informed that the prisoner-of-war conventions which the United States had signed were being violated by the United States in Vietnam and that the United States either through direct design or by accident had undertaken to use sadistic methods and methods of torture in order to obtain information in Vietnam.

Cross-examination about his connection with the overt acts brought out that although Raskin had turned in his own 4-F draft card at the rally outside the Justice Department, he did not view a draft-card–turn-in as a very meaningful or important thing: "That is, I thought it was, you know, in my view, silly." He added that when Coffin tendered the briefcase full of draft cards to McDonough, "I squirmed, but I stated no objection."

His purpose in accompanying the delegation into the Justice Department had been to demand an official inquiry, along the lines of the Warren Commission investigation, into allegations of war crimes in Vietnam.

I didn't think that the draft-card–turn-in was the issue, in my view the issue was the illegality of the war and the problem of war crimes.

So what I did after Mr. Waskow spoke to the question of evidence of a crime was at that point, after he had spoken, to say that it was my considered opinion that the question was the war crimes in Vietnam, and I said that I hoped that Mr. McDonough would report to the Attorney General that I hoped that a special committee would be appointed by the Attorney General to ascertain whether or not war crimes had occurred in Vietnam and whether or not this was in violation of American law.

That is my recollection, to the best of my knowledge, of what happened at that point.

An important question that may arise in the future for those who tend to get a little carried away at mass meetings was partially clarified during the cross-examination of Raskin: Does the government consider applause evidence of conspiracy?

Wall is questioning Raskin about the speeches outside the Justice Department: "Do you remember Dr. Spock next to Mr. Coffin applauding for a long time when that was being said?" Boudin leaps to his feet in a rage: "Objection! Objection! I didn't know that applause was a crime, and I want to come up before your Honor and argue this matter. I think this is *intolerable!*" "Stop that talk!" roars back the judge, and the lawyers troop to the bench.

Tempers are so high that we can hear most of what is going on up there. Boudin is repeating that "it is not a crime for a man to applaud, and it's improper to use this as an indication of conspiracy or a crime." The judge is countering: "You stood up with that unjustifiable remark, you can't holler before the jury 'it's intolerable'! If you do it once more, I'll deal with you. . . . Want this to be a repetition of the Dennis trial? Keep it in mind!"

Mr. Wall is allowed to ask the question, and now he proceeds to interrogate Raskin about his own applause after Coffin's speech: "Let me put it this way. Was your applause merely perfunctory politeness to Mr. Coffin or did you applaud in *agreement* with the position he was taking, and in *advocacy* of the same position?"

Somewhere betwixt and between, it seems:

A. Not in advocacy of the same position but certainly more than politeness.

Q. And then he went on to say, "and we pledge ourselves to aid and abet them in all ways we can." Do you agree with that statement?

A. To aid and abet young men who in good conscience—

The Court: No, no. Do you *agree* with the statement? Read the statement again.

Q. I will start from the beginning. "This is to publicly counsel these young men to continue in their resistance against the draft, to continue to refuse to serve in the armed forces as long as the war in Vietnam continues." You say you applauded that partly or mostly out of politeness rather than agreement with it?

A. Well, more than politeness, yes.

Q. More than politeness?

A. More than politeness.

Q. "And we pledge ourselves to aid and abet them in all ways we can." Were you associating yourself with that statement that he made?

A. Yes, and I would like to qualify that.

Q. All right.

A. Because my meaning of that would be that those who in good conscience had made up their own minds certainly deserved the moral support of older people. . . .

Raskin even outdid Mitchell Goodman as a Wall-irritant. At one point during cross-examination, Wall thundered forth: "Stop looking at your lawyer!" (implying illicit signaling between Raskin and who? Telford Taylor? Calvin Bartlett?). All defense lawyers rose as a man at this affronting insinuation. A moment later the judge was heard whispering urgently to his clerk, "Tell that son of a bitch to *cut it out!* He'll blow the case if he keeps this up, and get us all in trouble."

6.

Flagging courtroom spirits revived as Dr. Spock's case got under way. Preliminary to his own testimony were the surprise appearance of Mayor Lindsay, who came up from New York as a defense witness, and the buffeting of his several distinguished character witnesses by the judge.

There were oohs and aahs in the corridor when Lindsay was seen, accompanied by Leonard Boudin, striding toward the courtroom. "Isn't he handsome! If only there were some women on the jury, they'd all fall in love with him." To which Russell Peck, moving amongst the corridor throng, threw out a dexterous "Sorry about that."

Mayor Lindsay cast a wonderfully comical light on the whole conspiracy charge, for he seemed unwittingly to implicate himself as a full-fledged co-conspirator, or "detail man," as John Wall would say, in the planning of the Whitehall Street demonstration. He threw around all sorts of Taboo Words like "cooperate," "agree," "plan," with gay abandon. It soon became apparent that he had done considerably more to wilfully and knowingly combine, conspire, confederate, and agree with diverse other persons in connection with this event than had Dr. Spock. In fact, he had gone to some trouble to seek out Dr. Spock, apprise him of all the arrangements, and introduce him to the leaders of the demonstration.

Furthermore, the New York City police were in it up to their necks, meeting behind the scenes with David Mc-Reynolds of the War Resisters League and other organizers of the sit-in, mapping out routes, discussing policy and logistics, deciding on procedures to be followed, even agreeing down to the last details as to the exact spot on the sidewalk where Dr. Spock and the others should sit and be arrested.

The Mayor testified that he had been following the circumstances leading up to the demonstration very closely, and decided that he should "reach out for some of those who were involved, particularly Dr. Spock," to discuss the whole matter.

"Our police had already had discussions with some of the participants in regard to logistics, use of marshals, routes to follow, the areas around the induction center that could be used and not used, and I knew about all those discussions, of course, in great detail," he said. Having learned that Dr. Spock did not know about *any* of these plans and was not even acquainted with David McReynolds and the others, the Mayor decided to get them all together for a meeting at Gracie Mansion at which they could make thorough preparations for a peaceful rally to culminate in the arrest of Dr. Spock.

"Dr. Spock said he was delighted to cooperate," said the Mayor, "that he, of course, had a disagreement over the war in Vietnam, that he felt called upon to state publicly exactly what he thought and that this demonstration was a way in which he could express himself and that obviously, of course, he hoped very much it would be a peaceful and orderly demonstration—but he expected to be arrested, and he wanted that to be an expression of his dissent, but that he expected and hoped that it would be a quiet and orderly thing, that people would sit down at the appointed place and then be taken by the police in custody. That was the plan."

The Mayor and the demonstrators exchanged information about personnel for the march. McReynolds explained that his group had spent many hours "in setting up a structure of marshals that would be identified and whose job it was to cooperate with the Mayor's staff and with the police," and the Mayor in turn promised to furnish the names and telephone numbers of a special staff he had assigned to act as direct liaison between demonstrators and police.

"I told them," the Mayor said, "that I understood their concern about being left free to express themselves and we would protect that right. I told them that my concern, on the other hand, was about the stability [of the city]. I said that I could not tolerate any violence and that while we would make every effort to see to it that the demonstrators were allowed to state their case and to proceed along agreed-to channels of walking and marching, that I expected their full cooperation. . . ."

One other small worry was brought up by David McReynolds: "I recall him saying that he hoped that he would be arrested very promptly because it was very cold in December and he didn't want to have to sit on the pavement too long." This too was amicably arranged and nobody caught cold. "Marshals, arrest that man as a conspirator!" rumbled Dan Lang, as the Best-Dressed Politician of the Year stepped down from the witness chair.

7.

For some unfathomable reason known only to lawyers and judges, the ordinary rules of evidence are not only suspended but completely reversed when character witnesses take the stand. Hearsay evidence, which means pretty much what it sounds like, is normally not admissible in a court of law, that is, a witness may not ordinarily answer, "I heard him say . . ." (I have heard it said that there are thirteen exceptions to this rule, but these do not concern us here.)

A character witness may *only* give hearsay evidence and he must under no circumstances say anything about the defendant's character. He may only testify as to the defendant's general reputation in the community—in other words, to other people's opinions of the defendant. He may not discuss his own opinion of the defendant, nor how he arrived at it, nor even what he *believes* to be the defendant's reputation.

Often a judge will relax these rules and permit a character witness to testify within legal limits in his own way and style, but in Judge Ford's court, there were three standard set questions to which the character witness had to respond: 1. "Do you know if the defendant has a reputation in the community for veracity, etc.?" The answer here must be "Yes" or "No." (The human impulse to say, "Reputation? Well indeed! Of course he has, I should say so!" must be curbed.) 2. "Do you know what that reputation is?" Again, "Yes" or "No." 3. "And what is that reputation?" Here, a single unadorned adjective is called for, such as "Good," or "Excellent," although the super-bright character witness might get away with "Of-the-highest-order" spoken as one word.

This absurd routine is so far outside the normal way people communicate ("What do people think of so-and-so?" "Oh, he's a splendid chap, brilliant, the kindest man on earth . . .") that the poor character witnesses found themselves totally at sea in trying to say their piece, particularly since Judge Ford was far from well-disposed toward them.

Thus Dr. Dana Greeley, president of the American Unitarian–Universalist Association, witness for Michael Ferber, having weathered the first two questions, was asked by

Ferber's counsel: "And what is that reputation?" "I would say that he would be acclaimed very highly—" began Dr. Greeley, but the judge cut in: "No, no. Just good, bad, or indifferent, please, or whatnot." To which Dr. Greeley responded indignantly: "Excellent! Excellent, *not* whatnot."

The character witnesses for Dr. Spock, eminent leaders in medicine, education, and public health, some of whom had traveled thousands of miles to come and testify, fared especially badly at the hands of Judge Ford. He would first heckle them unmercifully and then gruffly order them from the witness stand like small boys who have failed to recite their lesson properly.

It would go like this:

Boudin is examining Professor James Dixon, president of Antioch College. He has elicited that Professor Dixon has known Dr. Spock for many years, has worked with him on public-health legislation, educational policy, and the like.

Boudin: And on the basis of all that, can you tell us whether Dr. Spock has a reputation in the community for veracity, for integrity, and for good character?

Professor Dixon: I can.

Boudin: And will you tell us what that reputation is?

Professor Dixon (enthusiastically): Dr. Spock's reputation is a person of extraordinary integrity, extraordinary independence of view . . .

Judge Ford (cross): No, what is the *reputation?* Is it good, bad, or indifferent?

Boudin (pacifically): The witness is going to be very brief, I think.

Judge Ford (crosser): Let him answer the question! It is a simple question. Let him answer it and we will get along. WHAT IS HIS REPUTATION?

Professor Dixon (puzzled, but trying): And a person who holds his convictions with great firmness and skill . . .

Judge Ford (*very* cross): *What* is his *reputation????*

Boudin (*very* sweet): Is his reputation for character, veracity, and integrity a good, bad, indifferent, or excellent reputation?

Professor Dixon (dimly tumbling to it now): Oh! An excellent reputation.

Judge Ford (grumbling): That's all I wanted to know. . . . Step down, sir.

Dr. Milton J. Senn, for twenty years Sterling Professor of Pediatrics and Psychiatry at Yale Medical School, is the next to walk this tightrope. He testifies that he had been closely associated with Dr. Spock over the years and knows him socially—but lets drop "we haven't seen each other for quite some time." Boudin is already in the middle of his next question ("On the basis of these associations . . ."), but Judge Ford has spotted it and interrupts: "Did you say you *haven't seen him for some time?*"

Dr. Senn: I would say within the last two years we have not met.

Judge Ford (with telling emphasis): *Not met at all!*

Boudin deftly pilots his witness past this shoal and establishes that Dr. Senn has met Dr. Spock hundreds of times over several decades, and that he knows what Dr. Spock's reputation is in the community; it is "excellent and without blemish."

Judge Ford: As you have known him?
Dr. Senn: As I have known him.

(The judge is clearly trying to implant the impression that Dr. Senn's information is out of date, so Boudin pursues this):

Q. Is this a reputation which he has *today?*
A. It is my belief, yes.
Judge Ford: No, no, "It is my belief."

(To Boudin, who has wheeled round, incredulous): Oh, go ahead, sit down.

But Boudin will not. The wrangle continues for a while with Boudin doggedly pursuing the witness's knowledge of Dr. Spock's *present* reputation, and the judge interrupting. Finally Dr. Senn gets out "Excellent!" and is hustled off the stand by Judge Ford with a barked-out "Step down, sir."

8.

There was much curiosity among the courtroom crowd about the judge. We learned he is an Irish Roman Catholic, a Democrat, that he had worked his way through Harvard at the turn of the century as a railway conductor and postal clerk, was a classmate of Franklin D. Roosevelt, that FDR had appointed him as a federal prosecutor in 1933, that he had served on the Boston City Council during and after World War I, that in 1938 he was appointed, again by FDR, to his present lifetime post as federal judge. Carol Liston, in one of her *Globe* "color" stories, wrote with understandable restraint (for after all she has to live in Boston), that "over the years, some observers of Ford's courtroom feel that his experience as a U.S. Attorney has left him with at least some noticeable sympathy for the prosecution's point of view."

How did he get assigned to this particular case, we wondered? I asked Russell Peck about this. Peck explained that he himself is responsible for parceling out the cases among the six federal judges, and that he does it entirely by lot. "The point is to have the assignment removed from anyone's personal choice, so that attorneys are not tempted to shop around for a given judge to sit in a given case."

The cases are divided into categories—criminal, tort, contract, admiralty, and so on. Each of the six judges gets an equal number of cases in each category. This is accomplished by putting their names into a series of numbered envelopes. If, for example, there were twelve tort cases to be tried, the envelopes in that category would number 1 through 12 and each judge would get two.

How do the judges' names get into the envelope? "I write them on slips of paper, shuffle the slips face down on my desk, or shake them in a hat, and then I pick them out at random and place them in the numbered envelopes." "Oh— in rather the same random fashion in which you assembled that jury panel?" Mr. Peck gave me a rueful-dirty look.

9.

At last it is Dr. Spock's turn. He seems a trifle too big for the witness chair—his appearance is at once ungainly and magnificent, like a great eagle in a too-small cage.

The rules of evidence are now shifted into reverse. Dr. Senn was chastised for saying "it is my belief," but Dr. Spock is *only* allowed to say anything about the war, and the circumstances that brought him into this courtroom as defendant at the bar, if he prefaces his statement with the Magic Words "I believed." (This is called "state-of-mind testimony"; the judge, having ruled out any evidence about the illegality of the war, allows the witness to say what he believed to be the facts.)

The judge admonishes him early on. Dr. Spock is explaining how he arrived at his present position on the Vietnam war, starting with how the United States first got involved. He is up to the Geneva Accords: "The Geneva Accords specified among other things . . ."

Judge Ford: Strike it out.
Boudin: What did you *believe* . . .
Judge Ford: I have said several times we won't go into the Accords of Geneva at all. They are not relevant to the issues in this case. He believed in them. That's it, please.

Boudin (doggedly): What did you *believe* they said? Don't tell us what the Geneva Accords were or their contents, just your state of mind.

Dr. Spock: I *believed* that the Geneva Accords specified that there was to be an election within two years . . .

Judge: NO!

Boudin: I am asking for his state of mind.

Judge: He said what the Geneva Accords *specified*.

Boudin: What did you *believe* it *signified*?

Now it is plain sailing, for Dr. Spock is allowed to answer: "I *believed* that it *signified* in substance that Vietnam was to be left to the Vietnamese people and there was to be no further interference from foreign countries and that their government was to be decided by an election in 1956."

If this was intended to put Dr. Spock off his stride, it did not work. The cumulative effect of "I believed," repeated over and over again in Dr. Spock's measured, indignant tones, was to add a dimension to his discourse about world events, so that it became more than a mere recitation of the facts as he saw them. It came through as the deeply felt credo of a profoundly compassionate and outraged man.

A sampler of Spock beliefs:

On the Tonkin Gulf Resolution: "I believed that our government was wrong in stating that the Tonkin Gulf Resolution was a substitute for a declaration of war.

"I also believed that the Tonkin Gulf Resolution was achieved by the Administration, was secured from Congress on the basis of misleading information.

"I believed that we had provoked the retaliation from North Vietnam, that our government knew we had provoked that attack and deliberately misled Congress in getting the Tonkin Gulf Resolution."

On violation of international rules of law: "The United States, I believed, has been deliberately destroying crops and foliage, which is forbidden by the Geneva Conventions.

"I believe that we have forcibly dislocated and put into what are essentially concentration camps between two million and three million South Vietnamese people, which is forbidden, that dislocation is forbidden, by the Geneva Conventions.

"I believed that we were destroying a country that had never intended us any harm. We have killed hundreds of thousands not only of fighting men of the Vietnamese forces, but we have killed hundreds of thousands of civilians, women and children. There are tens of thousands of orphans who will grow up to be delinquents because of lack of parental care.

"I believe that the United States has been carrying on a war that had no shred of legality and I think will blacken the reputation of my country for decades, if not centuries to come.

"In other words, my own belief is that this was a totally *outrageous* and *abominable* thing that the United States had been carrying on."

On loss of U.S. prestige: "I felt strongly that the U.S. had lost its leadership of the free world, and I believed from reading the foreign press that the United States is now despised by hundreds of millions of people who used to believe in the United States around the world."

On a pediatrician's view of the war: "Especially in relation to those twenty-three thousand young American dead, I have a strong feeling—what is the use of physicians like myself trying to help parents to bring up children, healthy and happy, to have them killed in such numbers for a cause that is ignoble?"

On the Nuremberg judgment: "I believed that it justified me and other Americans in opposing orders of any kind from its government which we believed would constitute crimes against humanity."

On the obligations of a citizen and husband: "I believe that a citizen was compelled to work against the war if he believed it was contrary to international law, and this gave me the belief that I was not subjecting myself to conviction on this basis. But I *did* have a belief that I ought at least to discuss it with my wife!"

During the direct examination of Dr. Spock, the judge relieved Mr. Wall of his prosecutorial duties and did virtually all the objecting for him.

Leonard Boudin is saying to Dr. Spock, "We will now come to the press conference of October 2. I'm not going to examine you in great detail about it . . ." Says Judge Ford: "Never mind making a speech, put the question, please."

Boudin icily demands to approach the bench on this. During the bench huddle he points out that he had merely made a brief preliminary remark of the kind made by several other counsel, and he adds: "Will your Honor note my exception to your Honor's statement to the jury?"

The judge leans toward the jury. "What I meant, members of the jury, was to have counsel put the question without any preliminary talk before the question is put. That was all. *And it is his duty to do so,*" he adds, glaring at Boudin in severe rebuke.

Sometimes the judge gets carried away by his own advocacy, as in the following bewildering exchange: Dr. Spock has just been stating his beliefs as to betrayal by the U.S. of its promise to abide by the Geneva Accords in establishing the puppet Diem government: ". . . and my belief was that this was particularly outrageous for a democratic country like the United States to do since President Eisenhower himself said . . ."

Judge Ford: Never mind Eisenhower. What you believe.

Boudin: What did you believe, Dr. Spock, with respect to what President Eisenhower had said?

Dr. Spock: That if they had been allowed to have their election, eighty per cent of the Vietnamese people would have voted for Ho Chi Minh.

Judge Ford: That is what Eisenhower said?

Boudin moves along to another question, but Judge Ford suddenly interjects reprovingly: "We refer to Eisenhower as *President* Eisenhower." Totally confused, Boudin: "But I thought *we* had . . ."

On the troublesome matter of "counseling," Dr. Spock unwaveringly explained that his own intention had indeed been to reach *everybody* with the message of the "Call to Resist Illegitimate Authority"—not just the older generation, not just the young men who had already made their minds up to refuse the draft, but also those draft-eligibles who were undecided.

"First, I thought the 'Call' and my signing it would have an effect on the population generally, older people but also younger people. It would be my way of saying to the American people, 'I believe that these young men who believe that the war is unjust are doing a patriotic thing, giving up their educational deferment. They are risking jail because they believe they're doing right by their country.' I believed it would be a new and effective way of saying to the government, 'We believe that the war is so wrong that we are going to publicly take a stand with these young men.' "

He also believed it would have an effect on young men, "on that group who had already acted in draft resistance . . . and on another group of young men who had already decided that the war was unjust but had not got up the courage to take overt action, this would give them the courage to take active steps in draft resistance.

"Then I believed in addition that there were many young

men who were evading the issue of the rightness or wrongness of the war, who preferred not to look into it, and that this would be a dramatic way of saying to them: Look, there are a number of young men and older people, too, who believe that this war is not only unjust but disastrous to this country. We invite you to listen to our views and to join us.

"So that I hoped that these people who had not faced the issue, even of making the decision in their own minds, would join us.

"I believed, on the other hand, that it is wrong for me to try to persuade anybody actively to resist the war. And I might point out that in all these things I was doing I was addressing the public generally. I was never in the business of counseling young men."

Lastly, a telling word about Dr. Spock's position on individual conscience versus the law:

Q. Did you base your claim of right to oppose the war upon your conscience or upon your view of the law?

A. I always based it on rule of law. I never felt I had to differentiate between law and conscience or fall back on conscience, because I always believed that a citizen must work against a war that he believes in good conscience to be against international law. This is the Nuremberg principle, which I believed is part of the United States law.

Mr. Wall, perhaps more than a little uneasy at the prospect of crossing swords with this adversary, laid aside his customary weapons—belligerence, sarcasm, indignation— in favor of a straightforward, almost conversational manner. Dr. Spock responded in kind, as though patiently trying to explain his views in simple terms to one who might be expected to have some difficulty understanding them.

There were certain antiwar tactics of which he did not

approve, Dr. Spock said in response to Wall's questions. He would not encourage draft-eligibles to flee to Canada: "I don't think that helps to end the war, it only solves *their* problem." He did not advocate destruction of Selective Service files, nor the forcible closing down of induction centers. "I think that doesn't stop the war, it is counterproductive in terms of public opinion, and likely to turn people against the peace movement." For the same reason he would not favor sending money to the Viet Cong.

On the other hand, he said, he "approved very much" of turning in draft cards, and would have gladly carried the fabrikoid briefcase full of draft cards in to the Department of Justice himself had he been asked to do so. He "would be glad if 500,000 men in the army or navy decided that the war was unjust and refused to obey orders." He wanted to encourage action on the part of "those who have decided that the war is unjust, but who haven't got up the courage to take active steps."

"And you also wanted to reach the young men who were evading the issue?" asked Mr. Wall. "Correct." "Well, don't you consider that an act of persuasion?" "Yes, in the sense of public education and encouragement," answered Dr. Spock.

What of the October 2 press conference—did not Dr. Spock realize that his famous name attracted an unusual number of reporters to such functions? "Right, that's why I try to go to so many press conferences, I was averaging three a week." Did Dr. Spock tell the Women's Strike for Peace in Philadelphia that getting 500,000 men home from Vietnam justifies civil disobedience? "Yes." And that the draft-card burners are the real heroes? "Correct."

Did he tell a newspaper reporter that those who are against the war should burn their draft cards and those that are in the military should refuse to go to Vietnam? Peering reflectively at his young interlocutor, Dr. Spock replied:

"Those are *approximately* my views. But I come to my views very slowly, and I express them very carefully, and I doubt very much that I said '*should* refuse.' I would never say 'should refuse'; everyone has to make up his own mind. I *hope* that many men will refuse to be inducted, and I *hope* that many men will conclude that the war is illegal and will refuse to obey orders, but that is not the same as '*should*,' or that I urged them to." "No, it certainly isn't," rejoined Mr. Wall, a trifle lamely.

The defendants have now all been heard from, but the battle for the jurors' minds and hearts is by no means ended. Now it is the turn of the experts, and only after they have had their say will the jurors retire to carry out the oath they took on the day they were empaneled: "Do you severally solemnly swear that you will well and truly try the issues between the United States and the defendants at the bar according to the law and evidence given to you, so help you God?"

4

Closing Arguments

1.

Three and a half weeks of trial, fifteen fat volumes of testimony. The jurors have sat (and sometimes slept) through this endless barrage of words and images flashed before them. Now come the summing-up arguments, a fascinating yet at times agonizing spectacle.

The final days of the trial belong to the lawyers, who must pick and choose from this vast amount of raw material, decide what to magnify, what to minimize, what to ignore altogether, how to weave a consecutive story from it all that will convey Innocence (or at least Reasonable Doubt) for the defense, Guilt for the prosecution.

As the moment for the closing arguments approaches tension builds up, one can sense it at the counsel table, it spills over into the audience. For the lawyers this is the culmination of all the months of pretrial work, the intensive concentration during the trial, the painstaking scrutiny of the daily transcript, the rushed, last-minute consultation with colleagues about possible approaches to the jury.

Each defense lawyer was allowed about an hour in which to summarize the three and a half weeks of testimony, and

Mr. Wall (because there is only one of him), about two hours. The differences of approach to the issues among the various defense teams that had dogged the trial from the beginning were dramatically highlighted by the closing arguments.

While certain common themes ran through all—the "conspiracy" of strangers, a conspiracy conducted entirely in public, the peaceful, nonviolent character of all the defendants' activities, activities protected by First Amendment rights of free speech—each lawyer stamped the finished product with his own indelible individual trademark, his own philosophical outlook.

It is second nature to a defense lawyer in any trial when addressing the jury to glow and vibrate with crusading belief in the justness of his client's cause, to quiver with indignant outrage at the preposterous allegations of the prosecution, and these lawyers to a man glowed, vibrated, and quivered, each according to his ability. It is also second nature to hack away at the prosecution's case, to pull out from the evidence every element of proof in his client's favor. These lawyers did that, too.

But does not the political trial impose a further obligation on the defense lawyer, that of forcing the jury to examine root causes, to think as they have never thought before about why this prosecution was brought, how the defendants got in this fix—to interpret for the jury a world that for them may be strange, unfamiliar, antipathetic, the world of political action? This is an exceedingly tough thing to do, within the confines of the record, the time allotted, and court procedure. Only Barshak and Boudin attempted it.

St. Clair followed the tried and true methods of criminal defense, garnished with reflections on the First Amendment. Homans, dedicated civil libertarian, spoke of love, hope, and moral courage. Barshak, nimbly treading just at the edge of forbidden territory, in his quietly impressive way, treated of the underlying issues of the trial. Bartlett mournfully developed the theme of the Little Man Who Wasn't There. Boudin with elegant skill sliced the conspiracy into shreds. Wall, effortlessly reaching for the lowest common denominator, couched his argument in terms of movie plots and speeding tickets.

James St. Clair, first to address the jury, early on fell dutifully in step with the Court's rulings. Observing that the Vietnam war is the first in our lifetime "about which there was any substantial question as to whether it was a proper war" (and that Mr. Coffin himself had served in both World War II and the Korean conflict), he added, "Now, as his Honor pointed out yesterday, this is an issue upon which people can differ. Some, no doubt, think it is a proper war. Some, obviously, think it isn't. His Honor will tell you that is not what is being tried here. We are not trying the war. We are not even trying the unconstitutionality of the draft act." Having summarily disposed of the war, proper or improper, St. Clair, seasoned trial lawyer that he is, proceeded to deal with the alleged crime in the customary fashion of his calling.

The experienced criminal lawyer knows how to construe the evidence to the best advantage of his client, how to anticipate and demolish in advance the likely arguments that will be made by his opponent, the prosecutor (for the latter always has the last word). For example, he will dwell upon the defendant's upright character: "Now, ladies and gentlemen of the jury, you heard my client's foreman testify here the other day. Let me recall to you what he said. 'Sober, reliable, a regular church-goer, always on the job.' Now, I ask you, ladies and gentlemen, is that a description of a *murderer?*" His alibi: "And didn't you hear his brother testify that as they were driving back from the church supper that evening he heard the town hall clock strike eight—

the very moment the prosecution claims the shots were fired?" The failure of the attempt: "If this was a murder attempt it was the clumsiest in history. The prosecution's own witness, the doctor who testified here, admitted that the victim may yet recover . . ."

To the distress of the spectators (and perhaps to Coffin himself), St. Clair bore down heavily on these themes.

On Coffin's character: "Is it likely that a clergyman, chaplain of one of the major universities of the world, with a distinguished military record, who was a trusted employee of the CIA for a number of years, would enter into a criminal conspiracy?" (Groans from the *Ramparts* readers in the audience.)

On his alibi: "If there *was* a criminal conspiracy among those present on October 20, Reverend Coffin didn't seem to participate in it. You may recall that after the demonstration some of the parties went to another meeting that night. Reverend Coffin didn't go. . . . The Reverend Coffin had nothing to do with the Whitehall Street incident, in fact he was invited to go and declined. He refused to participate because he did not believe in that form of demonstration. He believed in peaceful, orderly, serious-minded appeals to his government. . . . Coffin had always been against burning of cards." (Groans from the unindicted co-conspirators, for is not the inference that those who did participate, those who had burned their cards, were guilty while Coffin was innocent? That Spock and Goodman, who had been arrested at Whitehall Street, were not "peaceful, orderly, serious-minded" types?)

On failure of the attempt: "Let's see what the success was of this nationwide program of young people to turn in their draft cards. I hold in my hand a box three inches wide and about ten inches long representing the 'success.' According to my analysis there are cards of 253 individuals from this nationwide program. Can the government say with any persuasiveness at all that there is evidence in this case of *success* to prove the conspiracy? Certainly not in the turn-in of these few cards on the result of a nationwide program." "A draft card is turned in to the Department of Justice. What happens to it, and what *did* happen to it? It was sent to the local draft board, where the individual is subject to being reclassified 1-A as a delinquent. It doesn't hinder or delay the draft act; it accelerates it! One way to really get into the army quickly is to turn in your draft card." (Groans from the Resistance kids. St. Clair seemed to be pulling the rug out from under their whole movement as well as trivializing the often-stated dedication of his client to their cause.)

Next, Mr. Homans for Mike Ferber. While one cannot fault the lawyers for drawing on the evidence to demonstrate the nonparticipation of their clients in the alleged conspiracy, it was somehow discomforting to find splendid Mike Ferber disappearing from the scene like the Cheshire Cat as Mr. Homans listed for the jury all the places where Ferber wasn't, all the manifestoes he didn't sign, all the people he had never met, all the activities of which he had no knowledge. He was not at the October 2 press conference, was not chosen to go into the Department of Justice with the delegation, not a signer of the "Call to Resist Illegitimate Authority" nor of any of the Mitchell Goodman documents, and except for one casual encounter with Coffin in the Arlington Street Church, not acquainted with his co-defendants. It would, of course, have been most remiss of Homans *not* to point all this out, and it was not his fault that the net effect of the recitation was somehow demeaning to Ferber. Hard is the lot of a lawyer defending a conspiracy case where there was no conspiracy.

The redeeming portion of Mr. Homans' summation came at the very end—he tried so hard, and with such evident emotion breaking through his natural New England reserve, to find the words with which to convey to the jury his own high regard for his client: "Few are willing to brave the disapproval of their fellows, the censure of their colleagues, the wrath of their society. Moral courage is a rarer commodity than bravery in battle or great intelligence. Yet it is the one essential vital quality for those who seek to change a world that yields most painfully to change.

"You will recall one question I asked Mr. Ferber. I asked what did he mean when he said we must love our brothers, and he was a little embarrassed, as you must have noticed, and answered. I would suggest this is not a case of conspiracy, this is a case of love, of love for one's fellow man here in this country or abroad, and acting upon that, I would suggest you would find an explanation of Michael Ferber's actions, and I hope you will return a verdict that is just."

Listening to these arguments, I could not help wondering what tack the defense would have taken had the circumstances been somewhat different. Supposing these five, all dedicated to the cause of ending the Vietnam war, all part of the East Coast intellectual community, had been close friends, constantly in and out of each other's houses, meeting regularly to plan press conferences, demonstrations, mass mailings of Resist pledges? The indictment charges that the conspiracy started "on or about August 1, 1967." So here is Coffin, on the phone to Raskin in Washington, saying, "Can you come up to New Haven on or about August 1? Mike Ferber is going to be there, and Ben Spock, Mitch Goodman, all the guys." "What do you mean, *on or about* August 1?" says Raskin, who is a stickler for precision. The meeting is arranged, and from it flow all the other acts charged in the indictment: the five friends draft the "Call to Resist," send out notices for the October 2 press conference, agree that Ferber and Coffin shall be the principal speakers at the draft-card–turn-in ceremony in Boston on October 16, and agree that they would all meet in Washington on October 20 to confront the Attorney General with the draft cards. And supposing there were no minor differences over tactics between the five, they were all in complete agreement about the propriety of demonstrating at induction centers, burning draft cards, and the like —so what? I wondered. Would not the peace movement have benefited from the improved efficiency, the sense of united purpose that could have resulted from this different set of circumstances? And had this been the case, would they have been any the more "criminal"?

Ed Barshak's summation came as a surprise to everyone. He had been the quietest of all the lawyers during the trial, never one to jump up first with objections—perhaps the judge had hardly noticed him, and that is why he was able to get away with so much in his closing argument?

Explaining that he was going to present "a sort of non-legalistic approach," he plunged right in to Mr. St. Clair's proper or improper war: "The basic facts are really rather few in number. The first is an immense fact, which has been sitting in the atmosphere of this courtroom ever since we got here, but from which none of the witnesses can subtract anything, and that is the fact of the existence, back in 1967, during the time of this alleged conspiracy, of the war in Vietnam, and the tremendous disruption of feelings among people in this country.

"Some people reacted very strongly to what they considered the huge number of American troops halfway around the world supporting what they considered a sort of musical-chairs local government and with a tremendous, as they saw it, death and destruction of moral proportions, in their eyes.

"We wouldn't be here but for this basic fact: that this has been unlike any other war in which this country has ever been involved, a war which is tearing apart the American people, to say nothing of what it is doing to the people who live over there.

"That is the fact against which I suggest you have to judge the conduct of what people did."

Placing responsibility for preserving free speech squarely on the jury, Barshak told them: "It is one thing for the Court to tell you what is the law of this, that and the other thing, what is the law of free speech, what is the law of conspiracy and so forth. But what in fact is left over for free speech, what in fact is left over for the rights of us Americans, depends upon how *you* find the facts.

"What I'm saying is there is a danger, and you are the only ones who are in any position to do anything about it. There is a danger that juries could find facts in such a way that this tool of the law called conspiracy will eat up the area that you and I and everyone else has considered to be our right to associate with each other, to sign things, to go to meetings and so forth.

"If we aren't careful about that, then we are going to allow the law of conspiracy by virtue of the facts found by juries to swallow up what we all consider to be very important to us. . . . How the jury sees the facts makes the real determination in this country as to what we can and what we can't do. . . . I can't talk about the law, but the judge of course will. After you hear the rules, the question is whether or not you are going to characterize the defendants' actions factually as a criminal conspiracy or as allowed American conduct, allowed American association, allowed sitting down on the sidewalk for the purpose of violating a local ordinance, *you* are going to decide that, and nobody else can."

After giving a capsule account of Mitch Goodman's peace activities both before and during the period of the alleged conspiracy—including his coffin gambit on Fifth Avenue—Barshak delivered a warning: "It took courage for these gentlemen to state their positions diametrically opposed to what the Administration had been saying all along, they must have known they were running the risk of some people saying they would be unpatriotic.

"This notion of patriotism can be very simple in the totalitarian society. You just do what you're told—'Heil!'— and run and do it. . . . Since the time of Hitler the worst thing missing is the lack of conscience. It is seared in my memory. Maybe in some of yours, too. What I'm trying to say to you is if you are going to use common sense, as I know you are, be careful before you label as criminal intent an exercise of conscience by people like Mitch Goodman who, like myself, have a seared memory of what happens where there isn't enough conscience."

Raskin's counsel, Calvin P. Bartlett, listed what he called ten "lurid activities" with which his client had nothing to do: the Whitehall Street demonstration, the Yale Service of Conscience, the Arlington Street Church episode, a Spock press interview, the Goodman letter to the Attorney General, the meeting between Goodman and Coffin in New Haven, obstructing induction centers, sit-downs, picketing. "And finally, Mr. Raskin never in his life was present when a draft card was burned."

He pressed on (and this, it turned out later, was a telling point with the jury): "Have you, since you have been here for three weeks, seen on the TV screen or anywhere the voice of Marcus Raskin? Have you ever heard him make a speech on the many, many reels which you have seen? I submit the answer is No."

Another telling point: Raskin did not listen to the speeches of the others at the October 2 press conference because "they were boring." (Unhappy glances exchanged by some of the speech-makers in the audience.) Mr. McDonough had (as we all know by now) confused Raskin with Waskow as the speaker at the Department of Justice who pounded the table and demanded that the government accept evidence of a crime.

Mr. Bartlett, like Mr. St. Clair, dwelt ponderously on

all the top-secret stuff to which his client had once been
privy as incontrovertible proof of his patriotism: "Loyalty
—when you think that the information that Mr. Raskin had
on disarmament and other matters, the classified, top-secret
information given him when he was on the staff at the
White House and elsewhere, that one inch of disloyalty
or lack of patriotism in this man could have resulted in
disaster!" (Later, Raskin told me he found some of this
"shockingly embarrassing: I *urged* him to go slow on the
presidential confidence bit.")

Twinkling Boudin, reveling in his unaccustomed role
as trial lawyer, styled his address to the jury as "The Case
of the Missing Agreement." The "Call to Resist" was, he
said, the only concrete evidence of an agreement that deserved looking at, and the question for the jury to ponder
was: Does this document constitute a criminal agreement
setting forth criminal purposes? If so, what of the thousands
of other signers—Professor Robert McAfee Brown, distinguished professor of religion at Stanford; Professor
Samuel Goldberg of Harvard; Rabbi Louis E. Goldberg;
the poet Robert Lowell, to name a few? "Either the document is meaningless, or it contains an implication of criminal intent on behalf of all of these distinguished men."

Or is the document rather a political platform, "a public
manifesto or tract, the kind that were so familiar in the
days of Tom Paine, a campaign document, a statement of
beliefs"? Boudin led the jury through the "Call," paragraph
by paragraph, then summarized it as "an attempt by these
older men, who are watching the younger men go through
all these traumatic experiences, death, injury, fear, watching them go through all of these, watching some of them try
to extricate themselves from the terrible thing which we
older people have brought them to. . . . These older people
said, Why should we sit on the sidelines when these young
men are leading the battle? Let's at least come up in the rear.

The people who signed this are not the leaders or instiga-
tors. They are the admirers, and admiration is not yet
criminal in this city or in this country."

As Boudin was in full swing his moment at center stage
was turned briefly into the Case of the Facial Demonstration.
During all of the summations there had been a complete
hush over the courtroom, none of the usual whispered asides
just out of earshot of the marshals that marked the more
boring bits of the trial. Therefore a *frisson* of astonishment
ran through the spectators when suddenly the judge roared,
"No demonstrations! No facial demonstrations will be in-
dulged in here." The press, round-eyed, gazed apprehen-
sively at one another ("Was it *you?*" "Was it *me?*") and
Mr. Coffin half rose to ask, "Do you mean me, your Honor?"
"No," said Judge Ford, "that gentleman there," pointing to
Victor Rabinowitz, Boudin's law partner and the only
beard at counsel table. Rabinowitz: "Who, *me?*" Judge
Ford: "Yes. Go along." Boudin, with a courtly swiveling
movement, turned back to the jury.

What else did the government have on Dr. Spock? For one
thing, unlike Raskin, he listened to and applauded other
people's speeches. "Now really you must have some worry
about your case if you have to pinpoint attention to the
fact that one man is applauding another. I do not really
think that in our system of mass meetings, of publicity, of
demonstrations, that applause can properly be said to be a
constituent element of the crime of conspiracy." This got
to Mr. Wall, who rose to object: "There is no indication
that I said that the applause is proof of conspiracy." Then
why was it pointed out as an item of evidence? asked Boudin
evenly.

Where other counsel had performed a vanishing act
with their clients, emphasizing all the things they hadn't
done, perverse Boudin produced a huge chart to show
that the five public or quasi-public appearances of which

the government had accused Dr. Spock were only a minute fraction of his actual antiwar activity during the period of the alleged conspiracy. He had in fact attended about seventy other meetings, press conferences, and demonstrations. He was constantly on the go, all over the country, seizing every opportunity to speak against the war. What did he do after the October 2 press conference? He dashed off to another meeting in Long Island. And after the October 20 demonstration in Washington? He spoke at another demonstration at the Lincoln Memorial, covering both in one trip.

Again, where others had emphasized they spoke for one defendant alone, Leonard Boudin spoke for all: "You know I have the honor to represent Dr. Spock and Dr. Spock alone, but a sense of fairness in a lawyer's evaluation of the evidence gives me another sense, a sense of discomfort in merely asking for an acquittal for Dr. Spock. The same argument that I have made here to show the absence of agreement by Dr. Spock I think is equally applicable to all the defendants in this case."

And now Boudin turned the whole force of his personality directly on the jury—not pleading, not haranguing, just speaking very directly: "This is indeed a historical case which will go down, I think, in Anglo-American jurisprudence as an important case involving the fundamental liberties of the people in a period of national tension. In this country the findings of fact as to guilt are in the hands of the jury, persons to whom we entrust the liberties of our fellow citizens. This is particularly important, historically and today, as a barrier to an overzealous prosecution, a prosecution of political opponents of the government which is prosecuting.

"You have the historic function of determining the guilt or innocence of the defendant, the guilt or innocence of each one of these defendants. It is upon your final judgment and evaluation of the facts that we rely and depend. I thank you."

2.

Invariably, closing defense arguments engender a sense of high optimism among the accused and their friends. "Boudin made it all so crystal-clear, how *could* they convict after that?" "And the way the judge kept interrupting, and his facial-demonstration ploy! Surely the jurors are on to him by now?" There was hopeful talk of a hung jury, even of acquittal. But the Old Trial Hand was certain of the outcome, and inquired cynically, "What shall we do during those ten tense minutes while the jury is out deliberating?"

As Wall got into stride the optimism slowly leaked away. He was (we all thought) extraordinarily effective, his address to the jury dotted with colloquialisms, simple imagery, and homespun parables.

Mr. Wall's summation was as interesting for what it omitted as for what it contained. One might think that a prosecutor who has charged conspiracy to disrupt the draft in the middle of a war to which half a million American troops were committed (and in which young Americans were dying at the rate of hundreds a week) would feel honor-bound to cut loose with a bit of old-time flag waving. Where were our brave boys Over There, the gray-haired mothers and weeping sweethearts? Where were aid-and-comfort-to-the-enemy, subversive plots, the white feather, the threat to our way of life, the Yellow Peril?

Nowhere. None of these heart-tugging word pictures or erstwhile sure-fire appeals to red-blooded American patriotism figured in Mr. Wall's discourse, presumably because the Vietnam war was too generally unpopular to lend itself to that kind of thing.

Instead, Mr. Wall, one eye on the Gallup poll, played the

favorite themes of the moment: dangers of permissiveness, and law and order.

The government, benign but resolute patriarch, does not enjoy inflicting discipline, but sometimes regretfully finds it necessary: "As there may come a time in the government of individual families where permissiveness goes beyond the bounds of reason [a malevolent glare, here, at the hirsute trial fans], so, also, there comes a time in the government of nations when duly constituted authority must assert itself and face up to unwarranted challenges, no matter how unsought or how distasteful that confrontation may be."

Law and order versus anarchy: "If there is disagreement on policy, even on morality, as long as we can go to the polling booth and vote, I submit that is the proper way to do things, if we are not going to have *anarchy*. And sincerity can't be a defense. It can't be. Beliefs cannot be accepted as justification for conduct in violation of the duly passed law of the land. To permit that justification would be to say that whatever a person says his beliefs are is superior to the law of the land and would permit an objector to be a law unto himself. *Anarchy!*"

To help us through the complexities of the conspiracy law, Mr. Wall told about this terrific movie he once saw, *The Killing*, starring Sterling Hayden. In the movie, which is all about a conspiracy to rob a race track, various people were recruited by Sterling Hayden to help him in his plan: a bartender and a chess player were to start a fight as a diversion; somebody else was to shoot the favorite horse in the race; the getaway man, a policeman, was to drive off in his police car with the loot, and so on. "All members of the conspiracy. All agreed to disobey the law. All knew the purpose of this particular conspiracy was one to rob the race track. None or few knew each other."

Why did the government not prosecute the thousands of others whose activities had paralleled those of the five?

"It may be a poor analogy, but take the case of speed traps. You've got so many police. There is a speeding problem at a certain place. One police officer out there. He stops somebody. The fellow says, 'Hey, look, five guys just went by; why me?' " Because, Mr. Wall explained, "one of the reasons for enforcement of the law is deterrent to others—you can't get everybody in that speed trap, but you are going to get enough so that *everybody knows*. If it's a real bad speed trap and real danger to safety of the community, there comes a point where maybe you will have to have enough police out there to stop *everybody* who speeds." (Significant glances exchanged, here, by the many speeders in the audience.) "I submit it's a poor analogy, but when somebody says, 'Why me? Why me, and why not them?' maybe there are not enough police. Yet, maybe there are."

One must agree with Mr. Wall, it was rather a poor analogy, for the speed-trap cop operates in random fashion, he does not lie in wait for hours looking for Dr. Spock's car to flash by.

Mr. Wall's discussion of the defendants was an artful performance, perhaps a shade too artful as it turned out. He hardly mentioned Ferber at all, he eulogized Dr. Spock for his candor and forthrightness, sneered at Coffin, disparaged Goodman, and spent an inordinate amount of time savaging poor Raskin, whose wife at one point fled the courtroom in tears.

On Dr. Spock: "I submit to you he made a credible witness and a believable witness. And I submit to you you'd be warranted in finding that if he goes down in this case, he goes down like a man, with dignity, worthy of respect. . . . I submit to you that the defendant Spock on the stand was a man who appeared to be telling the truth, appeared to be hiding nothing." *But:* "I submit you could find on the evidence that the man convicted himself on the stand— that's for you to decide."

On Mr. Coffin: "Do you remember the defendant Coffin on the stand? He said he didn't know what aiding and abetting meant. Then I asked him if he remembered on the Contact radio program whether the following exchange took place:

Q. Do you think you'd really get a chance to state your case in open court? The prosecution hasn't helped people like Howard Levy particularly. Do you think you would have a chance?

Rev. Coffin: Actually, Levy had a good deal more of a chance than I would have thought. He did get a chance to make a good case against the war. But it might well be that a prosecutor would simply say, "Did you aid and abet these people in turning in their cards?" And I'd say, "Yes I did." And then the prosecutor might say: "Well, that's all the evidence we need."

"Those are Coffin's words on December 14. Contrast them with his words from that witness stand!

"Rev. Coffin says: You are a man of conscience. Don't surrender your conscience and I won't. . . . Is this country going to be tied to a string that is tied to Mr. Coffin's conscience? Is it going to be tied to a string even to the conscience of a man as sincere, as dedicated, as great, as Dr. Spock?"

On Goodman: "Mitch Goodman wrote to his congressman, he says, took an ad in the paper, went over to Lafayette Park and threw his discharge in a box and carried a coffin down Times Square. Big deal! Big deal! Does that give him a license now to break the law? I submit it doesn't."

Mr. Wall zeroed in on Raskin with elephantine sarcasm: "This great thinker, the head of some kind of brain factory in Washington . . ." "If you believe the defendant Raskin, that he didn't know anything about anything, didn't listen, just didn't know what the story was, just didn't know what was happening, of course you must find him not guilty." "Some of the defendants have testified that they had no intention to counsel, aid, or abet anyone. All except Raskin, I believe, who says he doesn't know anything from anything." "In a sense it's fortuitous, if you believe Raskin, the poor man who just happened to be in New York on October 2, just happened to be walking by the Justice Department on that day and decided to go in and talk to the Attorney General—it's fortuitous, and a terrible accident that he was indicted."

As to what Mr. Wall did or did not consider evidence of conspiracy, this got ever more muddling as he talked. Surely the defendants' signatures on the "Call to Resist" were evidence, since distributing the "Call" was Overt Act #1 of the indictment? But no. Discussing this document and the thousands who had signed it, Mr. Wall declared: "The government is not suggesting it is going to indict anybody for signing a piece of paper." And he seemed to have thought better of what he had said during the arguments on the motions about applause being evidence of implication in the conspiracy: "You will notice that nobody was indicted who merely stood by and applauded. . . . I think it is asking a lot, imposing on your intelligence to suggest that anybody in this, the most open society in the world, is going to be indicted for applauding. In questioning Mr. Goodman or Mr. Raskin on the stand I took very careful care to ask him whether the applause was perfunctory—I was getting the facts. . . ."

The closing portions of Mr. Wall's address were designed to set at rest any possible qualms the jurors might entertain that the government in bringing this case was something less than solicitous of First Amendment rights.

"Free speech is not an issue in this case. If you were to convict any of these defendants for talking about Johnson, talking about the generals, talking about Vietnam, you'd be doing a terrible injustice to them, to yourselves and to this country and the institutions under which we live. . . . You may disagree with the defendants, but by God, you are not entitled to convict them because you disagree with their political or moral or philosophical beliefs! . . . I submit to you, gentlemen of the jury, that these defendants and any person in the country can attack the law from every platform in America with impunity, but cannot under the guise of free speech nullify it by disobedience to its express provisions. . . .

"If they are guilty, say so. If they are not guilty, say so. In closing I just want to say this, and it's something you know and we all know, and that is that the government of the United States wins every case, every case in which justice is done no matter what the verdict happens to be. The government of the United States asks you to do justice under the law."

Judge Ford: Half past nine tomorrow morning, gentlemen. Half past nine.

5

The Charge and the Verdict

On several occasions during the closing days of the trial defense counsel emerged from behind the barrier looking exceedingly glum, suffering from severe and visible frustration. There was one exacerbating episode after another in the privacy of chambers, all revolving around the judge's charge, or instructions to the jury.

As the Old Trial Hand told me, these "instructions," in which the judge makes good his promise to lay down the law for the jurors, are the equivalent of a four-year law course crammed into one morning. He must define and clarify for the jury a score of complicated legal concepts, summarizing, in the form of "general instructions," principles (like the presumption of innocence) that govern all criminal cases, and stating in "special instructions" the law as it applies to the specific offenses charged in the indictment.

The content and wording of the charge is a matter of the greatest concern to the litigants, since this is the last and most authoritative word the jury will hear before they retire to their deliberations. In a case like that of the Boston Five, where the facts are not essentially in dispute, the law as laid down by the judge becomes *the* determining factor in the minds of the jurors. Moreover, it is of the utmost importance to the lawyers, whose closing arguments precede the judge's charge, to know exactly what position he will take on the legal issues involved. Consequently, the rules of the court require the judge to tell the lawyers in advance how he intends to instruct so they may shape their closing arguments accordingly.

Well before the end of the trial the contending lawyers submit to the judge their own proposed instructions, based on case law and precedent, couched in terms that express their theory of the case. At a conference in chambers the judge outlines the instructions he intends to use, the lawyers then argue for the adoption of their own proposals and object to those parts of the judge's charge with which they disagree. The lawyers will be on the sharpest look-out for errors of law in the judge's charge, for these are often their strongest points for appeal.

Judge Ford held such a conference on the morning of the closing arguments, but to the dismay of defense counsel he instructed the court reporter, for the first and only time during the trial, not to make a transcript of the proceedings. His reason, he said, was that he did not want the reporters to get wind of any of it (why, since the jury was locked up?). This put the defense at a severe disadvantage, for how could they object to portions of the judge's charge and, more important, properly prepare their own closing arguments without it?

Worse yet, the judge then informed them he would submit to the jury, in addition to the general verdict, "guilty" or "not guilty," a set of ten "special findings," in the form of a questionnaire to be completed by the jury in the event of a guilty verdict. This surprising announcement gave rise to an outraged howl of protest from all five defense counsel.

The questions in the special findings were put in this

way: "Question No. 1: Does the jury find beyond a reasonable doubt that defendants unlawfully, knowingly, and wilfully conspired, confederated, or agreed together and with each other and with diverse other persons to counsel Selective Service registrants to unlawfully, wilfully, and knowingly neglect, fail, refuse, or evade service in the armed forces of the United States and all other duties required of registrants under the Military Selective Service Act of 1967 and the rules, regulations, and directions duly made pursuant to said Act? Answer 'Yes' or 'No.' " And so on, down the list of the ten separate alleged objectives of the conspiracy charged in the indictment: conspiring to "aid" draft refusal, conspiring to "abet" draft refusal, "counseling," "aiding," "abetting" registrants to turn in their draft cards, etc.

In this mouthful, there is no provision for disagreement amongst the jurors, the Yes or No answer must be unanimous. Nor does it allow for any differentiation among the defendants, who are lumped together as a single entity.

In vain, counsel argued that this use of special findings in a criminal case, without the consent of the defendant, was unprecedented. Special findings are sometimes submitted to the jury in civil cases for the purpose of sorting out complicated issues. But in a criminal trial there is only one issue, guilt or innocence of the crime charged in the indictment, in this case a single count of conspiracy. Defense counsel urged that the jury has a historic right to reach its judgment for its own reasons, to vote its conscience free from the need to respond to the logic of a trial judge. The very phrasing of the questions would suggest guilt to the jury or tend to induce a compromise verdict, they said; in the rare cases in which special findings are used in criminal cases it is done only with the consent of the defendant and only when absolutely required for his protection.

Judge Ford, who like all trial judges does not relish the idea of reversal by a higher court, made it clear whose protection he had in mind: "Suppose they found them guilty, and so forth, and found them guilty of counseling. I may be wrong on the definition of aiding and abetting, but if they found them guilty of counseling, that would be enough to sustain the verdict."

Whence came the extraordinary proposal for special findings? In chambers, Telford Taylor remarked upon a curious circumstance: a series of sheets containing a request for special findings identical to those adopted by the judge had been distributed to defense counsel by the government the day *before* the judge had announced his plans to use them. Judge Ford's response: "They had prescience." He added, "It isn't a special verdict at all. There will be one verdict, and that will be guilty on the conspiracy count."

Word of these goings-on reached the press. Jack MacKenzie featured Judge Ford's prediction of "one verdict, guilty," in his Washington *Post* story, whereupon the judge ordered the court reporter to change the transcript to read, "There will be one verdict, and that will be guilty or not guilty on the conspiracy count."

The setting for the judge's charge is arranged as for a mystical communion between him and the jury. The formality and ritual that marked the trial are turned up a notch: bailiffs call for absolute silence. Once the jury comes in all doors are barred, there can be no comings and goings in the courtroom during this holy moment.

The judge binds the jurors to him in these words:

"Members of the jury, our duty is joint. There are two domains in which we serve. It is your duty to receive the applicable law from me, and it is my duty to explain it to you as correctly as I can.

"You must apply the law that I lay down. If I fall into error in laying down the principles of law, my error or errors can by reviewed in a higher court. If you apply your own law and make an error, it cannot be reviewed and corrected.

"Your domain is the determination of the facts . . ."

Defense counsel had submitted instructions bearing on the motives of the accused, such as Boudin's on criminal intent: "It is for the jury to determine the fact as to whether the defendants acted in good or bad faith, or with an evil or innocent intent. You may take into consideration the sincerity or insincerity of the defendants' belief that the war in Vietnam was illegal and that the draft was unconstitutional. If you find that the defendants sincerely and in good faith entertained such a belief, it is your duty to acquit. . . ." And on the nature of conspiracy: "A conspiracy connotes secrecy, artifice, fraud, concealment, and the like. In the absence of proof of such elements, you may not find a conspiracy on the basis exclusively of public statements."

Judge Ford, however, used virtually none of the instructions proposed by any of the defendants. Instead, he paraphrased John Wall's closing argument in these terms:

"Motive, no matter how laudable or praiseworthy that motive may be, cannot negate a specific intent to commit a crime. Good or innocent personal motive alone is never a defense where the act committed is an intentional violation of law—a crime. . . .

"When a statute has been knowingly violated, to show that a defendant had a good motive—such as dissemination of religious beliefs or the fulfilling, as he saw it, of a mission imposed upon him by the Deity, or his conscience—is no excuse whatsoever.

"There is no freedom to knowingly conspire to violate a law of the United States with impunity merely because one believes or doubts that the law is immoral or illegal or unconstitutional . . . a bona fide, sincere belief on the defendants' part that the Vietnam conflict and the conscription

of young men to serve in it was illegal, immoral, or unconstitutional, or a belief that the Selective Service Act was
unconstitutional, or a belief that they were protected by a
constitutional right of free speech, would be no defense or
excuse whatsoever to an intentional and wilful violation of
that law by the defendants, and such beliefs, members of the
jury, must not be considered by you in determining the guilt
or non-guilt of the defendants.

"Further, I charge you that if you should find from the
evidence that the defendants, or any of them, purposed to
test the law by conspiring to counsel, aid, or abet someone to
violate the law, then the fact that their purpose was to make
a test case is no defense to the charge here presented against
them ... the reason for such violation is immaterial to you in
your consideration of the question of their guilt or innocence."

His view of the conspiracy doctrine was identical with that
expounded to me by Van de Kamp: "The lack of success in
accomplishing the objectives of the conspiracy charged here
is incidental. . . . It is the agreement, not the success of the
plan, that is the important factor. . . .

"For two or more persons to conspire . . . to commit a
breach of the criminal law of the United States is an offense
of grave character which strikes a blow at the very existence
of law and order. . . .

"If an unlawful act is done openly and with public fanfare
or outward display and not in secret, it does not change in
any way the unlawful nature of the act. In other words, in
deciding whether or not these defendants had a criminal
intent, the fact that they made no attempt to conceal their
activities from governmental agencies is irrelevant and immaterial. . . .

"It is not necessary to establish a conspiracy to prove that
two or more persons met together and formally entered into
an unlawful agreement . . . if they intentionally and wilfully

worked together for a common purpose or purposes . . . it would establish a conspiracy. . . .

"A conspiracy may be shown even though the individual conspirators have done acts in furtherance of the common unlawful design apart from and unknown to the others. In a conspiracy all of the conspirators need not even be acquainted with each other and may or may not previously have met or associated together."

On Mr. Wall's speed trap: "It is no excuse or defense to those on trial that others not on trial or not indicted appear from the evidence to be implicated in the charge alleged in the indictment. . . ."

On conspiracy and First Amendment rights: "The government does not have to prove a conspiracy or an agreement to use force and violence. Let me remind you, members of the jury, that speech is a form of conduct; also, ideas may be communicated by conduct, and words may at times be keys of persuasion and triggers of action dependent on the circumstances and setting under which they are made."

On the special findings: "In addition to your general oral verdict, in the event that, and only in the event that, your single general verdict is one of guilty on the conspiracy charged, you will make and return special written and unanimous answers to ten questions. These special questions, members of the jury, will help to inform you as to the issues involved in this case." (Which we had thought had been the purpose of the four weeks' trial.)

"You may go now," Judge Ford winds up quite briskly, shortly after noon, and the jury files out to start deliberating.

Unaccountably, the atmosphere in the courtroom lightens and becomes increasingly jovial as the hours of waiting for the verdict go by. The journey is almost done, behind us, it is gala night. As at the last dinner at sea, seating rules are relaxed. Those of us who are still there, "sweating out the jury" as the lawyers call it, are allowed by the bailiffs to sit wherever we like: press, lawyers, resisters, defendants, wives, and supporters intermingle, swap trial reminiscences and guesses about what is going on in the jury room. Margot Lindsay has packed up the borrowed pew cushions, and she passes round some bottles of vintage Châteauneuf du Pape: "1966, really *quite* a good year." Mr. Coffin asks Russell Peck if there is a pingpong table anywhere in the building. There is, but we can't use it, Mr. Peck explains apologetically, because it is marked in evidence as an exhibit in a criminal case. "Then, shall we play charades?" "I thought we *had* been, for four weeks."

It is interesting to notice how relationships among the cast of characters have changed over the course of the trial. At the beginning, some of the accused seemed wary of each other, even hostile. They have now become firm friends, have come to like and respect each other in spite of disagreements over many philosophical and tactical questions. Goodman, the militant, would have liked to have dramatized the trial by taking the issues into the streets, to have conducted forums each day after court in which evidence from experts on the war, excluded by Judge Ford, could have been heard by press and public. Raskin was opposed to any such thing—on advice of his lawyers he even vetoed a press conference that had been called in the middle of the trial. Yet now, in this twilight zone of the trial, lion and lamb sit beside each other amicably discussing the forthcoming presidential elections. It almost seems as though the prosecution has inadvertently laid the foundation for a genuine "breathing together" of the five.

Surprising, to me, was the attitude of the press to the defendants, accustomed as I was to the uniformly hostile press that political defendants of the fifties had to put up with. The Boston *Globe* had given magnificent coverage to the trial throughout—between them, Anson Smith with his daily reports of the proceedings and Carol Liston, with her "color" stories, had done an extraordinary job of re-creating the courtroom scene for the reader. (Perhaps that is why the judge ordered the jury locked up, a move generally made to protect the defendant from the effect of adverse newspaper publicity on the jurors.)

Nationwide, newspaper coverage of the trial had been slim (with the exception of Jack MacKenzie's long and thoughtful pieces in the Washington *Post*); but this, I thought, was largely due to the fact that the events around which the trial revolved by now seemed ancient history. At the time of the overt acts, the autumn of 1967, the mounting confrontation between the antiwar movement and the authorities was front-page news everywhere. Senator Eugene McCarthy was not yet in sight, the re-election of Lyndon Johnson seemed a certainty. By the time of the trial, the Boston courtroom seemed a backwater; all eyes were on the events that Spock, his co-defendants, and like-minded "peace people" had helped to bring about: the candidacies of McCarthy and Robert Kennedy, the Paris peace talks.

As the hours of waiting go by, and the jury still does not return, press, defendants, and lawyers drift out, first to lunch, then to dinner. The press are furious over the judge's charge. What possible chance do the defendants now have for acquittal? The judge practically repeated everything the prosecutor said in his closing argument. Some of the defense lawyers unbend to explain what went on behind the scenes: John Wall knew all along exactly how the judge was going to instruct on the law, and he tailored his closing argument accordingly. However, all the better for our chances on appeal, they assure us.

At last, rustlings behind the barrier, comings and goings of bailiffs and clerk, indicate that the hour is at hand. The jury has deliberated for almost eight hours, and now the defendants are called back in. They stand at attention in their accustomed row while the jury announces its verdict.

The clerk, staring ahead: "Mr. Foreman, How Say You? Is William Sloane Coffin, the defendant at the bar, guilty or not guilty?"

"Guilty."

"Is Michael Ferber, the defendant at the bar, guilty or not guilty?"

"Guilty."

"Is Mitchell Goodman, the defendant at the bar, guilty or not guilty?"

"Guilty."

"Is Marcus Raskin, the defendant at the bar, guilty or not guilty?"

"Not guilty."

"Is Benjamin Spock, the defendant at the bar, guilty or not guilty?"

"Guilty."

(On the special findings, the jury found the four guilty of all charges but conspiring to "counsel" registrants to turn in their draft cards.)

The jury is now polled individually, each in turn, so we start the whole thing over again:

"Juror Number Two, How Say You? Is William Sloane Coffin, the defendant at the bar, guilty or not guilty?"

"Guilty . . ."

It begins to sound like a litany, sixty questions, sixty responses, about as long and as short as the minute in *Yellow Submarine*. The defendants stand there, straight and stiff with solemn and befitting Sunday-morning faces, "Good night, and good luck," says Judge Ford to the jurors, and it is all over.

Marcus Raskin, deeply upset, escapes through the lines of waiting reporters. "How do you feel about the verdict?" they say. "I feel good for myself and very, very bad for the others," he answers, his voice breaking. Dr. and Mrs. Spock kiss over and over again for the photographers. A weird jubilance prevails; eventually we all go to the Parker House bar. Raskin is there, and the Old Trial Hand plies him with drinks: "Cheer up, Raskin. If you're dissatisfied with the verdict, you can always demand a new trial."

Everybody cheers up, including Raskin. The bar is a huge gloomy place, enlivened tonight by the presence of the Spock trial cast, for whom a large table is set up in the middle of the room.

The band strikes up a waltz, Dr. and Mrs. Spock rise, bow formally to each other, and take the floor, looking for all the world like a honeymoon couple. There is a spontaneous standing ovation. First some of the people at Dr. Spock's table stand, then they are joined in thunderous applause by the groups at tables around the side of the room: Parker House bar regulars, traveling salesmen, Kiwanis convention types, middle-aged couples out for a night on the town—all clapping as though their lives depended on it, all for that brief moment co-conspirators.

6

The Sentencing

A few weeks later we were all back in Boston to hear Judge Ford declare that the defendants' crime had been "in the nature of treason" (a word never used in the trial, even by the prosecutor) as he sentenced them to two years in the penitentiary. In addition he announced fines of five thousand dollars each for the elder three, one thousand dollars for Michael Ferber, who surmised that he had been accorded the special student discount rate.

The sentencing ceremony in Judge Ford's court consisted of brief epilogues to the trial, in which the participants, judge, lawyers, and convicted conspirators, each strove in his own way to express what the four weeks' proceedings had meant to him. These came through as vivid and highly characteristic vignettes.

First defense counsel spoke in behalf of their clients.

James D. St. Clair: "The Reverend Coffin is an upstanding, honorable man, a family man. . . . Has there been a great deal of harm done by his acts? No evidence was presented that there were actual draft-card–turn-ins due to his actions. Whether we agree with him or not is another question. He was a leader in a substantial public debate on a substantial public issue. I plead for a suspended sentence. . . ."

William Homans: "Michael Ferber is an exemplary student, a man of impeccable conduct, of good family. He is one of a group who felt very frustrated in 1967 in their attempt to influence the government. This case indicates the nature of the system against which they struggle. . . . He has nothing to apologize for. His conduct is not the kind that is discussed in court as a rule. He's not a bank robber. His is an attempt to affect government policy."

Edward Barshak: "Law enforcement and the judiciary will be best served if this trial is treated as one of principle. If a prison term is not suspended, then this case will be viewed as an act of repression for public acts and public speeches."

Leonard Boudin, disdaining as superfluous any mention of the exemplary, impeccable, honorable, and upstanding character of his client: "This is an historic trial, a trial which, in terms of history, may prove to be as important as many of the cases which have come down over the years in the field of civil liberties and of free expression." Speaking of the thousands of signatories to the "Call to Resist," he quoted Edmund Burke's speech on conciliation of the American colonies: " 'It looks to me narrow and pedantic to apply the ordinary ideas of criminal justice to this great public contest. I do not know the method of drawing up an indictment against a whole people.' "

Next, Judge Ford called upon those of the defendants who wished to address the Court. Spock and Coffin declined, they would save their remarks for a press conference after the sentencing.

Michael Ferber: "Your Honor, I have nothing to say that might mitigate my punishment. I only wish to point out that I have been part of no conspiracy, but rather I have been part of a movement, a movement led by my generation.

This movement arose from our horror and disgust at what the United States is doing both at home and abroad. Apparently we have frightened some people in the government who have decided that what we have created out of love for what our country might be, must, out of fear, be called a crime. I cannot leave the movement; I will remain working in it. I have no regrets."

Mitchell Goodman: "This is a crucial, desperate moment in history. I feel deeply that much depends on us who are well along in our lives. We must understand the young people who are growing up. Part of my impulse to join this movement comes from my desire to achieve this understanding. Every young man today is growing up in the strangest period the world has ever known. Since the invention of the A-bomb and the H-bomb there is a new limit of life, a new condition of history. When I was growing up, no matter what happened, I always assumed that life would continue. This is the post-bomb generation. They grow up in a world that can be blown up any minute, that might end any minute. We must have compassion for them. They act from moral principle, from their view of the world and of history. I am compelled to give them my support."

Judge Ford positively outdid himself. "The government has charged in this case what amounts to rebellion against the law," he thundered, encompassing defendants, press, and spectators in an avenging glare. "The defendants have been found guilty of intentional and wilful violation of the law." Quoting remarks made in 1835 by a North Carolinian judge, he continued: " 'Rebellion against the law is in the nature of treason. The law deserves our obedience.' . . . High and low, the intellectual as well as all others, must be deterred from violation of the law, and I believe it was Justice Abe Fortas who stated in a recent publication, 'Lawlessness cannot be tolerated.'

"Where law and order stops, obviously anarchy begins.

"It would be preposterous to allow those who, as the jury found, conspired to incite Selective Service registrants to violate the law to escape under the guise of free speech."

The convicted conspirators, at last freed from the unnatural restraint of the past six months—"unlawyered," as Mitchell Goodman put it—spilled out of the courthouse like schoolchildren at the end of class. Thousands had turned out to greet them (for the lawyerly ban on demonstrations was now lifted), among them, Marcus Raskin, who had come up from Washington to join with his erstwhile co-defendants. There were banners everywhere: "Spock's my doc!" "JOIN THE COMMON CONSPIRACY!," announcing a meeting on the Boston Common, where yet another group of young men would turn in their draft cards in honor of the defendants.

Many of the unindicted co-conspirators were on hand to express their support. Noam Chomsky addressed the crowd: "In the light of the trial just concluded, one must be careful what one says at a press conference! Nothing that happened in court calls into question the sentiments expressed in the 'Call to Resist Illegitimate Authority.' Free men will continue to express and act on this belief."

Robert Lowell presented twenty-eight thousand signatures collected during the trial on a "statement of complicity" ("If they are sentenced, we will take their places") and declared: "When a state sends noncriminals to jail, then it is tending towards a police state. Our backs are to the wall. We fight for the honor of our country. We thank these men for their courage and strength of heart."

Coffin denounced the trial in words which summed it up for many of us: "The four-week trial of the Boston Five was dismal, dreary, and above all, demeaning. It was unworthy of the best of America.

"It was demeaning in the first place to the government. I had little quarrel with being indicted; in a way I had invited it. But the invitation read clearly: to test in court the legality of an undeclared war, the constitutionality of the draft law, and finally to test in court what is always and eminently worth testing—the limits of dissent guaranteed under the First Amendment.

"But what did the government do? It skirted the uncomfortable, it ducked the difficult, it refused the invitation. Instead of confronting the real issues, it availed itself of the sweeping provisions and paranoid logic of an outdated conspiracy law.

"Naturally it was demeaning to us to find ourselves held to account for what we did not do, and few I imagine are the frustrations comparable to those of having to argue a big case in a small way."

Part IV

The power of the jury on occasion to deliver an accused person
from both the police and the letter of the law is the sole reason
for its existence as an institution.

> George Bernard Shaw, *Everybody's*
> *Political Who's Who*

1

Twelve Tractable Men

The concept of trial by jury is such a familiar article of
our mental furniture that, like the kitchen stove or re-
frigerator, it is simply taken for granted. We have ceased to
inquire into its origins, whether it works as it should, to
what new and creative uses it could be put. We know from
history books that it is an ancient common-law right derived
from Anglo-Saxon law, we know from friends who have
served on juries roughly how it works in practice, and we
have seen juries in action in many a Perry Mason show.

Yet a number of fuzzy and erroneous ideas have grown up
around the jury trial. For example, it is widely believed that
the role of the jury during the presentation of evidence is a
purely passive one, that jurors must sit attentively but si-
lently throughout the testimony. Not true. Theoretically, a
juror may speak up at any point during the trial, may demand explanations: "But I didn't understand what the
witness was saying, I should like to ask him a few questions."
Of course he seldom does because he is rarely told he has
this right. Moreover the juror, having watched Perry Mason
in action, is not likely to depart so radically and abruptly
from tradition at the risk of looking like a fool, even though

214 THE TRIAL OF DR. SPOCK

he may sense that the other jurors are as confused as he.

Likewise erroneous is the assumption that jurors are forbidden by law to disclose how they arrived at their verdict. Once discharged, a juror may discuss the deliberations of the panel as freely as he wishes. Not infrequently grave miscarriages of justice have been averted by such post-trial disclosures.

And is the function of the jury limited to weighing the evidence and deciding the facts in issue—did or didn't he do it? The answer is not so easy, although the judge routinely *tells* the jury that this is so, not once or twice but hypnotically throughout the trial: "You are the sole judges of the facts. I shall instruct you as to the law." If one of the lawyers manages to sneak in a bit of law here and there, the judge is quick to admonish the jury to pay no attention. "*I* will tell you what the law is."

With juries so conditioned, conviction of the civil-disobedient is virtually a foregone conclusion. The facts are not generally in dispute, he has readily admitted to them. He does not deny that he burned his draft card, or refused induction, or committed trespass during a demonstration— or, in the case of the Boston Five, signed antiwar manifestoes, attended press conferences, handed over draft cards to the Justice Department. The jury, having listened to the uncontradicted evidence of the alleged crime, now hears the judge instruct them that the law says thus-and-so, from which they can only infer that a crime has indeed been committed. Congress has expressly forbidden the burning of draft cards, refusal of induction is a felony, there is a local ordinance against trespass. If two or more come to the conclusion that the war is illegal and the draft is wrong and *act* on that conclusion, that is a criminal conspiracy. Everything now falls neatly into place like a simple jigsaw puzzle: a) he did it, b) it is against the law, c) if laws can be broken with impunity, anarchy will result. The jurors' duty is now clear:

no matter where their individual sympathies may lie, how much they may agree with the defendant's views or how strongly they may feel that the law is unjust and should be repealed, they have no choice as conscientious, law-abiding citizens but to vote a guilty verdict. Is that all there is to it? they must wonder as, exhausted, enervated, they are at last thanked by the judge for being so attentive, and are dismissed, dropped back into their accustomed lives.

Perhaps that is not all there is to it. After the Boston trial, Joseph Sax, a young law professor at the University of Michigan, wrote an article in the *Yale Review* in which he makes a brilliantly reasoned argument challenging this concept of the jury function.

He develops the thesis that a jury has the right, and in some cases the duty, to ignore the judge's charge, to find according to its conscience, and by its verdict to nullify unjust laws, to repudiate unjust governmental policy. "At this prospect the editorial writers have already recoiled in horror," says Sax. "The way of civil disobedience is the way of anarchy, they solemnly intone, and millions nod their agreement. The virtues of unbending obedience to the law have not always seemed quite so obvious to Americans." He cites the Fugitive Slave Laws of 1850, and the stubborn refusal of citizens in New England and the Middle West to enforce them. Even when indictments were brought against individuals who had clearly broken the law by rescuing fugitive slaves, prosecutions were often unsuccessful: community feeling against the laws and in favor of the defendants ran so high that juries refused to convict.

Sax draws on both English and American legal history to illustrate his point. In eighteenth-century England, Fox's Libel Law was enacted, giving the jury the right to take the law into its own hands in cases of what today would be called civil disobedience—"to provide a check against the influence of bad judges in bad times," as a member of the House of

Commons put it in the debate on the bill in Parliament. Sax has plucked some nuggets from this debate which could have been made to order for the issues in the Boston trial.

The principle at stake was whether the jury could be told it had a right to refuse to enforce the law of seditious libel. This right was advocated by one M.P. because seditious libel cases involved "censures upon public men and the acts of government," creating a special danger of "political craft and oppression perverting justice." Lords Camden and Stanhope argued for "the right of the jury to take both law and the facts in their own hands" so that "juries might go according to their consciences in the law. . . . Some juries," they said, "were found resolute enough to disregard the instruction, and find a verdict for the defendant, others were overawed by the presence and perhaps the menaces of a magistrate robed, learned and dignified, and found a verdict against their consciences."

In America, the Founding Fathers came out for the right of jury nullification of repressive laws: "For example, in 1771 John Adams said of the juror that 'it is not only his right, but his duty to find the verdict according to his own best understanding, judgment and conscience, though in direct opposition to the direction of the court.' And Alexander Hamilton said in 1804 that the jury in a criminal case is duty bound to acquit, despite the instructions of the judge, 'if exercising their judgment with discretion and honesty they have a clear conviction that the charge of the court is wrong.' "

Sax concludes with an appeal that might well be heeded by those called to serve on future juries in cases involving civil disobedience: "It is time for us to come to terms with our own contemporary version of the seditious libel problem, and recognize, as our forebears did, that it will sometimes be necessary to protest an unjust law by violating it and putting the question of justification to one's fellow citizens. . . .

"Those who think resisters are tearing at the fabric of the society might wish to consider the possibility that a society is best able to survive if it permits a means for taking an issue back to the public over the heads of public officialdom: when it recognizes that a government may have so implicated itself in a wretched policy that it needs to be extricated by popular repudiation in a forum more immediately available—and less politically compromised—than a ballot box."

This is strong, persuasive stuff. Yet is it not also somewhat visionary? Could Professor Sax's ideas be made to work in a real case before a real live jury? On the face of it, it would seem the first requirement would be a jury that included at least some representation of those most likely to be receptive to a radically new approach to the administration of justice —intellectuals, blacks, liberals, the wretched of the earth. Our Boston jury seemed, from what little we knew of them during the trial, a most unlikely bunch to respond to such unorthodox views. Only later, after I had discussed the trial with some of them, did I feel that the Sax approach would not have been wasted and might indeed have made a difference to the outcome.

The jury was screened in advance by the government. Mr. Wall told me that the Attorney General's office had ordered an FBI check of all prospective jurors which would disclose not only any actual criminal record, but also, to the alert local G-man, any suspect behavior requiring FBI surveillance. So presumably none of those finally empaneled had himself ever fallen afoul of the law, or engaged in any activity (such as peace demonstrations) that might have attracted the attention of the FBI.

Defense counsel, of course, had no such access to the private lives and thoughts of the jurors. What slim information they did have, gleaned from the city directory, on educational background and occupation, was not encouraging: High school only, five. Some college, six. College degree, one. There were two self-employed, six white-collar, three blue-collar, one professional. Meat cutter, printer, hardware clerk, loan supervisor, technician, engineer, customer-service representative. "And I wanted mothers, beards, and eggheads!" groaned James St. Clair when he saw the list.

Jury-watching, jury-analyzing, jury-predicting was an ongoing preoccupation of press and spectators. "Juror Number Six kept his eyes shut during Dr. Spock's testimony." "Have you noticed how Juror Number One keeps staring at the defendants?" "How do they see Wall? As Boy Scout or Torquemada?" "Or as Mr. Clean, wrapped in the American flag?" "I swear a couple of them have been dead for two days, somebody ought to do a mirror test to see if they're still breathing." "Might as well read the entrails of a chicken as try to guess what they're actually thinking, if anything." Those twelve impassive faces tantalized, irritated, intrigued us throughout the four long weeks.

Everybody did a certain amount of informal polling of Boston types—waitresses, hotel clerks, bar-stool acquaintances—about what they thought of the Spock trial, in an effort to take the measure of the New England mind. The results were far from propitious. The range of views was narrow indeed, from "Dr. Spock may be a great doctor, but he's broken the law and he should take the consequences," to "They should all be hanged as traitors." The latter comment was made by a cab driver to a sagacious local judge and myself. "*There's* your reason for the government's choice of Boston as the ideal city in which to try this case!" remarked the judge. "In Washington they ran the risk of blacks on the jury, in New York they'd have had Jews. They can be *sure* of this Boston jury."

Long before the verdict was returned the courtroom crowd had pretty much sized up the jury as hawks and bigots who would surely be prejudiced against the likes of the defendants and all they stood for.

When Anson Smith and I managed to interview three of the jurors at some length, shortly after the sentencing, their responses came as the greatest surprise. All three were strongly opposed to the Vietnam war, all expressed the highest regard for the defendants as individuals and for what they were trying to accomplish—and all said they felt, after hearing the judge's charge, that they had no alternative but to find them guilty.

Why then did they acquit Raskin—what had he *not* done that the others had done? After all, Raskin was the author of the "Call to Resist Illegitimate Authority," he had been at the October 2 press conference, had not only participated in the Department of Justice rally and delegation but had turned in his own 4-F draft card. In what way was he less a conspirator than, say, Ferber, who had never so much as exchanged two words with any of the defendants except for Coffin? This remained something of a mystery. After talking with the jurors we were left with the impression that Raskin's acquittal stemmed not from any special merit that would distinguish his case from the others, but rather from a tacit desire of the jury to assert its independence, to vote, in some token way, its conscience. Could this spark be fanned into a flame, along the lines suggested by Professor Sax, the outlook of the political defendant might be profoundly altered.

2

"Guilty as Charged by the Judge"

At first, none of the jurors was willing to discuss the case with anyone. One or two made tantalizing remarks over the phone to Anson Smith as he sought appointments: "There was real solidarity between the men on the jury, we were proud of one another . . ." "It was a hard case, our duty to deal with a brilliant bunch of fellows . . ." "We had a hell of a problem to stay awake in the jury box on account of the air conditioning breaking down . . ."

In time, three agreed to see us. (To what extent these three were representative of the jury as a whole, we have no way of knowing. Lawyers have suggested to me that the very fact that they were willing to discuss their verdict sets them apart as more open-minded and flexible than the others.) We were after more than just an account of the deliberations. That month must have been a weird chapter in the lives of the twelve jurors and two alternates, suddenly seized from their familiar world of home, family, job to be plunked down in total isolation amongst complete strangers. What was the sequestered life like, how did they all get along together—did irritations and hostility develop among the twelve of them? What were the marshals like as custodians, and what was the mysterious "entertainment" mentioned by the judge when he ordered them sequestered?

Our first interview was with the only professional man of the twelve, a thirty-seven-year-old architect of Portuguese descent. Mr. A. lives an hour's drive from Boston in a suburb of more or less stately homes. His house is large and pretty, the walls covered with his own collages and paintings. His wife was present during the interview listening attentively and their five very well-behaved children were occasionally seen flitting through the back rooms. Mrs. A. told us later that she had raised them all by Dr. Spock's book, although her husband had never read it. It struck me as a European ménage.

The trial had been, for Mr. A., an unrelieved nightmare. Until the day we came to see him, some three weeks after the verdict was returned, he had not discussed it with a soul, not even with his wife. The sequestration order came as a shocking surprise: "It was very unexpected—I had no idea when I went to report for jury duty that it would be *this* trial. I'm not familiar with legal terminology, and the notice said 'petit jury,' so I thought it would all be over that morning, in a couple of hours—I was completely unprepared.

"I was working under great pressure at the time and I'd left things at the office, half finished, expecting to come back in the afternoon. I called the office at lunchtime, to say I'd be there later. That was the last time I called the office." Then started a strange peregrination: "Judge Ford said we could all go home and collect our belongings, but five minutes later he changed that, and said we couldn't go home alone, we should have to be accompanied by marshals. There was a shortage of marshals and cars so there were several jurors to a car—we drove half round the state to stop by the homes of the jurors. I left about 5 or 5:30, and called my wife to say I'd be coming for my things about 8 p.m. But I didn't get there until 11 at night."

The jury was quartered in the Parker House, a few blocks from the courthouse, in single-occupancy bedrooms, where they were guarded night and day. "We were permitted to call home once a day. The calls were monitored—a marshal was listening in taking notes. Our letters were censored. I had to write a business letter to my partner, about a three-page letter; the marshal read it, checked it, and then mailed it." The jury got one daily newspaper, the Boston *Morning Globe*, from which the marshals had clipped out all news about the trial. Television programs were also monitored, a marshal was always on hand to switch off the set if there should be a news flash. All telephones, radios, and television sets in the bedrooms were disconnected. "One night I wanted to hear the ball game on radio—they had to get the electrician to come and fix the radio, connect it, and by then the third inning was over!"

Mr. A. hated being separated from his family, he missed them terribly. Worst of all was the regimentation, the lack of activity, the constant waiting around. "It was atrocious," he said. "I normally lead a very active life—it was unbearable. I'm used to the pressure of the architect's office, and I do a lot of painting. I like to paint for hours at a stretch, uninterrupted—but serving on the jury the time was all cut up, fifteen minutes here, twenty minutes there.

"The daily routine went like this: At about 6:45 someone knocked on the door, we went to the common room and had juice. Then we waited twenty-five minutes for half of the jurors to go down in the elevator to breakfast. Then we'd wait for the other group to get down in the elevator. After breakfast we went back to our rooms; another twenty-five-minute wait, and we came down in the elevator again in two groups, and then walked over to the courthouse. At the courthouse, it was unbearable. Those continual breaks, bench conferences, and so on."

For exercise, Mr. A. would pace up and down the jury

room during the court recess; like a man condemned to live in a Bastille cell he measured its exact dimensions, 35 x 14½ feet, and figured that you had to walk it 150 times to make a mile, which he did for the first several days. The weekends seemed to drag endlessly. Once or twice they went to the movies or to a ball game or just for a drive.

Anson Smith and I were beginning to express our sympathy at this horror-tale of enforced incarceration when Mr. A. burst out with a remark that was truly startling in the circumstances: "I would kill myself if I ever ended up in jail in these conditions."

Yet in a way Mr. A. was glad to have been through the experience. He said he was particularly impressed "with the extent the Justice Department went to to preserve the rights of the defendants by keeping the jury away from all contacts with the outside." A strong feeling of camaraderie developed among the jurors, they all got along extremely well, there were no conflicts. As for the marshals, Mr. A. could not praise them enough: "They were fabulous. I was absolutely floored. I expected them to be crude and rough, but they were the most tactful people I ever met. One of them is writing an anthology of Chinese poetry—a very fine man, *very* diplomatic. They were with us all the time. The biggest surprise was the personalities of the marshals, their tactfulness."

Discussing how the jury arrived at its verdict, Mr. A. was curiously reticent on one or two points. He declined to tell us how many votes were taken, how the jury stood at various stages, and he seemed loath to say much about the reasoning that led to acquittal of Raskin. We asked at what stage the jury distinguished Raskin from the other defendants. "Speaking for myself, I felt that way from the start of the deliberations." Was the jury impressed by McDonough's testimony, in which he seemed to confuse Raskin with Waskow? "I don't know about the others. My own point of view was that Raskin, though a very outspoken critic of the war, did exercise judgment about draft evasion. To me, this was the key issue." He seemed anxious to change the subject and we talked of other matters. Later, we returned to Raskin; why the not guilty verdict? "The way Raskin himself was convincing was the point. Wall was forceful, and I don't like people who push other people around. Wall's mannerisms bothered me a lot. Some of the jurors thought him a great hero, and some didn't. I was just listening to what Raskin was saying."

And what of the conspiracy? At this point in our interview we got a glimpse of the doubts and distress that assailed Mr. A. in reaching a verdict, doubts that were, however, put to rest by the judge:

Q. What item or items of evidence did you find most compelling about the conspiracy?

A. (Here Mr. A. was silent for a full minute, clearly very upset, searching for a way to explain. Finally, and painfully, he spoke): I had great difficulty sleeping that night after the summing-up arguments. I sympathized very strongly with the defendants—I *detest* the Vietnam war. Also to some extent I think there is unfairness in the draft law. But it was put so clearly by the judge. It was a law violation—there's no way—it's a very fine point—the jury can't say, "Was he justified in violating the law?" If the judge had said, "If you find they were justified, find them not guilty," it would have been *beautiful*.

Q. How did the other jurors feel about the war?

A. I don't know how the others felt—they take things as they come—perhaps they don't think much about it.

Q. Were they hawkish or dovish?

A. I don't know.

Q. Wasn't Ferber's link pretty tenuous?

A. I think that's true. But that's one of the things the judge's charge helped to clarify.

Q. Could the conspiracy doctrine be a dangerous weapon? Did you think about this at all?

A. Yes, I did.

Q. Where does political action stop and conspiracy begin?

A. That's why I couldn't sleep the night before the verdict; I was concerned.

Q. What did you think of Dr. Spock?

A. He's very honest and straightforward, has lofty and commendable ideals.

Q. And Coffin?

A. A dynamic person, he must be a great speaker.

Q. Then . . . how could they be part of a criminal conspiracy?

A. I can't answer—I would have to go into a re-evaluation of all my own thoughts on the subject. It goes back to the judge's charge.

Q. Do you think the other jurors were aware of this fine line between freedom of speech and criminal conspiracy?

A. I don't know—I had a feeling they probably weren't. Even before the judge's charge, I felt the majority of the jury saw things in black-and-white terms—although one or two had the concept of this fine boundary. Several definitions—word definitions of legal terms—made it clear this was a conspiracy to aid and abet.

Q. Why did you exonerate them of the charge of "counseling"?

A. We couldn't see any evidence they actually counseled—that they said to a kid, "Why don't you turn in your card?"

Q. Yet you found them guilty of aiding and abetting draft refusal? And aiding and abetting nonpossession of cards?

A. They did aid and abet, indirectly. You can "aid" by addressing yourself to that issue.

Q. What did you think of the judge?

A. He was very fair-minded, sharp for his age, for an eighty-five-year-old man, although sometimes he couldn't hear too well. He was very friendly and kind to the woman from the draft board; she was so nervous, he put her at her ease, made her relax.

Q. But she was a prosecution witness?

A. True.

Q. What about when he interrupted Boudin's closing argument and told Rabinowitz not to "demonstrate"?

A. Rabinowitz had a habit of making faces (Mr. A. mimics Rabinowitz, rolls his eyes ceilingward in a Heavens-to-Betsy fashion).

If Mr. A. emerged as at once sensitive and reserved, intelligent yet strangely naïve, by contrast Mr. B., a printshop owner of Italian extraction, seemed self-assured, talkative, and worldly-wise. He also was beset by some of the doubts, and troubled by the moral dilemma, that poisoned life for Mr. A. during the trial.

While he found the sequestered life trying, it did have compensations: "We had entertainment—always of the best —food always of the best, martinis before dinner, the government spared no expense to see that our life was as pleasant as possible. I gained twelve pounds during the trial. We went to the best restaurants and so forth—but it was abnormal. Everything we did was checked—even going to the men's room, we were accompanied right into the room." He enjoyed kidding around with the marshals: "All phone calls were censored, a three-way line: the juror, his loved one on the other end, and a deputy monitoring everything. Once I called my mother and we were talking in Italian! The deputy was at a loss, he yelled Uncle, and called in an Italian-speaking deputy. I said, 'I also *spreche Deutsch!*' There was lots of tomfoolery, horse-play." He added complacently, "But morale was at the highest. I gathered from the deputies that this jury was as good as they come—an excellent cross-section of citizens, men of conviction, not easily swayed. Each was determined to render a fair verdict."

The clue to how this fair verdict was reached by the "men of conviction" was supplied early in our interview. We asked if there had been much disagreement amongst the jurors during their deliberations. "A certain amount. But our duty was clear-cut. We were charged by the judge to make our decision on our findings. It was as obvious to us as to anyone else that they were guilty as charged by the judge." "Did you say *'guilty as charged by the judge'?*" I repeated, startled. "Yes," answered Mr. B.

On the defendants: "Coffin's a hell of a nice fellow. Friendly, articulate. Here's a man willing to fight for people's rights—he went South with the Freedom Riders, was in the CIA—the type of man I admire." "Ferber? I admire him too. A youngster who didn't appear to have the manly physique of an Atlas, but mentally he was a giant." "Goodman has the courage of his convictions, he believes in giving kids guidance." "Dr. Spock is outstanding. He could spend a life of ease in the Caribbean Sea—he doesn't have to do what he is doing. His book is almost a bible." "Raskin—here's a man who has been exposed to the machinery of government. I worked in the State House, and saw things that turned my stomach. Raskin was exposed to enough to turn *his* stomach! He thought the war was outrageous. He's a sincere individual."

On the prosecutor: "A cocky young fellow, outspoken, dramatic, a Hollywood-type prosecutor. I wasn't too favorably impressed by him."

On crime and punishment: "I'm in agreement with what they're trying to accomplish—my friends were amazed I found them guilty; but they did break the law." "I don't have to stress where *my* sympathy lay. Like Raskin, I think it's a senseless war. But my personal views don't count." "I'm convinced the Vietnam war is no good. But we've got a constitution to uphold. If we allow people to break the law, we're akin to anarchy." "I personally feel the government has a weak case. But if the defendants had been found not guilty—we'd have chaos!" "Technically speaking, they were guilty according to the judge's charge. If there had been a different charge we could have voted differently— if he had said, 'Let's face it, they're entitled to their opinions.' " "There'd have been adverse consequences if they'd been found not guilty, you'd have thousands of people doing the same thing." "Wall said, 'We've got to nip this thing in the bud.' What did he mean? To put a stop to it. There could be all sorts of reverberations—chaos." "We based our verdict on 'Were they guilty?' no matter how weak the case, and it *was* weak. The government didn't have a strong case. Up to the judge's charge I would have found them not guilty."

On the judge: "Here's a strange thing: Wall's closing argument. The judge charged us along the same lines as Wall did. When Wall gave his closing, the judge almost corroborated his charge—he was in general agreement with the prosecution, which is obvious to anyone who followed the trial. I hate to say collusion, but there was similarity of opinion between the judge and Wall." "Judge Ford leaned toward Wall. But he tried to be fair. After all, he is employed by the federal government, they pay his wages—he couldn't be *for* breaking the law." (Canny Mr. B.! You have something there.)

On the acquittal of Raskin: "Prior to the Andretta Room conference, in the films of the mass meeting outside the Justice Department, we could barely see Raskin's head in the film. The only thing he did was to state his views on the Vietnam conflict—as a matter of fact he's written two books about it. He's entitled to his views on the war."

Mr. B. told us in some detail about the chronology of the deliberations. The foreman played a relatively passive role, taking votes and chairing the discussion. First they took a secret ballot, each juror writing his verdict on a slip of paper. In this first vote four jurors (among them Mr. B.) found all defendants but Raskin guilty, eight found them all guilty. "We had some discussion after that, because the judge did say that if there was a reasonable doubt we should find them not guilty." Then one of the jurors—and it turned out to be our Mr. A.—went to the blackboard and made a chart showing how each of the defendants was linked with the others. (Why did Mr. A. not tell us this? What deep-seated feelings of personal distress over his role made him shy away from saying anything at all about the chart, which was his idea, the votes, the sequence of the deliberations?) After some five and a half hours of discussion, the jury arrived at its general verdict. The foreman then polled the jurors as to the special findings.

Q. How did you arrive at the verdict?

A. Every one of the twelve was determined in his own mind they were guilty. We had stacks of evidence, draft cards, testimony, pictures—we deliberated seven and a half hours.

Q. How come you found Ferber guilty of conspiracy when he didn't know any of the others?

A. That's a point well taken. It wasn't *totally* a conspiracy. What Ferber did do was aid and abet.

Q. But the charge was conspiracy?

A. Yes, but conspiracy to aid and abet.

Q. Did you think that Ferber was party to this criminal agreement?

A. A conspiracy can be two people entering an agreement. Ferber aided and abetted young men after they'd made their minds up.

Q. What persuaded you there was a criminal agreement among the four you found guilty?

A. Not criminal agreement—*conspiracy*.

Q. You must have thought there was evidence they were in agreement. What about the "Call to Resist," was that a big thing?

A. No. Raskin wrote the original article, then it was rehashed by others—after it jelled he was quite ill, and his baby had some malady—the draft was not uppermost in his mind. About the conspiracy, somewhere along the line each defendant was connected. Ferber in Washington, Coffin in Washington, Spock in Washington—you can join these three on this point. And then again, how about convicting the Mayor of New York? Here's a guy who prearranged things—he's aiding and abetting too. The more I think of it, the more I think how ridiculous! All those police at Whitehall Street, Goodman and Spock obstructing traffic! A battery of newsmen, and a deputy tapped Spock on the shoulder and arrested him. A ludicrous thing—Goodman, in the background, ran up and said, "How about arresting me?" The whole thing's rife with technicalities. But, why I don't want to talk out of turn, Raskin only *talked*. I've spent some sleepless nights over this. Look at what happened to Raskin! He said, "I hate the Vietnam war," and he spends weeks and weeks defending himself in court.

What of the reaction of friends and family to the verdict? "I've got three teen-age sons, two are draft age—the draft is breathing down their necks. When I heard we were going to be locked up, late in the afternoon of the first day of the trial, a deputy accompanied me to my home to get my personal effects. My three boys were home—they were somewhat flabbergasted. They'd discussed these things with me before, we're generally in agreement. My second boy said, 'Give 'em hell!' And he was *not* referring to Spock, he was referring to the government." But when the trial was over, and Mr. B. explained it all to the boys, they felt that Dad had done the right thing: "They agreed with me, that these men did break the law. But the law should be changed. The draft law is discriminatory; it's obvious it should be changed." Not all the family was so easily persuaded of the justice of the verdict: "My sister said she thought it was a shame to convict them, but her husband shut her up pretty quick." (Mr. B., like Judge Ford and Russell Peck, has a generally low opinion of the ability of women to reason intelligently about such matters. We asked him what he thought of the government challenging the two women called to the jury box: "Don't misunderstand me, I love women. But we had a job to do, and who wants a woman, who thinks with her feelings about these things?")

Mr. B. himself betrayed some qualms about his vote: "The Saturday after the verdict I woke with a splitting headache, wondering if I did the right thing. The conspiracy law should be changed—technically you could call the Mayor of New York and thousands of his policemen conspirators. I can't fathom it out, it's beyond me."

And now outstanding Dr. Spock, that hell of a nice fellow Mr. Coffin, courageous Goodman, and mental giant Ferber are all up for a two-year stretch in the penitentiary. What did Mr. B. think of the sentences meted out by Judge Ford? "I was surprised—I'd expected a slap on the wrist, probation, no sentence. I thought the judge was very rough on them. There wasn't a man there who wasn't trying to better his country. If they are incarcerated, the government would be making a great mistake. I saw Raskin after the verdict, and I said, 'I hope to God Uncle Sam doesn't see fit to create martyrs out of these four ...'" "Then why did you vote them

guilty, knowing this might result in their being imprisoned?"
"I knew they were guilty when we were charged by the
judge. I did not know *prior* to that time—I was in full agreement with the defendants until we were charged by the
judge. That was the kiss of death!"

So we had come full circle.

Our third and last interview was with a semi-retired man-
agement sales consultant in his sixties who lives in a modest
house in the suburbs. In all ways an *homme moyen*, Mr. C.
came closest to my idea of the Average Juror. We have seen
him reflected as part of a percentage point in the majority
columns of innumerable Gallup polls. He is law-abiding,
kindly disposed toward his fellow man, and would be the
first to admit he is not given to undue mental exertion. His
twenty-four-year-old son will be coming up shortly for reclassification: "My boy's not for the Vietnam war any more
than anyone else is. He'll do what he can legally not to go.
But he told me he thought our verdict was right."

Like Mr. B., he was impressed by the unaccustomed lavish
living: "We went to Trader Vic's, Pier 4, Jimmie's Harbour-
side. We could have only two drinks with our dinner—I
think the limitation was set not because of the money side,
but because they didn't want it to seem the jurors were
going on a toot, if somebody had a few too many. On weekends we went up the coast in air-conditioned Mercedes Benz
buses, stopped at the Old Mill in Westminster." His son is
a Rugby football enthusiast, and it happened that his team
was scheduled to play on Memorial Day weekend, in the
middle of the trial. "I tried to talk up Rugby to the other
fellows on the jury, but couldn't get them interested. So
two marshals volunteered to take me out—I think they enjoyed it. Some of my friends out there saw me, with two men
guarding me, one on each side! My wife came down from the
stands and we greeted one another, but the marshals stood
right between us as we talked."

Mr. C. had a good word to say for everyone: "The marshals were a swell bunch of fellows, very pleasant, very nice. . . . Judge Ford is terrific, very fair, has a good sense of humor. . . . Wall was a real keen boy, had the whole thing on the tip of his tongue every minute, he knew just where all the exhibits were, where to lay hands on them, and he spoke right up so you could hear him. . . . The defense lawyers were outstanding, they all did a good job. . . . Coffin is sincere, he has no ulterior motives, I think he firmly believes this moral law is above the government law. . . . Dr. Spock's a very fine man. . . . Ferber is a bright young boy, very presentable. He might be better off doing some athletics instead of all that studying? He's a Phi Beta Kappa, must be smart. I didn't go for some of his buddies very much, that group we'd see lined up in the corridor every morning. But I'm very strong for the younger generation, I think they're terrific. . . . The jurors—it's interesting to me, these fourteen fellows who never saw each other before, of varying conditions and environments—we got on pretty well together, there were no flare-ups, everybody was friendly, sincere about their duty and responsibility. Nobody jumped on anyone else for disagreeing."

Of the acquittal of Raskin, he said: "There's no doubt in my mind he knew what was going on, but the general feeling was that Raskin is one of those real brains, a little bit on Cloud Nine—he said he was there but he didn't listen, he was thinking of something else. There's no doubt he's loaded with brains; I know people like that, they'll participate in a conversation from time to time but they're way off."

Mr. C.'s explanation of how he arrived at the guilty verdict was totally bewildering:

Q. How did you reach a decision?
A. The biggest discussion was not "guilty or not guilty," but what the judge meant by conspiracy. You can

interpret that in a lot of ways. The judge did outline it very clearly, but it's not what an ordinary layman would call conspiracy. You think of people sitting down together and planning it out step by step, but that's not the way the judge said it.

Q. How did you construe "conspiracy"?

A. Conspiracy involved—not necessarily all five together, but along with others known and unknown, to burn draft cards and interfere with induction centers.

Q. Did you decide the defendants conspired to burn draft cards?

A. It was too obvious! No question about that.

Q. But they were not charged with burning draft cards?

A. No, that's right, but they were aiding and abetting the kids to burn draft cards.

Q. But that's not in the indictment—it was conspiring to aid and abet refusal to serve, nonpossession of cards, hindering the administration of the act.

A. Well, they weren't all necessarily cards. There were a lot of letters and so on burned too.

Q. But where did "burning" fit in your scheme of deliberations?

A. Not *burning* so much an issue as the fact they turned them in. But the burning made more impression on you.

Q. Spock and Coffin both testified they were opposed to burning cards.

A. We didn't feel they were out there saying, "You go in and burn it!" But Coffin is a persuasive speaker.

Discussing the judge's charge, Mr. C. unwittingly spoke directly to the point made by Professor Sax: "Of course you wonder if you made the right decision; but the way the judge charged us, there was no choice. People I've talked with since the verdict are sympathetic to the actions of Spock and Coffin—they seem to think the jury should have been there to decide if the law is right or wrong, but we weren't there to decide that. You can't have juries deciding whether *laws* are right—there are certain laws on the books."

Again, we wanted to know how it felt to have sent these "fine, sincere, bright, presentable people" to prison:

Q. What did you think of the sentence?

A. I thought he'd give the maximum, myself. But I thought it pretty smart to do what he did. I doubt they'll ever spend time in jail—there's the appeal, which will last way beyond the election. But I think the appeal court will uphold Ford.

Q. But—if the appeal court upholds Ford, they'll go to jail?

A. I don't wish anyone to go to jail. I couldn't wish anyone of the caliber of individuals they are to spend two years in jail. But I think the sentence was right, and the verdict was right.

We could not shake him from this queer inconsistency, although we went back over it with him a few times.

Summing up his reaction to the experience, Mr. C. had this to say: "I think if everyone could serve on a jury it would be very helpful to the whole country. I've said this to a lot of people. With all the goings-on in this country, to me this jury trial renews my faith in the United States system— to see the conscientious feeling of those men, taken at random—their sincere feeling and hope they've done the right thing."

A vastly consoling thought: the American way. No danger here of the political dissident being dragged from his bed at gunpoint in the middle of the night and hustled off to some secret destination, there to be held without trial. No, in America he is properly indicted, admitted to bail, allowed counsel of his choice, and eventually found guilty by a jury of sincere and conscientious people like Messrs. A., B., and C.

3

Postscript

After the sentencing a cry went up against the judge from most of the newspaper and magazine correspondents who covered the trial.

In his Washington *Post* "wrap-up" story, John P. Mac-Kenzie wrote: "The trial of Dr. Spock was a disaster for all concerned . . . a deep embarrassment for the American system of justice. . . . Sixteen volumes of transcript tell part of the story, but they can never tell it all. They do not convey the manner in which 85-year-old Judge Francis J. W. Ford showed his disbelief in the defense case and his tolerance for the Government's. . . . The Judge's display of bias may not be enough in itself to overturn the convictions. But it demeaned the Federal bench and deprived the nation of a trial that was fundamentally fair."

No impartial observer of that trial would dispute Mac-Kenzie's characterization of the judge's behavior. What the lawyers thought of it, in the convoluted recesses of their legal minds, is another matter. As the Old Trial Hand told me, "I'd always *rather* have a clearly bigoted judge like Ford in a political case. A liberal judge will due-process you to death, your client will be found guilty anyway, and you won't have any good points left for the appeal." He added,

"In political cases the outcome is predetermined ninety-nine per cent of the time. Lawyers, judges, press, jury like to pretend—no, actually believe, *have* to believe—that it isn't so. But the important decision isn't made by the judge, much less the jury. It's made by the policeman, or prosecutor, or politician who decides who is going to be arrested and what the charge will be. This is true in all cases, much more so in political cases."

The sagacity of these observations was borne out by another trial which was taking place three thousand miles away at the same time as the Spock trial.

David Harris had stepped down from the presidency of the Stanford student body to devote himself to the task of opposing the war, and had become one of the major figures in the Resistance. In June, 1968, recently married to folksinger Joan Baez, he was on trial in San Francisco for refusing induction into the armed forces. The atmosphere in the San Francisco courtroom could not have been more different from what we had seen in Boston.

There were seven women on the jury, including a member of Women's Strike for Peace. The judge, short and sharp with the prosecutor, was courteous and well-disposed to defense counsel. He was particularly benign in his attitude to the defendant, and took occasion to declare from the bench: "Mr. Harris is motivated by the highest motives, and as such he makes a very outstanding appearance, and therefore it's a very difficult thing to find Mr. Harris a criminal under the circumstances. . . . I think he believes in what he is doing. and I think that stems from what he believes to be high motives. I respect him for it. I say so publicly."

Several of the women jurors were moved to visible tears and audible sobs when Harris took the stand to explain his conscientious reasons for refusing to be drafted.

The jury found Harris guilty, and the judge sentenced him to three years in the penitentiary.

Would Dr. Spock and his co-defendants have fared better

with David Harris's judge and jury? Evidently not. Perhaps there would have been louder sobs and wetter hankies, had this jury been called on to try the great doctor, but the outcome would have been the same, or worse.

What, then, of MacKenzie's conclusion that Judge Ford "deprived the nation of a trial that was fundamentally fair"? Is it not self-deluding to speak in terms of a "fair trial" in a politically motivated, politically timed, and politically organized prosecution? When applied to such a case, does not the cherished concept of due process of law, the foundation of our system of jurisprudence, become merely an elaborate sham to mask what is in reality a convenient device to silence opponents of governmental policies? If this is so, does not the demand for fair trial and due process in political cases simply help perpetuate the myth—should not the demand rather be, in the public interest, an *end* to political trials?

The fact must be faced that political prosecutions invariably produce unjust, often tragic results. Found guilty after a costly, often ruinous trial, branded a criminal if not a traitor, the defendant must seek his comfort in the thought that perhaps years later, after the hysteria of the moment has abated, an appellate court may reverse his conviction. Nor is there much solace for the rare defendant, like Marcus Raskin, who is acquitted, for, having gone through the ordeal and the expense of the court proceedings, his life and career disrupted, he is neither in the eyes of the public nor his own "vindicated." He has merely been lucky enough to slip through the net.

So it is the fact of political prosecution rather than the fairness of the court procedures that is crucial.

Thirty years after the execution of Sacco and Vanzetti, Professor Arthur Morgan of Harvard Law School, one of America's foremost authorities on the law of evidence, concluded his exhaustive review of the case with the comment,

"They were victims of a tragic miscarriage of justice." He was referring to unfairness in trial procedures—prejudice of the judge, prejudice of the jury. More to the point was the conclusion of his colleague, historian Arthur M. Schlesinger. For Professor Schlesinger, the Sacco and Vanzetti case was living proof that "myths to the contrary notwithstanding, judicial processes do not take place in a social void; judges are men, not gods. The strict observance of legal forms does not necessarily assure the accused of a fair trial."

A look at some of the more celebrated political trials of this century lends support to this view. Eugene Debs, Harry Bridges, Tom Mooney, the Rosenbergs and Sobell, and Alger Hiss all enjoyed every benefit but one of what we call due process of law. Their procedural rights were protected every step of the way: trial by jury, able, often distinguished counsel of their choice, interminable appeals all the way up to the Supreme Court—they were given every conceivable consideration, permitted to avail themselves of every legal remedy known to Anglo-American jurisprudence. In case after case, conviction after conviction, press and public never failed to point out with pride: "See what a marvelously fair trial we gave those scoundrels, those traitors!"

The one right they were denied was, of course, the most basic of all: the right not to be tried for dissent. For no matter how the formal accusation was styled ("perjury" in the case of Alger Hiss, "conspiracy to commit espionage" in the case of the Rosenbergs) behind these prosecutions lay the decision of government to move against what it deemed to be the threatening and discordant voice of opposition to the established order.

There is an enormous body of literature about these cases, volume after volume by historians and legal scholars who, in hindsight, vindicate the accused outright or cast substantial doubt on their guilt. It is interesting to note that the government has never bothered to counter these studies with its own polemic urging the validity of the guilty verdict in these trials. Perhaps the reason is that the government could not care less about the judgment of history, and even cares little about the final outcome of the political case on appeal, which could take two or three years if it goes all the way up to the Supreme Court. The government's purpose in prosecuting is more immediate: to stifle opposition to its policies, well served at the point of the guilty verdict. (Thus one of our jurors, Mr. C., may have "had prescience," as Judge Ford would say, when he remarked in his comfortable way, "I doubt they'll ever spend time in jail—there's the appeal, which will last way beyond the election.")

If the purpose of the political trial remains constant, the rationale changes with the times, expressed in rhetoric tuned to the popular fears and prejudices of the moment. In Sacco and Vanzetti's day, it suited the government's purpose to conjure up the spectre of gun-toting foreign anarchists. Tom Mooney was made to symbolize the emergent (not yet respectable) labor movement (on being sentenced, he said: "I am under sentence of death. Whatever may be the legal equivocation, the crime of which I have actually been convicted is not that of having thrown a bomb into a throng of innocent people . . . but that of having striven with what strength I had for the alleviation of industrial wrongs that labor has suffered and the establishment of the rights which naturally belong to labor."). Harry Bridges was attacked first in the right-wing press as an agent of English shipping interests trying to tie up American ports, and only later as an agent of an international Communist conspiracy. In the early 1950's, the Rosenbergs and Sobell were cast in the role of atomic superspies and offered up as sacrificial scapegoats to the anti-Communist hysteria of the day.

The case against the Boston Five was expressed, predictably, in terms of the favorite electioneering slogan of all three 1968 presidential candidates. Judge Ford's remarks as he pronounced sentence were already ringing in our ears, for we had heard them daily, for months, in the campaign speeches of Nixon, Humphrey, and Wallace: *"Where law and order stops, obviously anarchy begins."*

The Boston defendants were exceptional people (and who knows, the government may already have regretted tangling with them): charismatic, intellectual, solidly respectable white citizens. Their prosecution was clearly "political," so labeled by the press.

In this era of law and order, the Year of the Mace, the political trial in its myriad guises—as an instrument for crushing war resistance, the black rebellion, the student revolt—may not always be so easy to identify.

Is not the black in Watts or Oakland, flagged down for doing thirty in a twenty-five-mile zone, a political victim of the eternal warfare waged by urban police departments against the ghetto? He will get due process, if he bothers to appear in court, be found guilty of speeding, and fined accordingly (for he has clearly violated the traffic laws, which have been established for the protection of the public, both black and white). The next time he comes before a judge may be for uttering the word "motherfucker" in the presence of a policeman, thereby corrupting that policeman's morals (an actual case), and so it goes. Soon he is in more serious trouble—perhaps, discouraged with due process, he is caught with a concealed weapon, which he is carrying for what he conceives of as his own protection against the mothers. For this he will get a jury trial, and be sent to state prison. As the late Supreme Court Justice Robert Jackson said, "A prosecutor has more control over life, liberty, and reputation than any other person in America. He stands a fair chance of finding at least a technical violation of some law on the part of almost anyone."

This view of the law as a Pandora's box that can be

opened or closed at will by the prosecutor was candidly set forth by John Wall in his speed-trap analogy, and by John Van de Kamp when he said, "We wouldn't have indicted them except for the fact there was so much evidence available on film."

Was the prosecution of the Boston Five a lawful and orderly use of the immense power of the prosecuting authorities? In the middle of the Boston trial came comment from an august source: a short paperback book by Supreme Court Justice Abe Fortas, issued by the New American Library in May, 1968, with this message to the reader: "In the tradition of the American revolutionary press the Publisher presents CONCERNING DISSENT AND CIVIL DISOBEDIENCE."

The revolutionary tract was quoted by Judge Ford in pronouncing sentence, and its major points were paraphrased by the prosecutor in his summation to the jury. While it does not mention the case of the Boston Five by name, it does discuss the issues raised by the trial, in language curiously reminiscent of the memorandum that announced the establishment of Van de Kamp's special unit in the Department of Justice.

In effect it is the liberal argument for law and order, so sugar-coated with the rhetoric of tolerance and balanced impartiality that the full import of Justice Fortas's words only becomes apparent when examined in the context of some of his actions on the Supreme Court and as trusted adviser to President Johnson.

A trade union leader once told me that the wily labor arbitrator will often handle a ticklish case by "giving one side the language and the other side the decision," thus placating everybody. Justice Fortas does just that. He pays eloquent tribute to Negroes and the youth generation: "They have triggered a social revolution which has projected this nation, and perhaps the world, to a new plateau in the human adventure. They have forced open the frontier of a new land—a land in which it is possible that the rights and opportunities of our society may be available to all, not just to some. . . ."

He heaps praise on the college generation of today: "Young people have suddenly taken on distinctive character and quality. . . . There are the activists, the militants, who are passionately devoted to the cause of the Negroes and the poor. . . . They have programs, convictions, energy and initiative. . . ." He has kind words for the draft resisters, who are "seriously and honestly wrestling with the dilemma of rejecting not all wars, but their deep moral aversion to participation in a particular war." Their attitude, he says, is "entitled to respect, whether or not one agrees with it."

Respect, however, is about all they are entitled to, for "[the dissident] may be motivated by the highest moral principles. He may, indeed, be right in the eyes of history or morality or philosophy. These are not controlling. It is the state's duty to arrest and punish those who violate the laws designed to protect private safety and public order."

Yet while Justice Fortas seems to advocate the widest tolerance for all forms of protest short of violence and impairing other people's rights, within days after publication of his book he voted with the majority of the Supreme Court in upholding the conviction of David O'Brien for burning his draft card on the steps of the Boston courthouse. Does burning a piece of paper impair other people's rights, threaten the private safety or the public order?

Central to the Fortas thesis is that the "theory of the state insists that the individual must conform his conduct" to the government's decision to wage war until the government's position is changed. "The needs of the state for manpower to wage war are always critical. Its ability to muster the needed soldiers may be the measure of its ability to survive. . . . By participating in the particular war, the state takes the position that the war is justified and moral. This is a governmental decision of the utmost gravity. . . ."

What if the government, in taking this decision of the utmost gravity, has failed to conform *its* conduct to the United States Constitution and international law by which it is bound? In his lone dissenting opinion in the O'Brien case, Justice William O. Douglas said the Court should have ordered argument on the much broader issue of whether the military draft is permissible at all in the absence of a declaration of war, a question "upon which the litigants and the country are entitled to a ruling." Justices Douglas and Potter Stewart have repeatedly urged that the Supreme Court should investigate charges that the Vietnam war is being waged illegally.

But Justice Fortas's concern for law and order does not, apparently, extend beyond these shores, for he has consistently opposed such an investigation, and in his rulings on draft cases has consistently voted against giving a hearing to litigants who attempt to raise this issue.

What is Justice Fortas's own position on the war? His book is deceptive. One might well conclude from it that he is dovish, or at least neutral, and that his strictures against draft refusers are based entirely on his concern for obedience to the law. He says that "by the use of the powerful instruments of dissent by people opposed to the war . . . issues of vast consequence have been presented with respect to the war in Vietnam, and, without doubt, national decisions and the course of that war have been affected."

His own stand on these issues of vast consequence is described in a *New York Times* series entitled "The Vietnam Policy Reversal of 1968."* It is one of those fascinating accounts full of minuscule detail ("Mr. Rusk sent out

* *The New York Times*, March 7, 1969.

for sandwiches") in which we feel our eye is to the keyhole, observing the every move of those who wield ultimate control over our lives and destinies. Fortas, we learn, was one of "a secret council of trusted advisers" summoned by President Johnson six days before his abdication speech. These wise men, including Dean Acheson, McGeorge Bundy, Cyrus Vance, Arthur Goldberg, were falling like dominoes into the dove camp, "opposing further military commitments, advocating some way of getting out of the war." Not so Justice Fortas, one of a minority who persisted to the end in "holding firm in defense of a hard line."*

In a throwaway line buried somewhere in his book, Fortas says: "Most of our people recognize war as a savage inevitability in a world which is still far from being universally civilized." Which is just what Michael Ferber and his colleagues refuse to recognize.

Writing in the Boston *Globe,* Ferber gives his views on law and order: "Let us be clear that the generation of Resistance has plenty of respect for law and order, certainly much more respect than President Johnson has, whose war in Vietnam is illegal in a dozen ways, certainly much more than many policemen have, whose bias against black people and young people is notorious. There is nothing lawful and orderly about the way America arranges its political, economic, and diplomatic affairs, only a veneer of efficiency and stability. If the law must be broken, it will be broken in the name of justice and morality, without which law and order are mere tyranny. It will not be broken for the personal gain, prejudice, fear or megalomania that now dominate America's lawless society."

What can be done about the evil of political trials? In the wake of the Spock trial, a number of scholars began to

---

* For further discussion of Fortas's book, see *Disobedience and Democracy: Nine Fallacies on Law and Order,* by Howard Zinn, Random House, 1968.

raise this question. Ronald Dworkin, professor of law at Yale University, in an article entitled "On Not Prosecuting Civil Disobedience" published in *The New York Review of Books,* wrote: "In the United States prosecutors have discretion whether to enforce criminal laws in particular cases. . . . There are, at least *prima facie,* some good reasons for not prosecuting those who disobey the draft laws out of conscience. One is the obvious reason that they act out of better motives than those who break the law out of greed or a desire to subvert the government. Another is the practical reason that our society suffers a loss if it punishes a group that includes—as the group of draft dissenters does —some of its most thoughtful and loyal citizens. . . ." Joseph Sax, writing in the *Saturday Review,* speaks of the "miracle of prosecutorial discretion . . . criminality can be, and is, produced or ignored virtually at will by law enforcement officials." He urges that this discretion be exercised in favor of persons who, like the Boston defendants, "by advocating a form of passive resistance to governmental fiat, operate at one of the least abrasive levels of conduct. . . . This is not to suggest that passive resistance should always be insulated from legal sanctions, but merely that the society's willingness to tolerate such conduct should be much greater than for direct action."

While calling on prosecutors not to prosecute may seem a little like urging lions to stop eating Christians, it is likely that if enough people were moved to concern themselves with political trials everywhere, in their own communities or on a national level—and by learning about these trials were stung into action to demand a stop to them— prosecutors, who are after all only cogs in the political system, would be forced to call a halt.

As Sax says, "A substantial outcry by the press and the general public against the Spock trial would have gone far to stifle the prospect of other such prosecutions; instead, we got the widespread response that 'the law' left the government little choice but to proceed as it did. Sometimes more direct action may be required. Jurors may simply have to refuse to convict, or grand jurors to indict. An independent citizenry has its ways."

At the Spock trial, the government's message came over loud and clear: You are not as free as you think you are. Yes, of course you may sign a peace petition, you may have your name on a newspaper advertisement supporting draft resisters; as John Wall said, the government is not suggesting it is going to indict somebody for signing a piece of paper! You may go to that mass meeting, and applaud if you feel like it—do you really imagine that in this, the most open society in the world, anybody is going to be indicted for *applauding?* However, if you do all these things, you will be "kept under surveillance by the FBI as a general security precaution" (as Van de Kamp told me the Boston Five were), and should it happen to suit the government's purpose, you will then be prosecuted, and the petition, the advertisement, the mass meeting, and your applause will be solemnly paraded before the jury as evidence against you.

The last words are Dr. Spock's. At a press conference immediately after the sentencing, in a small room packed with reporters and TV cameras, he began to speak with his usual earnest warmth: "Judge Ford said that the law must be obeyed. We agree. I am not convinced that I broke the law; there was no evidence of conspiracy. Millions of Americans are opposed to the war. There is no shred of legality or constitutionality to this war; it violates the United Nations Charter, the Geneva Accords, and the United States promise to obey the laws of international conduct. It is *totally, abominably,* illegal. Johnson is not running again. He admits that the war is a mistake, yet the war goes on. I intend to go on working against the war."

And then suddenly the doctor seemed to lose the calm,

easy geniality that had marked his demeanor throughout the trial. He became enraged, a towering personification of wrath. It was as though the full meaning of the long ordeal he had just been through was at last borne in on him. Stretching out his huge arms as though to reach far beyond the room and embrace a whole nation, he cried out loudly, urgently: *"Wake up, America!* Wake up before it's too late! Do something *now!"*

Appendix

1. The Indictment

1/5/68
Sel. Serv.
50 USC app.
462 (a)

UNITED STATES DISTRICT COURT
DISTRICT OF MASSACHUSETTS

UNITED STATES OF AMERICA	INDICTMENT
v.	CRIMINAL NO.
WILLIAM SLOANE COFFIN, JR., MICHAEL FERBER, MITCHELL GOODMAN, MARCUS RASKIN and BENJAMIN SPOCK	(50 U.S.C. App. 462(a))

1. From on or about August 1, 1967, and continuously thereafter up to and including the date of the return of this indictment, in the District of Massachusetts, the Southern District of New York, the District of Columbia and elsewhere,

WILLIAM SLOANE COFFIN, JR.
of New Haven in the District of Connecticut,

MICHAEL FERBER
of Boston in the District of Massachusetts,

MITCHELL GOODMAN
of New York in the Southern District of New York,

MARCUS RASKIN
of the District of Columbia, and

BENJAMIN SPOCK
of New York in the Southern District of New York,

the defendants herein, did unlawfully, wilfully and knowingly combine, conspire, confederate, and agree together and with each other, and with diverse other persons, some known and others unknown to the Grand Jury, to commit offenses against the United States, that is,

a. to unlawfully, knowingly and wilfully counsel, aid and abet diverse Selective Service registrants to unlawfully, knowingly and wilfully neglect, fail, refuse and evade service in the armed forces of the United States and all other duties required of registrants under the Universal Military Training and Service Act (50 U.S.C. App. 451–471) and the rules, regulations and directions duly made pursuant to said Act, in violation of 50 U.S.C. App. 462(a);

b. to unlawfully, knowingly and wilfully counsel, aid and abet diverse Selective Service registrants to unlawfully, knowingly and wilfully neglect, fail and refuse to have in their personal possession at all times their registration certificates (SSS Form No. 2), prepared by their local boards, as required by the rules, regulations and directions (32 C.F.R. 1617.1) duly made pursuant to the provisions of the said Universal Military Training and Service Act, in violation of 50 U.S.C. App. 462(a);

c. to unlawfully, knowingly and wilfully counsel, aid and abet diverse Selective Service registrants to unlawfully, knowingly and wilfully neglect, fail and refuse to have in their personal possession at all times valid notices of classification (SSS Form No. 110) which had been issued to them by their local boards showing their current classifications, as required by the rules, regulations and directions (32 C.F.R. 1623.5) duly made pursuant to the provisions of the said Universal Military Training and Service Act, in violation of 50 U.S.C. App. 462(a);

d. to unlawfully, wilfully and knowingly hinder and interfere, by any means, with the administration of the Universal Military Training and Service Act, in violation of 50 U.S.C. App. 462(a).

2. It was a part of said conspiracy that the defendants WILLIAM SLOANE COFFIN, JR., MITCHELL GOODMAN, MARCUS RASKIN and BENJAMIN SPOCK would sponsor and support a nation-wide program of resistance to the functions and operations of the Selective Service System, which said program would include, but not be limited to, the interruption of the induction process at induction centers throughout the United States; the public counselling of Selective Service registrants to resist the draft, to refuse to serve in the armed forces of the United States, to surrender their valid Selective Service notices of classification and registration certificates, and the aiding and abetting of such registrants in such activities.

3. It was a further part of said conspiracy that on October 16, 1967,

the defendants WILLIAM SLOANE COFFIN, JR. and MICHAEL FERBER and other co-conspirators, some known and others unknown to the Grand Jury, will conduct and participate in a public meeting at the Arlington Street Church, Boston, Massachusetts, which said meeting would be attended by Selective Service registrants.

4. It was a further part of said conspiracy that at the aforesaid public meeting on October 16, 1967, the said Selective Service registrants would surrender possession of their valid notices of classification and their registration certificates.

5. It was a further part of said conspiracy that at the aforesaid public meeting on October 16, 1967, the defendant WILLIAM SLOANE COFFIN, JR. and other co-conspirators, some known and others unknown to the Grand Jury, would accept possession of the aforesaid notices of classification and registration certificates from the said Selective Service registrants for the purpose of tendering the same to the Attorney General of the United States.

6. It was a further part of said conspiracy that the defendants WILLIAM SLOANE COFFIN, JR., MICHAEL FERBER, MITCHELL GOODMAN, MARCUS RASKIN, and BENJAMIN SPOCK would accompany a large number of Selective Service registrants and other individuals to the Building of the United States Department of Justice, 10th and Constitution Avenue, N.W., Washington, D. C. on October 20, 1967, and participate in a demonstration of resistance against the operations and functions of the Selective Service System.

7. It was a further part of said conspiracy that at the aforesaid demonstration, valid notices of Selective Service classifications and Selective Service registration certificates surrendered and collected at various demonstrations of resistance to the functions and operations of the Selective Service System previously held in various communities throughout the United States, including those surrendered and collected at the aforesaid meeting conducted at the Arlington Street Church in Boston, Massachusetts on October 16, 1967, would be collected by MICHAEL FERBER and other co-conspirators, some known and others unknown to the Grand Jury, and deposited in a common repository.

8. It was a further part of said conspiracy that at the aforesaid demonstration at the United States Department of Justice the defendant WILLIAM SLOANE COFFIN, JR. would address Selective Service registrants and others participating and in attendance at such demonstrations, publicly counselling said registrants to continue in their resistance against the draft, to continue to refuse to serve in the armed forces of the United States as long as the war in Vietnam continued and

pledging himself and others to aid and abet said registrants in all ways possible.

9. It was a further part of said conspiracy that the defendants WILLIAM SLOANE COFFIN, JR., MITCHELL GOODMAN, MARCUS RASKIN and BENJAMIN SPOCK and other co-conspirators would enter the Building of the United States Department of Justice on said October 20, 1967, and would deliver to the Attorney General of the United States the aforesaid repository containing the said notices of classification and registration certificates.

OVERT ACTS

At the times hereinafter mentioned, the defendants committed the following overt acts in furtherance of said conspiracy and to effect the objects thereof:

1. During the month of August, 1967, the exact date being to the grand jurors unknown, the defendants WILLIAM SLOANE COFFIN, JR. and BENJAMIN SPOCK distributed and caused to be distributed at New York, New York, a statement entitled, "A Call to Resist Illegitimate Authority."

2. On October 2, 1967, the defendants WILLIAM SLOANE COFFIN, JR., MITCHELL GOODMAN, MARCUS RASKIN and BENJAMIN SPOCK held a press conference at the New York Hilton Hotel, Rockefeller Center, New York, New York.

3. On October 16, 1967, the defendant MICHAEL FERBER gave a speech entitled "A Time To Say No" at a meeting at the Arlington Street Church, Boston, Massachusetts.

4. On October 16, 1967, the defendant WILLIAM SLOANE COFFIN, JR., gave a speech at a meeting at the Arlington Street Church, Boston, Massachusetts.

5. On October 16, 1967, the defendant WILLIAM SLOANE COFFIN, JR., accepted notices of classification and registration certificates from Selective Service registrants at a meeting at the Arlington Street Church, Boston, Massachusetts.

6. On October 20, 1967, the defendant WILLIAM SLOANE COFFIN, JR., spoke at a demonstration of resistance against the operations and functions of the Selective Service System at the United States Department of Justice Building, 10th and Constitution Avenue, N.W., Washington, D. C., publicly counselling Selective Service registrants to continue in their resistance against the draft and to continue to refuse to serve in the armed forces.

7. On October 20, 1967, the defendant WILLIAM SLOANE COFFIN, JR., entered the United States Department of Justice Building, 10th and Constitution Avenue, N.W., Washington, D. C.

8. On October 20, 1967, the defendant MARCUS RASKIN entered the United States Department of Justice Building, 10th and Constitution Avenue, N.W., Washington, D. C.

9. On October 20, 1967, the defendant BENJAMIN SPOCK entered the United States Department of Justice Building, 10th and Constitution Avenue, N.W., Washington, D. C.

10. On October 20, 1967, the defendant MITCHELL GOODMAN entered the United States Department of Justice Building, 10th and Constitution Avenue, N.W., Washington, D. C.

11. On October 20, 1967, in the Andretta Room, United States Department of Justice, Washington, D. C., the defendants WILLIAM SLOANE COFFIN, JR., MITCHELL GOODMAN, MARCUS RASKIN, BENJAMIN SPOCK and other co-conspirators abandoned a fabricoid briefcase containing approximately one hundred eighty-five (185) registration certificates and one hundred seventy-two (172) notices of classification together with other materials.

2. Overt Act #1, "A Call to Resist Illegitimate Authority"

To the young men of America,
to the whole of the American people,
and to all men of good will everywhere:

1. An ever growing number of young American men are finding that the American war in Vietnam so outrages their deepest moral and religious sense that they cannot contribute to it in any way. We share their moral outrage.

2. We further believe that the war is unconstitutional and illegal. Congress has not declared a war as required by the Constitution. Moreover, under the Constitution, treaties signed by the President and ratified by the Senate have the same force as the Constitution itself. The Charter of the United Nations is such a treaty. The Charter specifically obligates the United States to refrain from force or the threat of force in international relations. It requires member states

to exhaust every peaceful means of settling disputes and to submit disputes which cannot be settled peacefully to the Security Council. The United States has systematically violated all of these Charter provisions for thirteen years.

3. Moreover, this war violates international agreements, treaties and principles of law which the United States Government has solemnly endorsed. The combat role of the United States troops in Vietnam violates the Geneva Accords of 1954 which our government pledged to support but has since subverted. The destruction of rice, crops and livestock; the burning and bulldozing of entire villages consisting exclusively of civilian structures; the interning of civilian non-combatants in concentration camps; the summary executions of civilians in captured villages who could not produce satisfactory evidence of their loyalties or did not wish to be removed to concentration camps; the slaughter of peasants who dared to stand up in their fields and shake their fists at American helicopters;—these are all actions of the kind which the United States and the other victorious powers of World War II declared to be crimes against humanity for which individuals were to be held personally responsible even when acting under the orders of their governments and for which Germans were sentenced at Nuremberg to long prison terms and death. The prohibition of such acts as war crimes was incorporated in treaty law by the Geneva Conventions of 1949, ratified by the United States. These are commitments to other countries and to Mankind, and they would claim our allegiance even if Congress should declare war.

4. We also believe it is an unconstitutional denial of religious liberty and equal protection of the laws to withhold draft exemption from men whose religious or profound philosophical beliefs are opposed to what in the Western religious tradition have been long known as unjust wars.

5. Therefore, we believe on all these grounds that every free man has a legal right and a moral duty to exert every effort to end this war, to avoid collusion with it, and to encourage others to do the same. Young men in the armed forces or threatened with the draft face the most excruciating choices. For them various forms of resistance risk separation from their families and their country, destruction of their careers, loss of their freedom and loss of their lives. Each must choose the course of resistance dictated by his conscience and circumstances. Among those already in the armed forces some are refusing to obey specific illegal and immoral orders, some are attempting to educate their fellow servicemen on the murderous and barbarous nature of the war, some are absenting themselves without

official leave. Among those not in the armed forces some are applying for status as conscientious objectors to American aggression in Vietnam, some are refusing to be inducted. Among both groups some are resisting openly and paying a heavy penalty, some are organizing more resistance within the United States and some have sought sanctuary in other countries.

6. We believe that each of these forms of resistance against illegitimate authority is courageous and justified. Many of us believe that open resistance to the war and the draft is the course of action most likely to strengthen the moral resolve with which all of us can oppose the war and most likely to bring an end to the war.

7. We will continue to lend our support to those who undertake resistance to this war. We will raise funds to organize draft resistance unions, to supply legal defense and bail, to support families and otherwise aid resistance to the war in whatever ways may seem appropriate.

8. We firmly believe that our statement is the sort of speech that under the First Amendment must be free, and that the actions we will undertake are as legal as is the war resistance of the young men themselves. In any case, we feel that we cannot shrink from fulfilling our responsibilities to the youth whom many of us teach, to the country whose freedom we cherish, and to the ancient traditions of religion and philosophy which we strive to preserve in this generation.

9. We call upon all men of good will to join us in this confrontation with immoral authority. Especially we call upon the universities to fulfill their mission of enlightenment and religious organizations to honor their heritage of brotherhood. Now is the time to resist.

---

send to: RESIST/Room 510/166 Fifth Ave./New York, N.Y. 10010

☐ I wish to sign "A Call to Resist Illegitimate Authority" and am willing to have my endorsement made public.

☐ I enclose a contribution of $_____ to support the work of RESIST. (Please make checks payable to RESIST)

☐ I am interested in organizing or joining a group in my community to support young men directly resisting the war.

name _____

address _____

city _____state _____zip_____

A PARTIAL LIST OF SIGNERS

Nelson W. Aldrich, Jr.
Edwin B. Allaire
Gar Alperovitz
Emilo de Antonio
Richard Ashley
David Bakan
Richard J. Barnel
Inge Powell Bell
Rev. Philip Berrigan, S.S.J.
Rev. James Bevel
Norman Birnbaum
Robert Bly
Samuel Bowles
Harry M. Bracken
Robert McAfee Brown
Robert Brustein
Henry H. Bucher, Jr.
Alexander Calder
Louisa James Calder
Haydn Carruth
Jerome Charyn
Noam Chomsky
Allen Churchill
Rev. William Sloane Coffin
Dr. Arnold M. Cooper
Robert Coover
Frederick Crews
Alfred Crown
William Davidon
Martin Davis
Jean Davidson
R. G. Davis
Stanley Diamond
Dr. James P. Dixon
Rev. Thomas Dorney, S.J.
Douglas Dowd
George P. Elliott
Lawrence Ferlinghetti
W. H. Ferry
Eliot Friedson
Dr. J. W. Friedman
Norman D. Fruchter
Allen Ginsberg
Rabbi Robert E. Goldburg
Mitchell Goodman
Paul Goodman
Norman K. Gottwald

Robert Greenblatt
Balcomb Greene
Barbara Guest
John G. Gurley
Roger T. Hogan
William Hamilton
Chester W. Hartman
Richard O. Hathaway
Jules Henry
Nat Hentoff
Edward S. Herman
Hallock Hoffman
James G. Holland
Leo Huberman
Karl Hufbauer
Dell Hymes
Christopher Jencks
Donald Kolish
Herbert Kelman
Roy C. Kepler
Fr. David Kirk
Herbert Kohl
Gabriel Kolko
Hans Koningsberger
Ivor Kraft
Jean-Claude von Itallie
Burton Lane
Christopher Lasch
Irving Laucks
Paul Lauter
Sidney Lens
Jerome Lettvin
Denise Levertov
Jack Levine
Robert Lowell
Elliott Lieb
Walter Lowenfels
Staughton Lynd
Dwight Macdonald
Herbert Marcuse
Kenneth O. May
Arno J. Mayer
Everett Mendelsohn
Seymour Melman
Thomas Merton
Ashley Montagu
Ira Morris

Barrington Moore, Jr.
Rev. Richard Mumma
Otto Nathan
Jay Neugeboren
Jack Newfield
Dr. Martin Niemoller
Michael Novak
Conor Cruise O'Brien
Carl Oglesby
Richard Ohmann
Wayne O'Neil
Grace Paley
Victor Paschkis
Linus Pauling
Bishop James A. Pike
Richard H. Popkin
Hilary Putnam
Philip Rahv
Anatol Rapoport
Marc Raskin
Peter V. Ritner
Henry Robbins
Gordon Rogoff
Philip Roth
Muriel Rukeyser
Robert J. Rulman
Marshall Sahlins
Franz Schurman
Richard Seaver
John R. Seeley
Wilfred Sheed
Stanley K. Sheinbaum

James Shenton
Philip Siekevitz
Edgar Snow
Theodore Solotaroff
Susan Sontag
Raphael Soyer
Dr. Benjamin Spock
Charles Stein
Grover C. Stephans
Elizabeth Sutherland
John M. Swomley, Jr.
Albert Szenl-Gyorgyi
Paul Sweezy
Daniel Talbot
William Taylor
Karl V. Teeler
Harold Tovish
Tomi Ungerer
William Vickrey
Gerald Walker
Immanuel Wallerstein
Brendan Walsh
James E. Walsh
Arthur Waskow
Howard Waskow
Anthony West
Gilbert White
Richard Wilbur
Sol Yurick
Robert Zevin
Paul R. Zilsel
Howard Zinn

3. Overt Act #3, Michael Ferber's Speech "A Time to Say No"

Statement by Michael Ferber
Service of Acceptance
Arlington Street Church
16 October 1967

We are gathered in this church today in order to do something very simple: to say No. We have come from many different places and backgrounds and we have many different ideas about ourselves and the world, but we have come here to show that we are united to do one thing: to say No. Each of our acts of returning our draft cards is our personal No; when we put them in a single container or set fire to them from a single candle we express the simple basis of our unity.

But what I wish to speak about now is what goes beyond our saying No, for no matter how loudly we all say it, no matter what ceremony we perform around our saying it, we will not become a community among ourselves nor effective agents for changing our country if a negative is all we share. Albert Camus said that the rebel, who says No, is also one who says Yes, and that when he draws a line beyond which he will refuse to cooperate he his affirming the values on the other side of that line. For us who come here today, what is it that we affirm, what is it to which we can say Yes?

To be honest we have to admit that we in the Resistance still disagree about a great many things, whether we speak out about them or not. For example, here we all are in a church, and yet for some of us it is the first time we've been inside one for years. Here we are receiving the help of many clergymen, and yet some of us feel nothing but contempt for the organized religions that they represent. Some of us, therefore, feel a certain hypocrisy in being part of this service.

But it would not surprise me if many of the clergymen who are here today feel some of the same contempt for organized religion that our unreligious or anti-religious brothers feel. They know better than we do the long and bloody history of evils committed in the name of religion, the long history of compromise and Erastian subservience to political power, the long history of theological hair-splitting and the burning of heretics, and they feel more deeply than we do the hypocrisy of Sunday (or Saturday) morning. Perhaps the things that made some of us leave the church are the very things that made some of them become ministers, priests, and rabbis, the very things that bring them here today. Many of them will anger their superiors or their congregations by being here but they are here anyway.

There is a great tradition within the church and synagogue which has always struggled against the conservative and worldly forces that have always been in control. It is a radical tradition, a tradition of urgent impulse to go to the root of the religious dimension of human life. This tradition in modern times has tried to recall us to the best ways of living our lives: the way of love and compassion, the way of justice and respect, the way of facing other people as human beings and not as abstract representatives of something alien and evil. It tries to recall us to the reality behind religious ceremony and symbolism, and it will change the ceremony and symbolism when the reality changes.

As a part of this service we will break bread together. We do this, however, not because some churches happen to take Communion; we do this for one of the root reasons for Communion itself: that men around the world and for all time have found it good to eat together when they are sharing in something important.

The radical tradition is still alive: it is present here in this church. Those of us who disregard organized religion, I think, are making a mistake if they also disregard this tradition and its presence today. This tradition is something to which we can say Yes.

There is another disagreement among us, or if not a disagreement then a difference in attitude toward what we are doing today. It is a difference that cuts through the other differences, perhaps because it is a little inside each of us, and it leads to a mistake that we are liable to make no matter how else we agree or differ. In religious terms, it is to dwell too much on the possibility of the Apocalypse; in political terms, it is to dwell too much on the possibility of a Utopian society. We must not confuse the ceremony and symbolism of today's service with the reality that we are only a few hundred people with very little power. And we must not confuse the change inside each of us, important though that may be, with the change that we have yet to bring about in this country and the world. Neither the Revelation nor the Revolution is at hand, and to base our hopes and plans on them would be a tragic blunder.

Maybe all of us—Leftists or Liberals, Reformers or Revolutionaries, Radical Religionists or Hippies—maybe all of us are apocalyptarians, I don't know. Surely something else besides a cold rational calculation of sociological options has brought us here to this church. And surely we ate in this church partly to celebrate the occasion of our noncooperation (and many of us will celebrate in a somewhat different way at parties with friends tonight). But let us not be deceived. The sun will rise tomorrow as it does every day, and when we get out of bed the world will be in pretty much the same mess it is in today. American bombers will continue to drop incendiary bombs on the Vietnamese people and American soldiers will continue to "pacify" their villages. The ghettos will continue to be rotten places to live in. Black and Mexican farm workers will continue to get miserable wages. America's schools will continue to cripple the minds and hearts of its pupils. And the American Selective Service System will continue to send young men out to the slaughter.

Today is not the End. Today is the Beginning.

This is the Beginning because, very simply, we have to dig in for the long haul. It is not going to be easy to change this country. To change it is going to mean struggles and anguish day in and day out for years. It will mean incredible efforts at great human cost to gain a few inches of ground. It will mean people dedicating their lives and possibly losing them for a cause we can only partly define and whose outcome we can only guess at. We must say Yes to the long struggle ahead or this service will be a mockery.

We are brought to a third difference among us. Earlier today Nick Egleson spoke out against the kind of resistance whose primary motivation is moralistic and personal rather than political. He is saying that we must make ourselves relevant to the social and political condition of the world and must not just take a moral posture for our own soul's sake, even though that too is a risk.

To some extent this argument depends on terminology rather than fact. Today we have heard our situation described in religious terms, moral terms, political terms, legal terms, and psychological terms. Very few of us are at home in all these different modes of speech, and each of us habitually uses only one of them to talk and think in. But what is happening today should make it clear that these different modes of speech all overlap one another and they often all say the same essential things. Albert Camus, who struggled in a more serious Resistance than ours, believed that politics is an extension of morality, that the truly moral man is engaged in politics as a natural outcome of his beliefs.

To return to Nick's concern, the real difference is not between the moral man and the political man, but between the man whose moral thinking leads him to political action and the man whose moral thinking leads him no farther than to his own "sinlessness." It is the difference between the man who is willing to go dirty himself in the outside world and the man who wishes to stay "clean" and "pure."

Now this kind of "sinlessness" and "purity" is arrogant pride, and I think we must say No to it. The martyr who offers himself meekly as a lamb to the altar is a fool unless he has fully taken into account the consequences of his sacrifice not only to himself but to the rest of the world. We cannot honor him for his stigmata or his purple hearts unless he has helped the rest of us while he got them.

So then what are we to do? We must look at ourselves once more. We all have an impulse to purification and martyrdom and we should not be ashamed of it. But let us be certain that we have thought through the consequences of our action in the outside world, and that these consequences are what we want to bring about. Let us make sure we are ready to work hard and long with each other in the months to come, working to make it difficult and politically dangerous for the government to prosecute us, working to help anyone and everyone to find ways of avoiding the draft, to help disrupt the workings of the draft and the armed forces until the war is over. Let us make sure we can form a community. Let us make sure we can let others depend on us.

If we can Yes to these things, and to the religious tradition that stands with us today, and to the fact that today marks not the End but a Beginning, and to the long hard dirty job ahead of us—if we can say Yes to all this, then let us come forward together to say No to the United States Government.

Then let our Yes be the loudest No our government ever heard.

4. Overt Act #4, Speech in Boston by the Rev. William Sloane Coffin, Jr.

October 16, 1967

Most words are dispensable. They can perish as though they had never been written or spoken. Some few, however, must forever remain alive if human beings are to remain human. "I love my city, but I shall not stop preaching that which I believe is true: you may kill me, but I shall follow God rather than you." and: "We must obey God rather than men."

Why are these words of Socrates and St. Peter so indispensable? Because in the first place they tell us that the most profound experience of the self is the experience of the conscience, and not as frequently suggested today the experience of private sensations and interior visions. And secondly, they tell us that because there is a higher and hopefully future order of things, men at times will feel constrained to disobey the law out of a sense of obedience to a higher allegiance. To hundreds of history's most revered heroes, not to serve the state has appeared the best way to love one's neighbor. To Socrates, St. Peter, Milton, Bunyon, Gandhi, Nehru, it was clear that sometimes bad subjects make good neighbors.

Let us remember these men were not out to destroy the legal order. By accepting the legal punishment they actually upheld it. Nor were they disrespectful of the law. They broke it as a last, not as a first resort. But they respected the law only, they did not worship it, and were determined to bend their every effort to the end that the law reflect and not reject their best understanding of justice and mercy.

And how can Americans so quickly forget their own heritage? Our Puritan forefathers came to these shores precisely because they would not surrender their consciences to the state! The Quakers in the Massachusetts Bay Colony were not only imprisoned but executed because they refused to obey the law. In Pennsylvania in 1750 John Wollman refused to pay taxes when Pennsylvania decided to arm against the Indians. And Washington, Hamilton, Jefferson, Adams were not only civilly disobedient but traitors all, until success crowned their efforts and they became great patriots.

Then in the 19th century Abolitionists again and again ended up behind bars, as of course did Thoreau with these incredibly modern words: "I am first of all a citizen of the world, and of this country only at a much later and convenient hour."

If only Americans could remember their own heritage they could at least applaud the spirit, even if they do not share the views, of those who here today are refusing to surrender their consciences to the state.

The issue *is* one of conscience. Let us be blunt. To us the war in Vietnam is a crime. And if we are correct, if the war is a crime, then is it criminal to refuse to have anything to do with it? Is it we who are demoralizing our boys in Vietnam, or the Administration which is asking them to do immoral things?

I have the highest sympathy for our boys in Vietnam. They know what a dirty, bloody war it is. But they have been told that the end justifies the means, that the cleansing water of victory will wash clean their hands of all the blood and dirt. No wonder they hate those who say "There must be no cleansing water." But they must strive, hard as it is, to understand that there *can* be no cleansing water if military victory spells moral defeat.

I have the highest sympathy too for those who back the war because their sons or lovers or husbands have died in Vietnam. But they must understand that *sacrifice in and of itself confers no sanctity,* that even if half a million of our boys died in Vietnam that would not make the cause one whit more sacred. (But how hard that is to understand when one's husband is numbered among the sacrificed.)

To us then the war is an issue of conscience. So too is the draft. For not only does the National Selective Act inexcusably defer the rich and better educated; it also insists that a man's conscientious objection be based on "religious belief and training."

Could anything be more ethically absurd? Have humanists no conscience? Why, many men become atheists because they think Christians are so inhuman that the only way to be a good humanist is to be an atheist. (Of course they are mistaken. Christians have always been the best argument against Christianity. But Christ is the best argument for it, and that's the argument that has to be met!) But it is absurd once again to say a man must be a believer in order to be conscientious.

Then despite numerous appeals by numerous religious leaders and groups, Congress last spring chose to recognize only the rights of conscience of the absolute pacifist. This too, as every good pacifist knows, is absurd. For the rights of a man whose conscience forbids him to participate in a particular war are as deserving of respect as the rights of a man whose conscience forbids him to participate in any war at all. This is an ancient Jewish and Christian tradition. Yet the tradition we honor the government steadfastly continues to dishonor.

So the war and the draft are both issues of conscience.

When an issue is one of conscience then surely it is one we may not wish to seek but it is one we cannot properly avoid—particularly the synagogues and churches. So what are they to do?

"Thou spreadest a table before me in the presence of mine enemies."

As men have always felt certain times to be more sacred than others, *i.e.,* the Sabbath, so also they have felt certain places to be more sacred, *i.e.,* the home, the temple, the church. And closely associated with these more sacred places has been the belief that there a man should find some sort of sanctuary from the forces of a hostile world. "Thou spreadest a table before me in the presence of mine enemies." These familiar words from the 23rd Psalm refer to an ancient desert law which provided that if a man hunted by his enemies sought refuge with another man who offered him hospitality, then the enemies of the man had to remain outside the rim of the campfire light for two nights and the day intervening.

In Exodus we read that the altar of the Tabernacle is to be considered a place of sanctuary, and in Numbers and Deuteronomy we read of "cities of refuge," three in Canaan and three in Jordan.

Then during the Middle Ages all churches on the continent were considered sanctuaries, and in some instances in England the land within a mile of the church was included. And according to the Justinian Code sanctuary was extended to all law breakers, Christian, Jewish, and non-believer alike, with the exception only of those guilty of high treason or sacrilege. Now if in the Middle Ages churches could offer sanctuary to the most common of criminals, could they not today do the same for the most conscientious among us? And if in the Middle Ages they could offer forty days to a man who had committed both a sin and a crime, could they not today offer an indefinite period to one who had committed no sin?

The churches must not shirk their responsibility in deciding whether or not a man's objection is conscientious. But should a church declare itself a "sanctuary for conscience" this should be considered less a means to shield a man, more a means to expose a church, an effort to make a church really be a church.

For if the state should decide that the arm of the law was long enough to reach inside a church there would be little church members could do to prevent an arrest. But the members could point out what they had already dramatically demonstrated, that the sanctity of conscience was being violated. And further, as the law regarding "aiding and abetting" is clear—up to five years in jail and a fine of ten thousand dollars—church members could then say: "If you arrest this man for violating a law which violates his conscience then you must arrest us too, for in the sight of that law we are now as guilty as he."

What else can the churches do? Are we to raise conscientious men and then not stand by them in their hour of conscience? And if there is a price to pay, should we hold back? Wasn't Cardinal Newman reflecting on the central symbol of the church, when he said, "Good is never done except at the expense of those who do it; truth is never enforced except at the sacrifice of its proponents."

But as the government is loath to have a moral confrontation with those aiding and abetting, the last word must go to those who today are engaging in a solemn act of civil disobedience which for many is an act of religious obedience. They are in the forefront of this battle.

Gentlemen, it is fitting that your action should take place within two weeks of the 450th celebration of the Reformation. For what we need today is a new reformation, a reformation of conscience. What you do today gives substance to the question: "What in our technological age shall it profit a man that he be able to fly through the air like a bird and swim through the sea like a fish, if he be not able to walk the earth like a man?"

You stand now as Luther stood in his time. May you be inspired to speak, and we to hear, the words he once spoke in conscience and in all simplicity: "Here I stand, I can do no other. God help me."

5. Overt Act #6, Statement Before the Department of Justice by the Rev. William Sloane Coffin, Jr.

October 20, 1967

What we are here to do is not a natural, easy thing for any of us. We are writers, professors, clergy, and this is not our "thing." But it must have been with precisely such people as we in mind that the poet Peguy wrote: "The worst of particularities is to withhold oneself, the worst ignorance is not to act, the worst lie is to steal away."

So we have come here to be with conscientious men in their hour of conscience; and because like them we cannot stand around with dry feet while wisdom and decency go under for the third time in Vietnam.

This week once again high government officials described protesters against the war as "naive," "wild-eyed idealists." But in our view it is not wild-eyed idealism but clear-eyed revulsion that brings us here. For as one of our number put it: "If what the United States is doing in Vietnam is right, what is there left to be called wrong?"

Many of us are veterans, and all of us have the highest sympathy for our boys in Vietnam. They know what a dirty, bloody war it is. But they have been told that the ends justify the means, and that the cleansing water of victory will wash clean their hands of all the blood and dirt. No wonder they hate us who say "There must be no cleansing water." But what they must strive to understand, hard as it is, is that there can be no cleansing water if military victory spells moral defeat.

We have the highest sympathy also for those who back the war because their sons or lovers or husbands are fighting or have died in Vietnam. But they too must understand a very basic thing—that sacrifice in and of itself confers no sanctity. Even if half a million of our boys were to die in Vietnam that would not make the cause one whit more sacred. Yet we realize how hard that knowledge is to appropriate when one's husband is numbered among the sacrificed.

The mother of a son lost in Vietnam once told me "My son used to write how much he and his company were doing for the orphans. But I used to answer 'If you want to help the orphans, son, you must stop killing their fathers and mothers.' "

Like this mother we do not dispute the good intentions, the good works of endless good Americans in Vietnam. But we do insist that no amount of good intentions nor good works, nor certainly government rhetoric to the contrary, can offset the fact that American policy in Vietnam, a policy devised by high-minded perhaps, but ideologically rigid and unimaginative men—this policy has run amok. The war is not only unwise but unjust, and if that is true then it is not we who are demoralizing our boys in Vietnam, but the government, which asks them to do immoral things.

As the war to us is immoral, so also is the draft. For the National Selective Service Act not only places the major burden of the war on the backs of the poor; it also confronts thousands of men with a choice of either violating their consciences or going to jail.

As the law now stands, for a man to qualify as a conscientious objector he must believe in God. Could anything be more ethically absurd? Have humanists no conscience? Why—and as a Christian I say this with contrition—some of the most outstanding humanists I know would think they were slipping from their high ideals were they to take steps towards conversion. As a Christian I am convinced it is a gross misfortune not to believe in God, but it is not automatically an ethical default.

Then despite numerous appeals by numerous religious bodies, Congress last spring chose to provide alternative service only for the absolute pacifist. This too is absurd, for the rights of a man whose conscience forbids him to participate in a particular war are as deserving of respect as the rights of a man whose conscience forbids him to participate in any war at all. This is the ancient Jewish and Christian tradition we honor. Yet the tradition we honor the government steadfastly refuses to honor.

So both the war and the draft are issues of conscience. And an issue of conscience is one a man may not seek but hardly one he can avoid.

We admire the way these young men who could safely have hidden behind exemptions and deferments have elected instead to risk something big for something good. We admire them and believe theirs is the true voice of America, the vision that will prevail beyond the distortions of the moment.

We cannot shield them. We can only expose ourselves as they have done. The law of the land is clear. Section 12 of the National Selective Service Act declares that anyone "who knowingly counsels, aids, or abets another to refuse or evade registration or service in the armed forces . . . shall be liable to imprisonment for not more than five years or a fine of ten thousand dollars or both."

We hereby publicly counsel these young men to continue in their refusal to serve in the armed forces as long as the war in Vietnam continues, and we pledge ourselves to aid and abet them in all the ways we can. This means that if they are now arrested for failing to comply with a law that violates their consciences, we too must be arrested, for in the sight of that law we are now as guilty as they.

It is a long-standing tradition, sanctioned by American democracy, that the dictates of government must be tested on the anvil of individual conscience. This is what we now undertake to do—not as a first but as a last resort. And in accepting the legal punishment we are, in fact, supporting, not subverting, the legal order.

Still, to stand in this fashion against the law and before our fellow Americans is a difficult and even fearful thing. But in the face of what to us is insane and inhuman we can fall neither silent nor servile. Nor can we educate young men to be conscientious only to desert them in their hour of conscience. So we are resolved, as they are resolved, to speak out clearly and to pay up personally.

6. The Role of the American Civil Liberties Union in the Case of the Boston Five

The ACLU's schizophrenic behavior in the Spock case may come as no surprise to those familiar with the history of the organization over the past few decades.

Long before the New Deal gave semantic context to the alphabet —NRA, CCC, NLRB, FCC—the ACLU had already become for millions of Americans synonymous with the defense of civil liberties. The American Civil Liberties Union has had and will have periods of greatness as a champion of political freedoms, but like many another crusading organization it had some shaky, even ignoble moments in the era of the cold war.

In the simple old days before the sixties, when the terms right wing, left wing, and center meant something that everybody recognized (namely, degrees of consanguinity to the Communist Party), the main targets of political repression were Communists and their alleged fellow travelers. Some ACLU leaders today concede that all too often, in that critical period, the organization ducked the onerous task of providing legal defense for these controversial individuals.

While never renouncing the principle of offering its services to all, regardless of political affiliation, it accomplished this in practice by setting impossible conditions—in the case of Communists, by requiring the defendant to pledge that so long as the ACLU was in the case he would not engage in out-of-court polemics or demonstrations, or seek to organize mass support for his defense, or encourage others to do so.

By the time of the Spock indictment, the old labels were no longer relevant (nobody, not even the prosecutor, suggested that the Boston defendants were reds), but the same sort of conflict arose in a different guise. There were those in the ACLU leadership who, while conceding that the indictment raised First Amendment free-speech issues, feared that these particular defendants would prove unmanageable, would insist on running their own kind of show in (and out of) court.

The American Civil Liberties Union role in the Spock case in four acts:

Act I. Two days after the indictments were handed down, Melvin Wulf, legal director of the ACLU national office, issued a press release blasting the indictments as "a major escalation in the administration's war against dissent" and announcing that the ACLU would put together a top defense team of lawyers to represent the defendants without fee.

Act II. At an emergency meeting the following week, the ACLU national board overruled its legal director and voted 11 to 4 not to involve itself in the Spock case. The minutes of the meeting state that several members argued "it would be intolerable for the ACLU to authorize a direct defense which is seen predominantly to rest on points which go beyond ACLU policy merely because they are seen as important by the defendant." (The "points that go beyond ACLU policy" are war crimes, the legality of the war, and the legality of the draft.) Following this meeting, the board issued a formal policy statement saying that it would not defend those who refuse to register for the draft because "we have assumed the draft laws are constitutional."

Act III. After this the roof fell in, according to Melvin Wulf, and a little palace revolution developed. "Some members thought the statement an egregious and damaging mistake—it made the ACLU look like a cop-out organization." Affiliates in New Jersey, New York, California, and Massachusetts demanded reconsideration and another board meeting was convened for March 2. By the narrow margin of 26 to 20 this meeting reversed the previous decision and specifically offered both legal and financial aid for defense of the Boston Five. The outcome was largely academic because by now, nearly two months after the indictment, most of the defendants had long since arranged for representation.

Act IV. Professor Joseph W. Bishop, Jr., of Yale Law School published an article in *Harper's Magazine* (May, 1968) in which he wrapped up the arguments against ACLU involvement. The gist of his position is that the ACLU should not have agreed to enter the case at the trial level—this could "well mean participation in efforts to convert the proceeding into a propaganda trial of the Johnson administration"—but should have confined its activities to an *amicus curiae* brief on appeal, and only then "if ACLU believed that the defendants' advice to young men created no clear and present danger to the Republic."

However, Mr. Bishop (who says he believes American policy in Vietnam to be "mistaken, although not immoral") uses up most of his space in *Harper's* in an unaccountably ferocious attack on Mr. Coffin. He starts off with honeyed words: "Coffin is handsome, articulate, charming, humane, sincere and courageous." But it develops that what Mr. Bishop is really after is Mr. Coffin's *conscience,* which becomes, after he has dragged it about and worried it for a while, a sort of loathsome excrescence with an almost independent life of its own, like a tapeworm or poltergeist: "a handsome, blond, six foot conscience" . . . "an efficacious substitute for analysis of problems which he calls conscience," "his conscience is likely to reach positions in one soaring bound." "The Divinity's built-in conscience regulator is sadly unreliable; even the best consciences do not all point in the same direction at the same time."

In one of his bouts with Mr. Coffin's conscience, Mr. Bishop writes: "The Newspeak of 1984 called it bellyfeel. Does the Government of the United States pursue a policy which is pronounced by Coffin's conscience to be wrong? Then the Government's authority ceases ipso facto to be legitimate, and he is privileged and indeed obliged to disobey its laws—'confront it' in the cant of the movement."

John Wall, the government prosecutor, picked up this thought in toto and paraphrased it as follows in his closing argument to the jury: "They claim to be intellectuals. I submit to you you'd be warranted in finding they don't think. They feel. It's bellyfeel, or gut reaction. They feel something is wrong or right. They feel it and they act on that feeling in their conscience. Is this country going to be tied to a string that is tied to Mr. Coffin's conscience?"

A Note on the Type

The text of this book was set on the Linotype in a typeface called Baskerville. The face is a facsimile reproduction of type cast from molds made for JOHN BASKERVILLE (1706–75) from his designs. The punches for the revived Linotype Baskerville were cut under the supervision of the English printer George W. Jones.

John Baskerville's original face was one of the forerunners of the type style known as "modern face" to printers—a "modern" of the period A.D. 1800.

This book was composed, printed, and bound by The Haddon Craftsmen, Inc., Scranton, Pa. Typography and binding design by Kenneth Miyamoto.